The Technological Study of Books and Manuscripts as Artefacts

Research questions and analytical solutions

Edited by

Sarah Neate
David Howell
Richard Ovenden
A. M. Pollard

BAR International Series 2209
2011

Published in 2016 by
BAR Publishing, Oxford

BAR International Series 2209

The Technological Study of Books and Manuscripts as Artefacts

ISBN 978 1 4073 0767 1

© The editors and contributors severally and the Publisher 2011

COVER IMAGE *Front cover image shows a miniature from Bodleian Library manuscript MS Douce 195 fol. 1r, reproduced with permission from the Bodleian Libraries, University of Oxford.*

The authors' moral rights under the 1988 UK Copyright,
Designs and Patents Act are hereby expressly asserted.

All rights reserved. No part of this work may be copied, reproduced, stored,
sold, distributed, scanned, saved in any form of digital format or transmitted
in any form digitally, without the written permission of the Publisher.

BAR Publishing is the trading name of British Archaeological Reports (Oxford) Ltd.
British Archaeological Reports was first incorporated in 1974 to publish the BAR
Series, International and British. In 1992 Hadrian Books Ltd became part of the BAR
group. This volume was originally published by Archaeopress in conjunction with
British Archaeological Reports (Oxford) Ltd / Hadrian Books Ltd, the Series principal
publisher, in 2011. This present volume is published by BAR Publishing, 2016.

Printed in England

BAR titles are available from:

              BAR Publishing
              122 Banbury Rd, Oxford, OX2 7BP, UK
EMAIL   info@barpublishing.com
PHONE +44 (0)1865 310431
FAX   +44 (0)1865 316916
              www.barpublishing.com

Contents

Introduction. The Book as a Material Object ii
A.M. Pollard, Richard Ovenden, Sarah Neate & David Howell

Part One: Manuscript Research Questions

Chapter 1. Curatorial Issues and Research Questions: Current Research on
Western Medieval Manuscripts and Oriental Manuscripts in the Bodleian Library 3
Emilie Savage-Smith, Sarah Neate & Richard Ovenden

Chapter 2. Conservation Issues and Research Questions: the Role of Analysis in Book and Manuscript
Conservation 9
Sarah Neate & David Howell, with contributions from Cheryl Porter & Nicholas Pickwoad

Part Two: Introduction to Manuscript Analysis Techniques

Chapter 3. Principles and Methods of Analysis in Archaeological and Manuscript Studies 17
Sarah Neate & A. M. Pollard

Chapter 4. Framing Analytical Research Questions 25
Mark Clarke

Chapter 5. Defining Methodological Problems: a Case Study on Paint Analysis and the Technological
Study of Manuscripts 31
Nicholas Eastaugh

Part Three: Analytical Solutions to Manuscript Research Questions

Chapter 6. Paper Degradation and Conservation: Overview of Recent Research (2000-2010) 37
Matija Strlič

Chapter 7. Investigating the Structural Integrity of Historical Documents using X-ray Diffraction
Techniques 47
Kate Thomas, Lee Gonzales & Tim Wess

Chapter 8. Advanced Optical Imaging Methods for Investigating Manuscripts 55
Haida Liang

Chapter 9. Analysis of Pigments on Manuscripts by Raman Spectroscopy: Advantages and Limitations 67
Lucia Burgio

Chapter 10. Non-destructive Ion Beam Analysis Techniques for Book and Manuscript Studies 77
Geoff Grime

Chapter 11. Provenancing Parchment, Leather and Paper using Stable Isotopes 85
A. M. Pollard & Fiona Brock

Chapter 12. Scientific Approaches to Dating Historical Documents 91
A. M. Pollard

Introduction: The Book as a Material Object

A.M. Pollard,[a] Richard Ovenden,[b] Sarah Neate[a,c] & David Howell[c]

[a] Research Laboratory for Archaeology and the History of Art, University of Oxford
[b] Department of Special Collections, Bodleian Library, University of Oxford
[c] Conservation and Collections Care, Bodleian Library, University of Oxford

The book (by 'book', in this context, we mean any portable object whose prime purpose is to convey documentary information, including both images and text) is, in our view, a much-neglected artifact in the spectrum of objects which constitute the material cultural heritage. There is, of course, a long history reaching back to the Greek and Roman periods in Europe and the Near East (and longer in China and other parts of Asia) of the book as a conveyor of information from the past. In comparison, the history of the study of the book has been a rich area for academic study since the Renaissance, growing with an increasing crescendo during the late 19th and 20th centuries to the current period, where 'The History of the Book' is an active branch of many traditional academic disciplines. Current academic trends have provided a great interest in the book as a cultural object, with many journal articles, monographs, academic conferences, and scholarly groups concentrating on the field.[1] Much of this academic liveliness has been fostered by the availability of the primary resources for these studies – printed books and manuscripts – in digitized form readily available over the web. A key problem has emerged, however: this academic study, increasingly driven by these digitized corpora, has not always been matched by a thorough knowledge of and grounding in the book and manuscript as a physical object. Scholars, especially the younger generation of graduate students, are able to immerse themselves more than ever in images of books and manuscripts. There is a danger, however, that this burgeoning research interest will not be matched by a deep level of understanding, knowledge, and familiarity with the materiality of the texts and images that they encounter.

Clearly, the 'History of the Book' and its related disciplines must be grounded in a full understanding of the carriers of their content. Authenticity of historical evidence is a crucial factor in any area of academic study. For example, if by physical examination, a book can be shown not to be 'genuine' (i.e., not of the period purported), then the information contained cannot be accepted as valid (for example in the case of the Hitler diaries). More subtly, if a book can be shown to be either later than the event described, or to contain later additions or amendments, then the information contained has to be interpreted in the light of this artifactual 'life history'. The attribution of a medieval manuscript, for example, to a particular locality (a particular religious house, secular scriptorium, or University setting) will have major implications for a broad range of cultural, historical, and intellectual studies.

Books are usually complex multi-material artifacts. Since the 15th Century, books have tended to be printed (using inks made from a range of organic materials) on paper (made from processed organic material), bound in leather (an organic biopolymer). Prior to this, Western books consisted principally of paper or parchment, but a range of other organic materials such as papyrus, leaves and bark were also utilized as writing substrates. They were inscribed by hand using a range of inks, and often illustrated in colour using a wide range of pigments, the preparation and use of which reflect not only the exploitation of the natural environment throughout antiquity and the medieval period, but also the technological development associated with glass making and metal working. The analysis of such artifacts is a challenge to modern analytical science, partly because of the complexity of the object, and partly because of the strict requirement in many institutions for the analysis to be non-destructive. Moreover, such complex three dimensional artifacts can present serious challenges in terms of preservation of the physical evidence. Most of the materials used are prone to alteration or decay, and the use of books over time causes mechanical degradation of the bindings. In some cases, as with iron gall ink, for example, individual (and integral) elements of the composite book will accelerate the degradation of the whole object, leading to loss of the information contained within. As such, many of these objects are in need of conservation treatment. Such work needs underpinning by an understanding of the interaction between the various materials and their environment, and the mechanisms involved. Although the individual components (e.g., paper, parchment) have been much studied, there has been less focus on the composite artifact.

In order to develop this activity in a specifically technological direction, we have brought together a national and international cluster of researchers who have studied the various components of the book as object, with the aim of sharing expertise, generating new interactions, and promoting interdisciplinary collaboration between researchers from the arts and humanities and those from science and heritage science disciplines. This volume documents discussions which took place between March and November 2009 at workshops and symposia organized by the

---

[1] see for example the web site of the Society for the History of Authorship, Reading, and Publishing, http://www.sharpweb.org

BookNET Research Cluster. We would like to express our thanks to everyone who participated in the activities of the Cluster, and gratefully acknowledge support provided by the Science and Heritage Programme, which is jointly funded by the Arts and Humanities Research Council (AHRC) and the Engineering and Physical Sciences Research Council (EPSRC).

Part One:
Manuscript Research Questions

Chapter 1

Curatorial Issues and Research Questions: Current Research on Western Medieval Manuscripts and Oriental Manuscripts in the Bodleian Library

Emilie Savage-Smith,[a] Sarah Neate[b,c] & Richard Ovenden[a]

[a] Department of Special Collections, Bodleian Library, University of Oxford
[b] Research Laboratory for Archaeology and the History of Art, University of Oxford
[c] Conservation and Collections Care, Bodleian Library, University of Oxford

Introduction

Research libraries contain millions of documents which have travelled through space and time to find their place on their shelves. These documents are frequently found in book form: individual pages bound together to preserve their contents in sequence, and to protect them from weather, wear and tear, and other forms of damage. But these 'books' also come in variant formats: sometimes as scrolls or folding portfolios, or as hinged groupings of other organic materials than the most commonly found substances of paper and parchment. As such, these documents are complex constructs which are often formed over lengthy periods of time, and with the involvement of many participants in their creation and evolution. Papermakers, scribes, illuminators, rubricators, bookbinders, and subsequent editors, censors, readers and owners may all have left the traces of their craft or trade, or otherwise of their interest in the volume. Pinning geographical location onto the individual components of such a complex object, at any given time in its history is therefore a further layer of complexity and difficulty.

Unravelling such questions has often been the task of the curator of a research library to undertake. They will often work closely with others to try to answer these questions: conservators are often the first ally of the curator, but members of the book trade, and individual scholars are often compelled by the same instincts as the curator in developing a detailed and nuanced understanding of books and manuscripts as historical artefacts of material culture. Such questions apply equally to manuscripts as to printed books, which can often betray as much complexity as manuscripts, with the additional difficulty of the involvement of printers, compositors and other related elements of the book trade. The scientific approaches which are detailed below promise to expand the armoury of the curator in investigation of the richness and complexity of the book.

Curatorial research questions and investigation methods

Of the 10,000 manuscript volumes from medieval Europe held in the Bodleian Library, most are written on parchment with only later ones, from the later 13th century onwards, on paper. Conversely, more Oriental manuscripts are written on paper, palm leaf and birch bark than parchment. However, whilst Western and Oriental manuscripts may differ materially and stylistically, the curatorial research questions are often similar. It is desirable both to conduct detailed studies of individual objects for the purposes of cataloguing, interpretation, and in the general support of researchers, and in so doing to be able to interpret the results with reference to the wider framework of related collections of objects.

The curatorial study of manuscripts often relies heavily on interpretations of the textual evidence, and on a stylistic analysis of the distinctive characteristics of script and decoration, with additional evidence provided by the study of line management, paper type, pricking and quires.[1] Most Western medieval manuscripts do not say when or where they were made, although some manuscripts have a scribal *colophon*, a statement written by the manuscript scribe, stating when and where the manuscript was copied, and often giving other details relating to the production of the manuscript, such as the scribe's name and the commissioner. As an example, the *Oppenheimer Siddur*, an owner-produced Hebrew prayer book held in the Bodleian Collections as shelf mark MS Opp. 776, has a colophon which states in Hebrew:

"I finished this prayer on the first day of the fourth month in the 231st year in the sixth millennium, according to the Creation era [28 June 1471]. I am Asher ben Rabbi Yitzhaq who requests this. It is my wish that my sons and the sons of my sons will pray to God with it..."[2]

Even where a colophon is not present, dating and localisation of an individual manuscript can often be determined to within half a century without scientific analysis, on the basis of comparison of script to known dated manuscripts. Illuminated manuscripts offer more information again, and can often be dated to decade, and even provenanced, on the basis of the decorative clues provided by the iconography or the particular style of the illumination. For example, the Northern Italian city of Ferrara, a major centre of manuscript illumination during the Renaissance period and the origin of the Ferrarese school of painting, produced illuminations which were characterised by a very distinctive floral style.

Where a colophon is not present, the output of stylistic dating is often a relative chronology rather than an absolute date, but combined with other evidence such as watermarks, annotations and inscriptions, offers a way of sorting groups of objects which can be more accurate than many scientific dating

---
[1] A quire is the basic structural unit of a medieval manuscript, comprising several folios folded together to create one smaller section of the text block.
[2] Colophon translation from Wijsman, 2009

methods. This is because the issue of dating is not a question which is solely materially focussed. Since stocks of material might have been held before they were used, and some types of manuscript such as palimpsests[3] clearly document the reuse of older materials, the textual evidence provided within a volume may provide a more accurate estimation of the date of manuscript *manufacture* than the actual material date of the writing surface. Equally, bindings and other organic materials (which may be thought suitable materials for scientific dating) may not be original to the manuscript and may have been added much later. So where can scientific analysis help curatorial research? The answer to this question lies in understanding what we *don't* know about the manuscript production process, and what may not be documented within a manuscript.

Potential applications of scientific analysis: selected case studies

Dating

Where there is insufficient evidence within a manuscript to provide a reasonable estimation of date, it may be beneficial to investigate the use of scientific dating techniques. One example of a potentially useful application of scientific dating methods would be for dating of the Bodleian Library's *Bakhshali manuscript* (MS Sansk. d.14). This is an extremely fragmentary Indian mathematical text of uncertain date, written on birch bark, which contains what *might* be the earliest documented use of the mathematical 'zero'. Estimations of the manuscript's age, as determined by mathematics and language scholars, vary between 200 AD and 1100 AD (see O'Connor & Robertson, 2000), but as yet no confirmation of the date of the manuscript has been possible.

Several manuscripts are also known to have more than one colophon, or evidence which suggests that the colophon is not genuine. Could analytical methods detect falsification of colophons by means of differentiating between the original ink and that used by a forger? An example is another manuscript held by the Bodleian Library, MS Marsh 137, which contains a false title page and colophon (dated 765/1363, but actually 17th century, a copy of the *Aphorisms* by Maimonides), illustrating the fictitious attempts by a copyist to create a provenance for the manuscript. This, of course, requires for comparison the testing of colophons/inks/papers whose age and place of production are secure using other criteria. Another Bodleian Library manuscript, MS Marsh 144, has two colophons, one of them giving a very early date which, if correct, would make it the earliest illustrated Arabic manuscript known to be preserved today. Can analytical investigation provide evidence that the ink used for the either colophon is contemporaneous with the text?

Provenance and localisation

The issue of localisation can be demonstrated with reference to two other manuscripts held by the Bodleian Library: MS Canon. Liturg. 383 and MS Can. Or. 62. MS Canon. Liturg. 383 is a Christian manuscript, written in 1470, and known to have been produced in Ferrara. The most famous manuscript to be produced in Ferrara was the Bible made for Duke Borso d'Este (see Johnson Wright, 2003 and van Boxel, 2009). MS Canon. Liturg. 383 is also richly decorated, having been produced for a Canon in Rome. MS Can. Or. 62, meanwhile, is a Hebrew Bible with Aramaic translation. Although the origin of the manuscript is unknown, the floral style of the decoration suggests that it may also have been produced in Ferrara. If pigment characterization can provide evidence that the Hebrew manuscript *was* illuminated in Ferrara, perhaps by the same workshop which illustrated MS Canon. Liturg. 383, we would not only have the means of locating the manuscript, but also of proving a direct cross-cultural social and economic interaction between two distinct religious groups.

Object biographies

The term 'provenance' also relates in a much wider sense to individual object biographies in addition to their region of production; the issues of ownership, the particular circumstances of manufacture, modifications or augmentations such as the later addition of gold leaf or amendments to the text. Whilst a colophon may provide documentary evidence relating to *some* of the circumstances of manufacture, there may be no corresponding evidence relating to other aspects of manuscript production, or the subsequent movements and ownership of the manuscript. An example of this is the previously cited *Oppenheimer Siddur* (MS Opp. 776), which, though known from the colophon to have been copied by Asher Ben Yitzhaq for his own private use, does not state who produced the illuminations. However, aspects of the manuscript's artwork and codicological features suggest that the scribe also may have been the illuminator. Could analytical assessment of pigments provide evidence to support this hypothesis? This is an interesting question, as there is evidence in many other Hebrew illuminated manuscripts that illustrations and painting were completed by non-Jewish illuminators (Wijsman, 2009).

Changes made to a manuscript during the course of its history can also add additional significance, and the Bodleian Library holds several examples of books commissioned or owned by royalty and leaders. This includes one manuscript, MS Hunt 264, which was commissioned by Saladin[4] in the 12th century and illustrates weapons and techniques of warfare. Investigation of faint inscriptions (either faded naturally or deliberately erased) can also provide clues to manuscript ownership and, although these can be difficult to see with the naked eye, may provide additional evidence for interpretation within an historical framework. Bindings are yet another aspect of the codex;[5] they present a different and complex set of features requiring examination, were often made using a number of different material types, and may have been added in a completely different geographical location to the original manuscript. Bindings are also often not contemporary with the manuscript itself. At present, one barrier to studying the bindings is the inability to interpret what can be observed- for

---

[3] Palimpsest: a writing surface which was deliberately reused, with the original text partly or completely erased before being overwritten.

[4] Saladin was the ruler and defender of Egypt during the 12th century European Crusades

[5] A codex is a bound manuscript volume (in comparison to other manuscript structures such as rolled papyri or scrolls).

example understanding the significance of observable patterns of sewing holes. This is particularly the case where rebinding has produced 'composite' manuscripts in which several individual manuscripts have been bound together. What were the circumstances for this? Who did it and why? Can studying the method or the materials used provide any evidence of where and when rebinding may have taken place? Many an Islamic codex is a hybrid of material, trimmed, rebound over the centuries, and often arranged in no apparent logical sequence. Could analysis indicate if individual separated folios may originally have been related?

Addressing wider curatorial issues using scientific methods

Moving on from a discussion of analytical techniques for investigating individual manuscripts, a much wider-ranging issue that could significantly benefit from scientific investigation relates to the organisation of manuscript production. This focus would undoubtedly inform any scientific assessment of individual manuscript provenance and localisation issues such as those discussed above. In order to understand how manuscript production was organised, it would be beneficial to have a method by which we can *sort* the individual materials used in manuscript production. That is, a method that will be able to distinguish between different manuscript workshops (assuming their materials *did* differ). The goal of such research is the definition of regional (or even individual) workshops. We want to know if there are sufficient measurable differences between inks, pigments, skins and papers of workshops at different locations and times to allow for meaningful differentiation between their products. If so, then we want to establish modern reference standards for medieval inks, papers, and pigments using dated and/or signed and located manuscripts, after which, it is hoped, we can then determine the probable time and place of production of an undated manuscript.

The identification and differentiation of workshops would, in turn, have major implications for our knowledge of the exchange of not only ideas, techniques and technologies, and the time required for them to reach one region from another, but also of the movement of the books themselves. There are implications for the analysis of products made by immigrant professional scribes. For example, if a scribe travelled from one region to another, the script from the home location might be maintained, while the writing materials and forms might change as the copyist adapted to the new locality.

In the Islamic world, medieval sources inform us that papers often had specific names, usually associated with a city of production, some more prized than others. Are such distinct types of paper evident? So far, we have not been able to identify them. There are obvious *visible* differences between various types of papers over time, but there has been no alignment with a workshop or even between the two great divisions of Arabic script, the Maghribi script associated with North Africa and al-Andalus and that used in the central and eastern realms. One of the things codicologists wish to know is whether scientific analysis can provide us with a more refined categorisation of papers than is now available through analysis of laid lines, chain lines, fibre distribution and watermarks. Papers used for certain high-quality illustrated 15th-century manuscripts from Shiraz (e.g. London, British Library, MS Add. 7759) have been described as 'Chinese paper'. Is there any analytical evidence to support this? Another aspect of such investigations would be characterisation and identification of products used historically to tint paper. Is there a wide divergence between tinted paper used in medieval codices and 19th-century North Indian paper tints? Are the tinted papers occurring in codices of treatises different from those employed in single-sheet miniatures?

Art historians have a slightly different perspective, for they are aiming to identify the palette of individual painters on the basis of signed and dated paintings or drawings (usually single-sheet miniatures) executed in ink and pigments and gold on paper, drawn by a particular artist, or connected by tradition or attribution with that artist. These paintings were usually never intended for inclusion in a codex but instead were destined to be in collections and bound into an album (sometimes now dispersed between different libraries). The single-sheets of non-codex material are easier to work with in terms of the application of available technologies, but the historical information potentially gained from them differs somewhat from that obtained from bound codices.

Analytical and interpretational limitations

Any investigation of collection-level research questions such as those relating to trends in manuscript production needs to take into account the interpretational limitations which are inherent in such studies. There are many features of manuscripts that we do not presently understand, and these complicate enormously the analysis of whatever data we obtain through technological analysis. We do not know if in fact there *was* a noticeable difference between the pigments, inks, and papers of different workshops. How much of it was shared and how much of it was distinctive to a particular time and place, we do not know. Such information, of course, is something we hope to learn by the application of science.

We also know little about the deterioration of a single batch of medieval ink or pigment over time, and since the inks/pigments were compounded individually and by hand, there could be great differences between batches. The attempts so far to apply scientific analysis to miniatures have been patchy (that is, just testing whatever is at hand) and have produced some confusing results. For example, J. D. MacArthur working at the research laboratory in the Louvre analysed the pigments of three miniature paintings that were signed by the same artist, and dated, but the elemental analysis of the pigments varied so much between the paintings that he could in no way imagine them to be the work of the same workshop not to mention the same artist.[6] In addition, we have no way of knowing how many times a scribe might have made a new batch in the course of copying a manuscript. We do not know how much within-

---

[6] This result was reported orally by Dr J. Duncan MacArthur (Department of Physics, Queen's University, Kingston, Canada) to the International Colloquium on the Scientific Analysis of Islamic Manuscripts, held at the University of Oxford in July of 1994. He was at that time conducting research at the Laboratoire de Recherche des Musées de France, Palais du Louvre, Paris.

page or within-codex variation (and hence within-workshop) there might be. For example, is it to be assumed that there is a constant and uniform method of mixing inks and pigments during the production of a manuscript? Is it to be assumed that contamination from dampness or soiling is insignificant? How valid are such assumptions? These and similar ideas should be foremost in our minds as we consider ways of applying modern scientific technologies to the analysis of historical manuscripts.

Analytical procedure

The aims and requirements discussed above reflect those of an historian or palaeographer wishing to apply scientific techniques to manuscripts. In this section, some procedures which might achieve those aims are outlined—based, to a large extent upon findings arising during a year-long grant from the Wellcome Trust in 1993-4 which funded a collaborative investigation between the Bodleian Library, (Department of Oriental Books and Manuscripts and the Department of Conservation) and the Scanning Proton Microprobe Unit of the Nuclear Physics Laboratory into the feasibility of using Particle Induced X-ray Emission (PIXE) analysis on an historical study of dated Islamic manuscripts. The same Wellcome Trust grant supported the subsequent International Colloquium on the Scientific Analysis of Islamic Manuscripts held in Oxford 7–9 July 1994.

Prior to undertaking examination of the manuscripts themselves, the Wellcome feasibility study and accompanying international conference concluded that four procedures should be carried out with whatever technology is selected, in order to demonstrate that the technique can produce satisfactory and reliable data of use to historians and codicologists:

1. Tests need to be conducted regarding the short-term and long-term residual effects of the technique upon the papers, ink, and pigments. It must be demonstrated that a technique does not cause potential damage to the material being tested. By definition, there will be some form of microscopic (or molecular) change, but whether *any* change is 'damage' needs to be addressed and consideration should be given to deciding what degree of change is acceptable. For example, in the early 1990's it was noted that PIXE sometimes produced brown spots at the test points which then faded to the naked eye; but these target areas were accidentally discovered to fluoresce when placed under ultraviolet light. Controlled experiments need to be conducted to further understand what is happening. Some pigments seem to interact with PIXE (saffron, for example). In other words, will the expected historical gain outweigh any change (harm) to the document? We, of course, hope it will.

2. A double blind experiment needs to be conducted with the chosen technique(s). Modern papers from different moulds and of different materials, on which there is writing in modern inks (both commercial and hand-made inks of different batches and recipes), and similarly with pigments, should be grouped and scrambled in a manner *unknown* to the technician operating the equipment *and* the person analysing the results, in order to see if the technique in question could sort the papers, inks, and pigments into the correct sets on the basis of their elemental composition as revealed by the technology. This is, after all, what the historian and codicologist is wanting.

3. Modern papers on which different inks and pigments were applied, should then be exposed to artificial aging or to contamination by other substances to see if test results are affected by these changes.

4. Test results need to be replicated in different laboratories. Material should be taken between laboratories using the same techniques in order to establish a 'standard' by which equipment can be calibrated.

Once those qualifications are met and everyone is satisfied with the ability of the technology to deliver usable data, then and only then (it was concluded) should work begin on manuscripts.

Whatever the project and whatever the technique, a team consisting of codicologists and historians as well as a statistician *must* be part of the design and running of the project. Additional problems arise if deliberate selectivity of 'suitable' manuscript material is undertaken prior to analysis. While physically analyzing full-page paintings or dis-bound single sheets may be easier (given the configuration of the equipment), they present in a certain way a more complex set of problems as far as sampling methods are concerned. Unless the research project is being designed by an art historian looking at single-sheet paintings, the examination should not be limited to loose sheets—for this completely skews the results when the aim is to study the production of codices. In order to build up a collection of usable data, the next step, if you are studying codices, is to begin by analysing only manuscripts securely dated by standard palaeographical methods. Testing should be confined to areas believed to be part of the original text (not marginalia, repairs, etc). Codices, of course, require a special cradle for holding the volume in a position for the testing to be conducted. A suitable cradle was designed for the Bodleian Library in 1993-4 by the Scanning Proton Microprobe Unit, under the supervision of the Conservation Department of the Bodleian, following but modifying a model designed earlier at the PIXE laboratory in Florence.[7]

For each manuscript selected, a visual morphology must be recorded—employing the naked eye, a hand lens, and oblique light to record physical features. Such information is then to be correlated with whatever physical tests are made. However, care should be taken to ensure that the descriptions of each item from a codicological or palaeographic viewpoint do not become so detailed that the project comes to a halt. Priority should be given to the recording of paper structure: thickness,[8] translucency,[9] laid lines, chain lines *and* distinctive letter forms

---
[7] For a photograph of the cradle, see Jarjis 1996, p. 103
[8] Using a micrometer on undamaged folios and recording the upper and lower range of several readings.
[9] The opaqueness, or translucency, of the paper can be assigned a value on the Sharp Scale of Opaqueness. The latter is a recently devised method (named

Watermarks, when present, should be recorded as precisely as possible.[10] All of this information should be stored securely along with photographs of sample writing, the colophon, and distinctive features of the manuscript. At present there are few on-line databases but it is to be hoped that these will soon be developed on a larger scale.[11] When they become available, data relating to the materiality of the manuscripts could equally be recorded in the database alongside the relevant codicological information.

Project design

The *design* of analytical projects is fundamentally important to the long term success of any programme of technological analysis. Here the statistician is as important as the codicologist and the scientist. The codicologist can determine critical parts of a manuscript, the statistician determines the nature and size of the sample and the natural variation of the population so as to produce confidence in the results, the scientist determines the scientific technology to be employed. Whatever the questions posed for the investigation, a statistician must be involved at all stages in order to assure that the results have a historical validity. The determination of what type of samples and how many are taken is crucial to obtaining a result that is statistically significant. This might involve total random sampling, carefully controlled points, or a combination of the two. To date, the application of scientific techniques to books and manuscripts has been most fruitful when a specific question is asked. For example, the Florence laboratory used PIXE to test the hypothesis that the ink in Galileo's notes on motion correlates in elemental composition with his dated letters, revising the *order* in which the letters were written, not their actual *dating* (see Giuntini *et al.* 1995; Lucarelli and Mandò, 1996: 650-652). In the initial phase of any new project, it might be wise to begin with a similar, rather specific problem, to see if the technique can be successfully applied.

Conclusions

The textual and stylistic study of manuscripts often enables a complete assessment of the age, provenance and cultural origins of individual manuscripts held in library collections, and renders scientific investigation unnecessary in many cases. However, there are many isolated occasions where issues of dating, localisation and significance cannot be resolved using existing curatorial methods, because evidence contained within the manuscript is either incomplete, contradictory or ambiguous. Where this is the case, the use of scientific techniques could be of significant benefit in answering these questions. There are, however, much wider ranging questions which could be addressed using scientific techniques. Historians and codicologists primarily want to know if there are sufficient measurable differences between inks, pigments, and papers of workshops at different locations and times to allow for meaningful differentiation between their products. To achieve this, we must *first* make certain that the assessing technique is capable of detecting *significant* differences between products, in order to ensure that the results are meaningful. The technique must also have a sufficiently low error term, must be globally applicable, and, if conducted *in situ*, must produce no damage to the material being tested.

Acknowledgements

The authors would like to thank Martin Kauffmann, Gillian Evison and Piet van Boxel from the Bodleian Library, and Suzanne Wijsman, University of Western Australia, for reviewing the text and providing helpful comments.

References

Giuntini, L., Lucarelli, F., Mandò, P. A., Hooper, W. and Barker, P. H. 1995 Galileo's writings: chronology by PIXE. *Nuclear Instruments and Methods in Physics Research B* **95**, 389-392

Jarjis, R. 1996 Ion-Beam Codicology: its Potential in Developing Scientific Conservation in Islamic Manuscripts. *The Conservation and Preservation of Islamic Manuscripts: Proceedings of the Third Conference of al-Furqān Islamic Heritage Foundation, 1995* (London: Al-Furqān Islamic Heritage Foundation, 1996), 93–117.

Johnson Wright, A. 2003 *The Bible of Borso d'Este: Christian Piety and Political Rhetoric in Quattrocento Ferrara.* Ann Arbor, Northumberland.

Lucarelli, F and Mandò, P.A. 1996 Recent applications to the study of ancient inks with the Florence external PIXE facility. *Nuclear Instruments and Methods in Physics Research B* **109/110**, 644-652.

van Boxel, P. 2009 The Virgin and the Unicorn. In *Crossing Borders; Hebrew Manuscripts as a Meeting Place of Cultures*, Chapter 5. Bodleian Library exhibition accompaniment edited by Piet w. van Boxel and Sabine Arndt. Bodleian Library, Oxford.

Wijsman, S. 2009 The Oppenheimer Siddur: Artist and scribe in a 15th century Hebrew prayer book. In *Crossing Borders; Hebrew Manuscripts as a Meeting Place of Cultures,* Chapter 6. Bodleian Library exhibition accompaniment edited by Piet w. van Boxel and Sabine Arndt. Bodleian Library, Oxford

Woodward, D. 1990 The Correlation of Watermark and Paper Chemistry in Sixteenth-Century Italian Printed Maps. *Imago Mundi* **42**, 1990, 84–93.

---

after its originator, Henrietta Sharp) by which the translucency of paper can be categorized in terms of the number of folios required before the outline of a dowel held behind the folio(s) is no longer visible when illuminated from behind with a constant light of 60 watts at an approximate distance of 15 cm.

[10] A simple 15-watt light bulb technique employing photographic paper was devised by David Woodward; for an example used on Bodleian Library MS Pococke 110, see Jarjis 1996, p. 109.

[11] In 2000 the University of Oxford Computing Centre supervised the production of a proto-database that formed a Master's dissertation (Weilan Tang, *Islamic Codicological Database & Imagebank – Pilot Project*, MSc dissertation, University of Portsmouth, 2000). This effort was not in the event put on-line, but it could form a starting point for such a database. One on-line codicological database which is currently under construction is Sfardata, the searchable database of the Hebrew Palaeography Project of the Israel Academy of Sciences and Humanities. This can be accessed at http://sfardata.nli.org.il/sfardataweb/frmLogin.aspx

Chapter 2

Conservation Issues and Research Questions: the Role of Analysis in Book and Manuscript Conservation

Sarah Neate[a,b] & David Howell[b]

With contributions from Cheryl Porter[c] & Nicholas Pickwoad[d]

[a.] Research Laboratory for Archaeology and the History of Art, University of Oxford
[b.] Conservation and Collections Care, Bodleian Library, University of Oxford
[c.] Thesaurus Islamicus Foundation & Dar al-Kutub Manuscript Project, Cairo
[d.] Ligatus Research Centre, University of the Arts, London

Introduction

In the conservation profession the number of scientific analyses carried out on different types of object and in different environments varies greatly. In easel paintings for instance, it is almost routine to analyse pigments and binders. It is not uncommon for textiles to undergo dye analysis as well as fibre identification. In archaeology and archaeological conservation, analysis is often fundamental to unlocking the information contained in many different types of artefact. Knowledge of materials and their state of decay can often influence both interventive and preventive conservation strategies. For instance, knowing whether a textile is cellulosic or proteinaceous may dictate the choice of detergent and suggest a suitable pH for wet cleaning. Items known to contain silver may need to be kept in an environment where there is no hydrogen sulphide present, whilst different types of photographic film need to be identified prior to storage because cellulose nitrate film is extremely flammable and requires special storage conditions.

For a number of reasons, however, the field of manuscript and paper conservation has not embraced analysis to the same extent, despite the huge range of materials and the interesting questions that could be addressed. Rather than dwell on why this should be, perhaps it is more important to outline the reasons why we should consider the analysis of this type of material, and the issues which need to be considered when dealing with valuable manuscripts.

Why analyse 'book' material?

The textual and stylistic content of manuscript material has long been the main focus of curatorial research into book material, with a particular and understandable focus on manuscripts which were written by hand before the advent of the printing press. Such manuscripts, which are typically of medieval origin or earlier, are of course getting older and may require intervention by a conservator in order to ensure their survival. The key to successful intervention is to understand the materials on which manuscripts are written, allowing them to be treated successfully (ie. preventing active damage from progressing further), repaired sympathetically, in a way which takes into account material stresses and the impact of degradation mechanisms, and to enable provision of a storage environment which is most appropriate for the specific materials used. Alongside this, the identification and further investigation of the materials and methods used to create the manuscript may provide further information about the circumstances of manufacture, allowing books to be viewed as historical artefacts as well as conveyors of textual information.

The study of books as objects falls well within the professional remit of the conservator for two reasons. Firstly, the use of analytical techniques to investigate the materials present is merely an extension of the close material assessment performed during a conservation treatment. Secondly, since the conservator's responsibility is to ensure the long term preservation of manuscripts which are held in the library environment, they are ideally placed to advise on the implications of different analytical procedures on the safety of a manuscript and to suggest ways of minimising damage. However, because analysis in this field is so under-developed, it is perhaps regarded with a degree of suspicion and scepticism; all too often, when analysis is conducted on library material, the results take so long to arrive that they are no longer relevant to current research questions, and other solutions will have been found to solve particular problems. Opportunities have also not been made to investigate objects, and answers have not been forthcoming for this reason. This makes it difficult for end users to formulate questions which analysis could help answer, and to see where the information would be usefully applied. We have a kind of "chicken and egg" situation: until we start using analytical techniques we cannot provide information, but until we see the worth of that information it is difficult to justify the analysis. This is especially the case where there is any risk of damage to manuscripts.

Conservation challenges

For analysis to be undertaken successfully within libraries, it must be justifiable within the wider remit of the library to preserve and understand the items in the collection. It must also be performed in a manner which is acceptable to the conservation department, which is charged with maintaining the integrity and condition of the objects in its care. Many libraries (more so than museums and art galleries) have a strict, non-interventive approach to conservation. Conservation ethics dictate that nothing should be done that doesn't necessarily need doing, and that any intervention should be reversible. It can be difficult to fit analysis within this.

Attitudes and policies can only be changed by providing sound evidence to support the benefits of analysis, and the processes used must shield the manuscript as far as possible from accidental damage caused by handling and analysis. Analysis of small samples of material taken from the manuscript is possible in some cases (such as when bindings have been removed and replaced during conservation treatment), but for visible, decorated areas of a manuscript, non-invasive analysis is often pursued as the preferred option, despite the constraints involved. Since non-invasive analysis requires the use of analytical equipment directly on a manuscript, there are more rigorous controls associated with this analytical approach. There should be as little physical contact as possible between the analytical instrumentation and the manuscript, and there should be no obvious physical damage resulting from the analytical process, or alteration of any of the structures and compounds contained within. Because of high insurance costs and personnel requirements involved with transportation of high value manuscripts, *in situ* analysis can often only take place within the library setting.

There are also budgetary issues to consider. When resources are limited it is much easier to justify expenditure on improving an object's environment or repairing it than performing analysis. Budget holders need to be persuaded that analysis represents good value for money; that as a result of analysis we now have knowledge that may have required years of curatorial research, or answers which could not be provided by other means. We want to know that our objects will last longer because analysis proved they were made of a particular material requiring special treatment; that we can 'use' an object differently because we analysed the risks. There has to be a cost benefit or intellectual payback. Additionally, any analytical equipment which is purchased by libraries needs to be directly applicable to a wide range of material in order to be cost effective. It should either cater for different manuscript formats- for example bound manuscripts, large format maps, single sheets and fragile materials such as papyri- or be capable of bulk condition assessment of the largest groups of objects, such as open shelf and lending collections (i.e. non-Special Collection material). The 'mass analysis' of collection material for the 'general good' is perhaps most easy to justify, but is usually expensive and time consuming. Mass condition analysis is usually only associated with large funded projects on paper-based materials such as Survenir,[1] but can be extremely useful for justifying treatments, directing funds and for generally improving conservation management and planning. At the other end of the spectrum, extra-ordinary analysis on individual items can be justified on the basis of manuscript importance and significance, and can be useful in generating funding to allow remedial conservation treatment and/or exhibition.

There is therefore a role for analysis within conservation. Book and paper conservation is a highly developed specialism, but there is much to be learnt about compatibility of materials, especially the use of modern materials in conservation, and the application of new technologies. This relies on the adoption of a scientific approach rather than the traditional craft dominated approach. The major remits of the conservation profession are to maintain the integrity of an object, and to understand the materials present in an object and treat them appropriately. With Special Collection items particularly, every object is absolutely unique, representing a different context of production and a different object history. Every effort needs to be taken to preserve this uniqueness; this is the underlying principle of conservation. Knowing what it is made of, how and when it was made, and how these parameters compare with objects of a similar type can enhance the apparent significance of a book or manuscript. Analysis can therefore do more to add to an object's significance and well-being than it risks taking away, with increased intellectual access to collection materials and knowledge dissemination to a far wider and more varied audience. In this way, other aspects of manuscript 'value' can be explored. It is worth noting here that 'damage' is a risk in all areas of object interaction and access, and that risk from sampling or analysis should not be taken in isolation; in the library environment, recalling a manuscript from its storage location, providing it to readers who may support it inexpertly, displaying in an exhibition and loaning to other institutions are all aspects of day-to-day manuscript interaction which can cause damage, yet this damage is deemed acceptable because it can be monitored and controlled. This approach can equally apply to the analysis of manuscripts.

Analysis logistics

In order for analysis to be successfully achieved, there are certain procedural and communication stages that are absolutely necessary and which if not adhered to will cause problems later on. It is important, for example, that both development of the research question and liaison between curatorial staff, analysts and conservators takes place prior to analysis being agreed. This ensures that the analysis is necessary to answer the research question posed, and involves specifying an area or particular deposit which is suitable for analysis, in order to analyse the appropriate place. A visual assessment of the object is useful to assess condition and suitability of the object to undergo either sampling or *in situ* analysis, and also to indicate the presence of factors such as over-painting or varnish layers which may hinder the analysis.

Where samples are removed from a manuscript for analysis, there is no direct risk to the manuscript during analysis. As such, this approach can be safer for the manuscript as a whole, but will inevitably involve the removal of a small section of material. In this case, visual assessment of the object will determine if sample removal is possible with an acceptable aesthetic impact on the manuscript (where possible, samples should be taken from less visible areas of the manuscript). The logistics of sample taking should then be discussed with curators and other interested parties, with permission sought prior to sample removal using agreed methods.

In situ analysis requires a considerable amount of planning and preparation before analysis can commence, including:

- Development of an analysis plan

---

[1] See Chapter 6 of this volume

Sequential progression through a written plan during analysis will ensure that all of the areas of interest are investigated, minimising the need to reanalyse (and therefore re-handle) at a later date. It can also be useful to plan analysis by placing a transparent melinex© grid over a photograph of the object for recording and annotation purposes. The logistics of analysis are also an important consideration at this point; how the object should be supported, what equipment should be used and in what order, who is responsible for object safety, where the object will be stored when not in use and what the instrumental settings should be, if this is a necessary concern. All personnel should understand their role and the role of the others involved. The safety of the manuscript can be compromised by those involved getting in each other's way, and duplicating processes increases both the time and money involved. Analysis can be extremely expensive and the more streamlined the operation, the better. At this point, permissions may need to be obtained from the curator to remove the object from its usual location, as well as informing anyone who may have a vested interest in the object.

- Scenario testing ('Dummy run')

If the equipment has not been used before, or the operator has no experience with handling and analysis of manuscript material, it may be useful to test the equipment and the protocol first using low value material such as modern parchment samples or a mass-produced (non-collection) book of similar size to the object requiring analysis. This is also useful in the case of very large objects and complex three-dimensional structures, where placement under analytical equipment may involve more than one person. At this stage, it might become obvious that the proposed analytical work is not going to be feasible for some other reason, for example equipment failure or lack of personnel. In this case, the manuscript itself can be left undisturbed until analysis can be rescheduled.

- Equipment preparation

Some analytical equipment requires a particular 'set-up' or calibration procedure to be undertaken prior to analysis. Any action of this nature should be performed before the manuscript is laid out ready for analysis, to prevent unnecessary exposure or accidental damage.

Following analysis, it is important that the results are communicated as soon as possible to interested parties, and that they are interpreted if necessary within the historical context so that the significance of the results can be understood. This is of major benefit in justifying analytical work which has been done, and enabling future analytical work to be conducted. An analytical report should be kept on file and be readily available for researchers to access.

Conservation research questions

Analysis of pigments and inks - Cheryl Porter

Of all scientific research questions applied to 'book' material, the analysis of pigments on illuminated manuscripts is perhaps most often reported in the scientific literature. The reason for this is that the research appeals to a number of audiences. To a chemist, maybe working outside a heritage environment in a University department, carrying out analysis is an academic challenge. The development of *in situ* analytical techniques and the validation of the analysis is very often an end in itself. This is no bad thing, but most people working in the heritage sector want something else, some other sort of information that would lead to a better understanding of the book and its history. For archaeologists and art historians, analysis and comparison of the pigments on manuscripts with those on other objects promotes the integration of library artefacts within the wider cultural heritage and allows deeper investigation of mutually interesting research questions, such as pigment provenance and trade, technological development of pigment manufacturing techniques and temporal and regional patterns of pigment usage.

An important reason that conservators need to analyse colour is for the purpose of exhibitions: ideally, the conservator should have some input not only into how the book will be exhibited, but also which page of the manuscript will be exhibited. In order to be able to advise on this, it is imperative that some information about the way that colours behave and react in an exhibition situation is understood.

For example:

- Orpiment, that most reactive of colours has a tendency to fade in light. Not only that, but it can also become chemically reactive in high relative humidity (RH)[2] and react with other colours.
- Red lead is known to fade to pink and then to a cream colour in slightly high RH.
- Organic colours will fade quickly, and the closer a colour is to the yellow end of the spectrum, the faster it will fade – so any manuscript page designated for exhibition should preferably be one without any organic yellows.

Then there is the question of treatments. It is important to know what it is on your manuscript that might react to any treatments that involve changes in pH.

After more than 20 years of research and analytical experience in the field of analysing colour in manuscripts, I think I can speak with some authority about the relative merits of the various analytical machinery and techniques. I believe I was the first person to use Raman Spectroscopy for pigment analysis in manuscripts (see Porter, 1992), and I have continued to use Raman, as well as XRF, UV- Visible spectroscopy, infrared photography and other 'non-destructive' tools. I have now come to the conclusion that the least harmful method is for a qualified conservator to take micro-samples for analysis. Let me explain this: it is not good enough simply to have access to a machine that can analyse 'non-destructively', because in

---

[2] Relative humidity (RH) is a term which describes the relationship between the moisture content of the air and the temperature, since warm air can hold more moisture than cold air. It is expressed as a percentage which relates to the maximum amount of water that the air can hold at a given temperature; therefore an RH of 100% means that the air surrounding an object is saturated with moisture. To decrease the RH, either the air temperature must be increased or water removed from the air.

reality these are rarely feasible and hardly available tools for manuscript study. The most important consideration when carrying out *in situ* or 'non-destructive' analysis is that the manuscript can be positioned comfortably, without causing strain or damage to the binding or any part of the manuscript structure. I have often been shocked to see how manuscripts are manipulated during these 'non-destructive' analytical sessions and it is a sad fact that in these situations, the results obtained and the machinery used very often take precedence over the needs of the manuscript itself. The potential for damage in these situations is far greater than is generally thought, especially if there is no conservator present to defend the manuscript.

After speaking at this BookNET Research Cluster symposium, it was interesting that many of the experts present felt that the simplest and least destructive methods for analysis were those commonly defined as 'destructive'. In all honesty, who knows what are the long-term effects of lasers and other high frequency analytical methods on organic materials? In short, I think that the safest and best way to proceed is to take micro-samples – so small that they can hardly be seen by the naked eye. In this case, we know precisely what 'damage' we are doing, and if the work is done sympathetically, by an experienced conservator in an area where the colour is already in difficulty and shedding from the page, I would whole-heartedly support the method.

There are also areas that 'non-destructive' analytical methods cannot address. In the main, these involve organic colours and binders. In my opinion, it is precisely the analysis of these components that is providing the most useful data for manuscript historians and for manuscript conservators. An important methodological and interpretive issue to mention is that, although there are several research projects being conducted on colour in manuscripts, there appears to be no co-ordination of the results and consequently, limited benefit for the conservator or for anyone else who might benefit from the information gathered. It would be useful for us all if some sort of databank could be established for the results of this research.

Skin and parchment: species identification – Nicholas Pickwoad

An investigation of the analytical methods which might be used to identify animal species, age at time of slaughter, methods of parchment preparation and geographical origin would greatly benefit the assessment of animal skins used in the manufacture of books. There is a perceived chasm in our knowledge of the origins of the skin materials used in the construction of books, and my own work has revealed how little we know about the sources of the skins used for both writing and printing on and for bookbinding. The literature is full of more or less well-informed speculation, with animals such as deer, seals and reindeer offered as alternatives to the more typical calf, sheep, goat and pig, but not necessarily with any scientific justification. Clearly perceptible differences in the skins from the same species of animal may be the result of both manufacturing processes as well as the breed and origin of the animal whose skin has been used, but these differences are often difficult for the non-specialist to define. Indeed, the identification of the main animal species used is often unreliable.

The ability to be more precise about the origins of the skins used would aid in the localisation of books and bindings, would throw light on the trade connections that must have existed in support of the book trade and how the manufacture of books interacted with different practices in animal husbandry. It could also explore how the production of animal skins as parchment, tanned or alum-tawed products was tailored to meet the demands of the book trade or *vice-versa*. There is evidence, for instance, in the use of small pieces of coloured skin as sewing supports that bookbinders were using skins made for another purpose, such as tailoring or glove-making, where colour would have been desirable. The identification of dyestuffs and other colouring materials could form part of any research project and help with the more accurate description of books.

Information on the manufacturing processes used and the effect these had on the appearance and handling characteristics of the skins might allow us to understand why, for instance, so many Oxford bindings of the later sixteenth and early seventeenth centuries are bound in dark brown calfskin – was it because of a stylistic preference or a local availability of leather made in a particular way? Was the increasing thinness of the skins used through the seventeenth and eighteenth centuries the research of changes in husbandry or the shaving or splitting of the skins? Did binders have access to skins from animals of different ages to suit different sizes of books? These are questions which is it hoped such a research project could help to answer.

"Reading" unopened books and scrolls

The ability to "read" unopened books and scrolls using techniques such as CT scanning, MRI scanning and X-Ray microtomography would have many uses in conservation. There are many instances where parchment pages have fused together as a result of incorrect storage conditions, or where an excavated manuscript is so friable that any attempt to open it would result in considerable material loss or structural damage. Books equally can be damaged by fire and other unplanned events, and can suffer restricted access through past 'treatments', as is the case with medieval manuscripts in heavily glued nineteenth-century bindings. Another source of hidden written and printed material, access to which poses a substantial threat to the preservation of bindings, is what is known as 'binders' waste', that is leaves or fragments of earlier material incorporated into bindings as endleaves, linings or, more especially, board laminations, and which are often visually inaccessible in the bindings.

A possible research area would therefore be an investigation of different techniques to see what might be of use to the bibliographical world. With greater definition, for instance, it may be possible to produce an image of the cross-section of a bound parchment manuscript which would allow it to be collated without being opened. This would provide a means of assessing the construction and significance of a manuscript in order to justify expensive treatments.

Condition assessment

The condition of objects is routinely 'measured' by visual examination. But quite often in conservation assessments of organic material the measurement of pH is routinely carried out. If this were to be carried out to accepted 'standard' protocols, the tests used would be destructive, and require quite significant amounts of material. Over a number of decades, several safer and non-destructive tests have been developed using increasingly small contact areas and very small amounts with water (since the tests have to be conducted in an aqueous environment). Whilst this could pedantically be described as 'destructive', because ions from the object have to be solubilised in order for the measurement to be taken, this minute intervention is considered to be worthwhile for the value of the information gleaned.

More sophisticated non-destructive methods such as Near Infrared (NIR) spectroscopy and X-Ray Diffraction have been used for monitoring degradation, perhaps most successfully in the Survenir project. These techniques are difficult and expensive to develop, and the finished 'product', either a piece of equipment or a sophisticated database, are expensive to access and currently outside the budgets of most institutions. These techniques offer real opportunities for developing conservation management and planning tools, useful for justifying treatments and directing funds. However there either needs to be more funding to develop more cost effective alternatives, or funding to provide grants to enable the purchase of expensive 'equipment' for condition assessment of library material.

Assessing interventive treatments

Over the last two decades there has been a gradual change in emphasis from interventive conservation research (ie. developing novel techniques for stabilising objects), to preventive research (ie. research into the effects of the environment and pollutants on object longevity). This is partly driven by an increasing desire to be less interventive and leaving the objects as much as possible as they are, partly by a number of instances where intervention has been ill-advised and harmful to objects, and partly because preventive actions are seen to be better for the greater good of the collection as a whole rather than focussing on the needs of individual objects.

But most collections house a great many objects that are already 'broken' in some way and although preventive action can slow down or prevent further damage it cannot undo damage that has already happened. For this reason we still need to carry out interventive treatments, but we must ensure that they are appropriate and safe. To that end the analytical evaluation of objects before, during and after treatment is essential, but sadly rarely available or implemented. Of note are the European funded projects, Inkcor which investigated the stabilization of Iron Gall ink, and PaperTreat evaluating mass de-acidification techniques on paper based material.[3] These projects demonstrate how analysis allows the success of different conservation approaches to be assessed and enables the development of new, more effective techniques for use on library material. There is the added advantage that research does not need to be performed directly on library material or in the library environment; modern materials can often be used in conjunction with accelerated aging techniques, and research can take place elsewhere, experimentally, but directly influencing the conservation strategies for the future.

Conclusions

The discussions held during meetings of the BookNET Research Cluster were intended to provide a statement for the current state of research and to develop a research framework for future study into the materiality of the book as a physical object. The remit of conservation, meanwhile, is to understand the material held in collections and preserve it for future access; a remit that can be directly benefited in certain areas by the controlled use of analytical techniques in order to allow deeper understanding of the materials we conserve. The conservation research questions listed in this paper can be divided into two main research areas: archaeometric research- ie. that which links with other, wider areas of heritage and archaeological materials research and provides a means for identifying, locating and investigating the materials used to create books- and those which concentrate on monitoring and assessment of the physical objects themselves in order to allow future interpretation to take place or to direct funding appropriately. What does not emerge from the account of discussions above is the amount of debate, some of it quite passionate, about the merits and necessities of sampling and 'destructive' testing. Whilst many participants were keen to promote analytical study of the book, some participants in the discussion were absolutely and fundamentally opposed to any type of sampling for whatever reason and pointed to past unsuccessful attempts as their rationale. Others argued the benefits in terms of useful information and progressing the profession for a very small 'loss' of material, which was argued to be less destructive than attempting to conduct complicated analysis *in situ*. There were a variety of opinions as to how much information could be elucidated by analysis that couldn't be obtained by simpler non-destructive means. Another body of thought suggested that by waiting for longer the analytical procedures would be improved and even tinier samples would be required. This initiated a much more open debate on the use of our collections and their purpose. As digitisation becomes much more prevalent, the book as a medium for words is all but redundant. The book as a source of information about when things were written, how objects were manufactured, how materials were traded and transported, and use of different materials in different workshops and regions is an area ripe for discovery.

Whichever analytical approach is pursued in individual cases, it must be stressed that studying the materiality of books has to be done responsibly, with real collaboration between analysts and library staff, and sharing of results. The research questions investigated by analytical means must have sufficient scholarly merit to justify the methods employed, and be discussed with conservation staff and other interested parties to ensure that

---

[3] see Chapter 6 of this volume for further information

the benefit of the results obtained outweighs any risk to the objects.

References

Porter, C. 1992 Laser Raman spectroscopy- a tool for non-destructive pigment analysis of manuscripts. *The Paper Conservator* **16**, 93-97

Part Two:
Introduction to Manuscript Analysis Techniques

Chapter 3

Principles and Methods of Analysis in Archaeological and Manuscript Studies

Sarah Neate[a,b] & A. M. Pollard[a]

[a.] Research Laboratory for Archaeology and the History of Art, University of Oxford
[b.] Conservation and Collections Care, Bodleian Library, University of Oxford

Introduction and background: analytical techniques used in archaeological studies

The use of chemical analysis in archaeology has a long and distinguished history, stretching back at least as far as the 18th century. It has also involved some of the great names of European science, such as Michael Faraday, Marcelin Bertholet and August von Kekulé. Initially applied as a method of answering the apparently simple question 'what is this object made from', research has expanded into a range of more challenging questions such as 'how was it made?', where was it made?', and 'what was it used for?'. Perhaps most challengingly of all, it is now part of the general enquiry about why an object was made, how was it used, and how it played a role in the material culture of a particular society. Most of the early applications consisted of the analysis of archaeological objects made of inorganic materials (e.g., metals, glass, ceramics, lithics), but from the mid-19th century onwards the scope was broadened to include organic materials – initially amber, but subsequently ivory, jet, and bone. From there it was a natural extension into biomolecular archaeology, studying collagen, DNA and amino acids in bone, and a wide range of organic residues found in, for example, ceramic cooking vessels. From the early part of the 20th century, chemical analysis was also applied to landscape archaeology to ascertain the location of human activity by the enhancement of phosphorus in the soil, and this has subsequently been extended to multi-element soil maps, and also amino acid distributions as evidence of repeated human activity. For a general introduction to archaeological chemistry, see Pollard and Heron (2008, chapter 1).

In the early days of chemical analysis, all such activity was by its very nature destructive. The main method of analysis up until the 20th century was gravimetry, in which a part of the object is dissolved and the various constituents precipitated out sequentially and weighed. A sample, and sometimes the whole object, had to be sacrificed for knowledge to be gained. With the arrival of instrumental methods of analysis from the 1930s onwards, sample requirements have been gradually reduced until now microanalysis using laser ablation (removing a microscopic amount of material) is now routinely available. Some investigative methods are still essentially destructive – particularly if spatial information is required, such as the metallography of a metal artefact, or a cross-section through pigment layers on a wall painting. In these cases a small sample is removed, mounted and polished for optical or electron microscopy. Even here, however, there is a move towards minimising damage, through the application of non-invasive 3D imaging techniques such as neutron radiography.

As a consequence, the standards of acceptability for invasive sampling have changed dramatically over the last forty years. Gone are the days when the analysis of a Bronze Age copper halberd required the object to be sawn in half. Sampling is still a matter for discussion with curators and conservators, and the preference is always for non-destructive means of analysis where possible; however, in archaeological research it is acknowledged that sampling is sometimes inevitable, and is routinely performed to answer certain questions. The general acceptability of sampling in the context of archaeological research results from a recognition of the increased need for analytical techniques to provide answers to research questions which cannot be obtained by other means. Since the vast majority of archaeological objects represent the only evidence for a period of prehistory for which there is no documentary record, the material record becomes not only the best source of information for technological development, trading patterns, and other aspects of materiality, but also proxy evidence for the identity and ideology of a society. It is therefore incumbent upon us to maximise the evidence we can extract from the material remains of past cultures, and chemical analysis is one of the tools which is employed.

Analytical priorities in archaeological materials research

In the second half of the 20th century, in an attempt to minimize the damage to museum objects, strenuous efforts were made to re-design commercial instruments (or even build new designs from scratch) to enable as far as possible the non-destructive analysis of whole objects. Nowadays this is less necessary, since most commercial instrumentation requires minimal sampling, as discussed above. In many ways, therefore, the analytical priorities for archaeological analysis are no different from any other form of material analysis, apart from the fact that, as in forensic science, one must be conscious at all times of the potential unique and irreplaceable nature of the sample. In archaeological, just as in any other materials science, therefore, the selection of equipment for analysis is determined by four main factors, although cost and availability are inevitably also a consideration:

- Spatial resolution
- Analytical sensitivity
- Diagnostic capability
- Repeatability/analytical reliability

Spatial resolution is a critical factor if the compositional variation across a surface (e.g., a cross section) is important, and is related to the diameter of the analytical beam employed (e.g., the size of the electron beam in an electron microscope).

A resolution of 5 microns implies that the beam is capable of analysing an area around 5 microns in diameter, which means that the instrument can distinguish the compositions of particles as small as 5 microns, or between adjacent areas about 10 microns apart. This is an important consideration in the analysis of heterogeneous structures such as metallographic sections, or paint cross-sections.

Analytical sensitivity is a measure of the smallest amount of a particular element the technique can measure. It will depend on the element itself, and the matrix that it is in. Most techniques have wide variations in sensitivity between elements, often depending systematically on the position of the element in the periodic table, but sometimes on other factors. It is usually expressed as a figure such as 0.02%, or 30 parts per million (ppm), depending on the concentration range of the element being measured, and represents the smallest amount of that element which can be detected in that particular type of sample.

Diagnostic capability refers to the ability of a particular instrument to measure a particular element, isotope or molecule with sufficient sensitivity to be able to answer the analytical question posed. It is therefore dependant not only on the analytical sensitivity, but also on the context of the question. For example, it would be pointless to try to measure the "trace element" composition of a pigment if the technique used is not sensitive enough to detect trace elements. Equally, the investigation of complex organic residues is best furthered using methods which allow the determination of molecular structures rather than elemental composition, since organic materials and deposits often consist of a very limited range of elements arranged in different ways within a molecular structure. This is simply to state, therefore, that the method employed should be capable of giving the required answer.

Repeatability and analytical reliability are factors which are a conflation of the measurements of accuracy and precision. Crudely speaking, precision is the degree to which repeated measurements on the same sample give the same answers (which over a long period of time can be termed repeatability), whereas accuracy is the degree to which the answer is close to the 'correct' value. A reliable technique is both precise and accurate.

Sample preparation is often necessary prior to analysis, as this allows separation of the investigated material from any other materials it was associated with on the object, as well as processing to remove any potential contaminants. Grinding or polishing a sample to regularise the morphology ensures accurate, predictable collection of data to enable both qualitative and quantitative analysis of the elements and/or molecular structures present in a sample. The quality of the analytical data produced is often directly in proportion to the amount of sample preparation carried out in advance. For example, determining the elemental composition of a completely unprepared corroded metal surface might be meaningless if the corroded surface is not representative of the bulk composition of the metal beneath.

Overview of archaeological analysis methods

The equipment and procedures used to analyse materials in archaeological contexts can be broadly divided into four main categories:

- Visual
- Molecular and structural
- Elemental
- Isotopic

Within each of the four categories of analysis, different configurations of analytical equipment may be available. These will provide the same type of information, but may have practical advantages or disadvantages when used to analyse different materials. No single method provides all the answers, and it is important to recognise that the use of several different techniques allows initial results obtained by one method to be confirmed by another. Although non-invasive methods are in general to be preferred, the use of more invasive procedures enables a more complete characterisation of the material. This is the balance that has to be struck when analysing museum material of any kind. A more in-depth description of the analytical methods described below and their application to archaeological material can be found in Pollard *et al*. (2007).

Visual analysis

Visual analysis techniques use the observations of a trained person to interpret the material present, and identification is usually made with comparison to reference samples of similar materials.

Techniques for visual analysis

Visual identification methods are commonly used in archaeological analysis for categorisation and recording purposes; typological studies where objects of similar style are grouped together, and for fibre and pigment identification using a microscope. For precise pigment identification, it is *not* sufficient to identify a pigment solely by eye using a standard light microscope, as a very limited range of observations can be made using this method. Instead, polarised light microscopy (PLM) is often used. This is a very specific technique used in geology to investigate the optical characteristics of crystals and mineral pigments which can exhibit specific internal reflections when viewed under polarised light. In many cases these patterns can be highly diagnostic of the mineral phase present. In order to conduct PLM analysis, small pigment samples are dispersed on a microscope slide in a medium which has a high refractive index, and observations on the optical properties of the particles are compared to standard reference collections such as the Pigment Compendium (Eastaugh *et al.*, 2005). Using this method, it is possible to identify different phases or mixtures of pigments and other materials which are present in the dispersion, and to inform the interpretation of later analyses.

Molecular and structural analysis

These techniques are able to distinguish between complex molecules which contain a mixture of atoms, or between materials which contain the same atoms arranged within different three-dimensional structures. Several techniques exploit the fact that specific structures and clusters of atoms will respond in a characteristic way to the input of energy, and therefore many analysis methods provide a qualitative "fingerprint" spectrum of the compound, which can be compared to reference spectra of known materials and hence identification made.

Techniques for molecular and structural analysis

Infrared (IR) spectroscopy

Infrared spectroscopy has a long history as an analytical technique, and is available in two main forms. Fourier transform infrared (FTIR) spectroscopy is the predominant infrared spectroscopy technique used in archaeological applications. An infrared energy source is directed at the sample, and different parts of the molecules within the sample absorb this energy at different wavelengths. This causes the bonds between the atoms to vibrate and rotate, in a way which is characteristic of both the atoms present and the particular way in which they are bonded together. By studying the frequencies of the primary radiation which are absorbed by the molecule, it is therefore possible to deduce the nature of the molecule. Vibration can only be induced in certain types of material and this technique is unsuitable for the identification of pure metallic structures, as well as some smaller, simpler molecules. Its main use is in the characterisation of organic materials – fabrics, papers, parchment, adhesives, resins and waxes, and some inorganic and organic pigments. Near-infrared (NIR) spectroscopy is a separate technique which uses a slightly different wavelength range of infrared energy to excite a sample, resulting in less specific and much weaker signals, but which can be combined with statistical analysis to provide a large range of data which can incorporate several variables, including both the chemical and physical properties of the sample. As a result, it has recently been successfully applied to the analysis of paper degradation in heritage contexts (see Chapter 6 of this volume).

Raman spectroscopy

This technique records the Raman effect - a phenomenon known as the "inelastic scattering" of laser energy, where certain molecules absorb energy at one frequency but emit it at another. These frequency shifts are measured and compared to reference spectra. The technique is often referred to as Raman microscopy, as the primary instrumentation used for analyses on archaeological and cultural samples incorporates a microscope attached to the spectrometer for accurate positioning of the laser. This method of analysis is used primarily for the identification of inorganic (ie. mineral) pigments, but other forms of the technique, such as Fourier transform Raman spectroscopy using a near infrared laser and surface enhanced Raman spectroscopy (SERS) have also been investigated and used for the identification of some organic pigments and binders.

X-ray diffraction (XRD)

This technique characterises a compound by measuring the extent to which an X-ray beam aimed at a sample is diffracted by the crystalline components of the material, and comparing these diffraction patterns with a comprehensive library of natural and artificial compounds. Laboratory XRD usually requires a small sample (a few milligrams) to be removed, so it is strictly minimally destructive. However, where micro-sampling is permitted on manuscripts, XRD has been used successfully to investigate the extent of collagen degradation within the pages of parchment manuscripts including the Dead Sea Scrolls (see Chapter 7 in this volume).

Separation techniques

Separation techniques are used to identify organic materials such as lipids in oils or amino acids in proteins, and can therefore be used to identify binders or organic pigments and dyes, or residues impregnated into archaeological materials such as cooking vessels. A device known as a chromatograph is designed to separate organic molecules as they pass down a column (carried by either a gas or a liquid), as a result of the different retention capacity of the lining of the column for different components. As each compound passes out of the column, it is transferred to another instrument (usually a mass spectrometer) for detection. Two commonly used separation techniques are 'Gas chromatography – mass spectrometry' (GC-MS) and 'High performance (or high pressure) liquid chromatography – mass spectrometry' (HPLC-MS).

Elemental analysis

These techniques are used to identify the chemical elements present in a material, but give no information about the arrangement of these atoms in a molecular structure. Some of these techniques work by directing a high-energy beam, often in the form of electrons or X-rays, at the sample, and stimulating the emission of characteristic X-rays from the elements in the sample. Others use the emission of light energy from atoms that have been promoted to a higher energy state by the input of heat.

Techniques for elemental analysis

X-ray fluorescence (XRF)

An X-ray beam is directed at a sample, and is of sufficient energy to eject electrons from within the individual atoms of the sample. These ejected electrons can be from one of several electron 'orbitals' which surround the nucleus of the atom. Each orbital contains electrons with identical energies. When one electron is ejected from an inner orbital, another electron from a higher energy orbital fills the vacancy, transferring to a state of lower energy. As an electron drops to the lower energy state, the energy difference is released as an X-ray with energy characteristic of the process which has created it. The pattern of characteristic X-ray energies allows the identity of the atom to be determined (usually automatically using computer software). The number of X-rays emitted (intensity) is a measure of the number of such atoms present in the sample.

Scanning electron microscopy (SEM)

This technique is analytically very similar to XRF, with the main difference being that an electron beam is used as the energy source. Since electron beams can be steered and focussed more easily than X-rays, this opens up a whole range of imaging and mapping options. An image of the sample can be viewed during the process, allowing microstructure to be observed and the analytical beam to be directed to particular areas of the sample. SEM comes in a wide variety of configurations for different purposes – some are more suited to microanalysis with limited imaging capability (often referred to as electron microprobe instruments), whereas others are designed for better imaging. In particular, a recent development using low vacuum technology and larger chambers has enabled the imaging and analysis of relatively large unprepared samples. This technique is particularly suited for museum samples, and is referred to as environmental scanning electron microscopy (ESEM). Where SEM is combined with X-ray analysis as described above, the technique is often referred to as 'scanning electron microscopy- energy dispersive spectroscopy' (SEM-EDS) or 'scanning electron microscopy- energy dispersive X-ray analysis' (SEM-EDX).

Proton Induced X-Ray Emission (PIXE)

PIXE is a method of ion beam analysis, which works in a similar way to XRF and SEM, but records the characteristic X-ray emissions which are stimulated by the excitation of the sample with a proton beam. Protons are larger and heavier than electrons, and are deflected less by the interaction of the beam with air and the sample. This allows a much smaller spot size to be maintained, and higher precision which allows depth analyses to be performed as well as highly accurate trace element identification (see Chapter 10 of this volume). In order to accelerate the proton beam, a high-energy input is required. This is provided by a particle accelerator. This is a large instrument, but if it has an external beamline the sample can be presented to the beam in air and without sampling, making the technique non-destructive, but not non-invasive (the high energy protons may result in damage to the object if not carefully controlled).

Inductively-coupled plasma - optical emission spectroscopy (ICP-OES)

A sample, often in liquid form, is introduced into an extremely hot gas, or plasma, torch at temperatures around 8000°C. The atoms in the sample are instantaneously excited (ie. their electrons are promoted to higher energy states), and on de-excitation the atoms emit radiation (usually in the visible or ultraviolet spectrum) which are characteristic of the elements present, and the intensity of which is proportional to the amount of that element present. These instruments can also be fitted with a laser ablation sampling chamber (LA-ICP-OES), where a laser is used to remove a microscopic sample from the surface of the object requiring analysis.

Laser ionisation (or laser-induced) breakdown spectroscopy (LIBS)/Laser-induced plasma spectroscopy (LIPS)

This is similar in principle to the ICP-OES described above, but the instrumentation is more compact and can be made transportable. A laser is used to ablate a microscopic sample from the surface of the pigment, which is heated to form plasma. As the plasma cools, characteristic wavelengths of UV, visible and near IR light are emitted. These are recorded optically as above, allowing elemental identification which can be extremely sensitive (see Giakoumaki *et al.* 2007).

Synchrotron analysis

A synchrotron is a particle accelerator which is capable of accelerating an electron beam to energies far beyond the scope of traditional laboratory equipment. The synchrotron takes the form of a large ring containing the high energy electron beam from which different types of electromagnetic radiation (X-rays, infrared, etc) are "tapped off" at individual stations around the ring. The extracted radiation is directed along beam lines towards the analytical instrumentation which enable analysis by all of the traditional laboratory materials characterisation methods, including FTIR, XRF and XRD (which are then referred to as S-XRF, etc.). The advantages of using a synchrotron as the energy source are, as with PIXE, a high beam intensity which can be focussed down to a tiny spot and extracted from the beamline to enable non-destructive analysis of whole objects in air with high sensitivity. Because of the high energy, 3D imaging of solid objects is also possible. The main disadvantage is that the sample has to be taken to the instrument, although it is also possible that some damage may occur to fragile materials as a result of the high energies used. Careful sample selection is therefore required.

Isotopic analysis

Many chemical elements occur naturally as a mixture of isotopes (atoms with identical chemical properties but different masses). With isotopic analysis, the aim is to look specifically at elements which display natural isotopic variability- lead, for example, has four stable isotopes, which occur naturally in different proportions depending on natural factors such as the geographic source of the material. Isotopic analysis methods characterise a material on the basis of the exact ratios of the different isotopes. This allows much deeper investigations of materials to take place, such as provenance studies which can indicate where a raw material was sourced (see Chapter 11 of this volume). This knowledge is helpful to the understanding of the trading of materials between different cultures and regions. Radiocarbon dating is also an isotopic method of analysis, since it quantifies the ratio of carbon-14 to carbon-12 which is left within organic materials, and uses this as a basis for determining the age of that material (see Chapter 12 of this volume). Isotopic analysis methods are an extension of elemental analysis, using equipment which is capable of separating the elements found in a material and recording the precise proportions of different isotopes of the same element present.

Techniques used for isotopic analysis

There are many types of mass spectrometry used in analytical chemistry, each of which are designed for a particular application. The main instrumental division is between those designed to measure the light stable isotopes (hydrogen, carbon, nitrogen, oxygen and sulphur), and those suited to the heavier, radiogenic isotopes (strontium and lead). A third branch of isotopic studies involves the detection of organic molecules by attaching a mass spectrometer to a separation device (either a gas (GC-MS) or a liquid chromatograph (HPLC-MS)), which allows the individual separated components to be identified.

Some common techniques for *in situ* analysis of manuscripts

Not all analytical techniques have been, or could be, adapted for *in situ* analysis on manuscripts. This is because *in-situ* analysis precludes the use of any separation and sample preparation techniques, which would enable contamination to be removed and aid identification of different layers of materials. The scientific equipment and procedures which are applicable to the analysis of manuscript pigments *in situ* cover only three of the four main categories discussed above:

- Visual
- Molecular and structural
- Elemental

There is currently no realistic method available for *in situ* isotopic analysis of materials on manuscripts, and the range of equipment available within each category of analysis is also limited. As a result, visual analysis methods are relied on to a greater degree than with studies of archaeological objects. Equipment used for each type of analysis is similar in principle to those used for the study of archaeological materials, but the methodology employed and the degree of information which is obtainable will differ significantly. Because no sample preparation or extraction techniques can be performed prior to analysis, the results obtained using *in situ* methodologies are *qualitative* (ie. they can tell you what is present, but not how much); *quantitative* results can only be provided using more invasive procedures. It is important to realise that interpretations drawn from qualitative data are inherently limited. Even such apparently straightforward results such as the presence/absence of a certain element or mineral are constrained by the sensitivity of the technique employed.

***In situ* visual analysis techniques**

Optical microscopy

Using open architecture instrumentation and table stands (where the microscope head and eyepieces are mounted onto an extending arm), high resolution microscopic examination can be used to investigate and assess the surface of a manuscript without the need to take samples. However, it is *not* possible to use *in situ* optical microscopy techniques for pigment identification on the basis of appearance. For pigment identification using a microscope alone, sampling must be conducted to allow either polarised light microscopy (PLM) or a technique known as fluorescence microscopy, which is capable of identifying a limited number of pigments and dyes which exhibit characteristic visible fluorescence (glow) under certain lighting conditions such as when illuminated using ultraviolet (UV) light.

Photography techniques

Simple reflection and photography techniques using different wavelengths of light such as IR and UV can be used in conjunction with visible light to investigate and record the surface of a manuscript as it responds to the incident light (see Mokretsova (1997), for an overview of photographic methods and applications). These techniques are widely used in conservation to characterise the material components of objects, including under-drawings and areas of retouching, repair and addition.

Reflectance spectroscopy

The most common application of this technique in manuscript studies is for pigment and ink analysis. Light is focussed onto a pigment deposit, and a reflectance spectrum is recorded which shows the wavelengths of light which have *not* been absorbed by the pigment. The spectrum produced is indicative of the pigment present, and can be compared to spectra produced by known pigments. At least in the visible light region, the technique can be considered to be a digital rendering of the visual comparison process, which increases its accuracy by allowing a less subjective comparison between different deposits. The utilisation of other wavelengths of light such as NIR to record spectral reflectance information alongside visible reflectance increases the available information and can show distinct differences between different pigments of the same colour. Thus, the blue pigments azurite and smalt can be easily differentiated on the basis of their spectral response to NIR light between 700 and 1000nm wavelength (see Liang et al. 2008: 35 cf 36). However, the technique cannot always provide unequivocal identification, and may be better utilised for comparative purposes, for example to monitor fading or colour change caused by light exposure.

Multispectral and hyperspectral imaging

These are more sophisticated techniques, which use as their base the principles of photography and reflectography using IR, visible and UV light sources. The process is refined to include multiple wavelengths of light from each region of the electromagnetic spectrum (see Fischer and Kakoulli, 2006), meaning that it is possible to record images of a document using a range of wavelengths, allowing the collection of multiple levels of information about the object for the assessment of damage, under drawings, faded text, over painting and alterations, in a single analysis. The techniques are often used in conjunction with reflectance spectroscopy for the collection of UV, visible and near IR spectral information about individual pigment deposits (see Chapter 8 of this volume).

***In situ* molecular and structural analysis techniques**

Infrared spectroscopy

A variety of equipment modifications allow spectra to be collected *in situ* and in reflection rather than transmission (see Derrick *et al.*, 1999). Microscope attachments for the FTIR spectrometer are now available, and different accessories can be used in conjunction with the microscope for analysis in reflection mode - enabling, for example, attenuated total reflection (ATR) and specular reflectance to suit different types of deposit. However, the use of microscopes can limit the size of manuscript which can be analysed *in situ*, and are best suited to single pages. It is also possible for FTIR and NIR spectroscopy to be conducted using equipment which delivers the energy to the object using fibre-optic probes.

Raman spectroscopy

Various equipment types have been developed for portable *in situ* analysis via fibre optic probes, though the most commonly used instrumentation is the Raman microscope, as this has better stability, focussing and spatial resolution than most fibre-optic solutions (see Chapter 9 of this volume).

X-ray diffraction

Portable XRD instrumentation suitable for *in situ* analysis is a very recent addition to the analytical toolkit, to the extent that very few instruments are commercially available. Those which are available are usually more suited to geological field analysis and require samples to be inserted into the portable equipment. Some reported '*in situ*' XRD actually appears to describe analyses which have been conducted on unprocessed, detached fragments of a manuscript, rather than being truly *in situ*; however, 'proper' *in situ* instrumentation is available for use in some institutions. More recently, instruments have been developed by several different institutions for the analysis of pigments, often in combination with XRF (Chiari and Sarrazin, 2008; Gianoncelli *et al.*, 2008). Non-destructive *in situ* XRD is also possible using a synchrotron, which can provide an extremely intense and highly focussed beam of X-rays to identify pigments on a manuscript without sampling, although a manuscript would need to travel to the nearest facility in order for analysis to take place. There might also be difficulties in presenting the sample to the beam, but in principle it is possible to produce a two dimensional map of the pigments on a manuscript surface, or the extent of collagen degradation within the pages of a parchment manuscript.

In situ elemental analysis techniques

Chemical spot tests

'Spot testing' is commonly used in conservation as a means of identifying certain materials or assessing condition. It usually involves applying a tiny amount of an 'indicator' substance to a very small area of an object (or a very small sample), in order to observe a visible chemical reaction which is indicative of the substance which is present. In paper conservation, the most commonly used tests are for determination of paper pH and to identify the presence of iron, which will suggest that an iron gall ink has been used on the manuscript. Both of these tests can be performed easily using manufactured test strips. These are placed on the object with a tiny amount of water (often the test paper itself need only be slightly damp). Test papers used in conservation contexts will also have been tested for colourfastness to ensure that the indicator substance will not bleed onto the material being tested.

X-ray fluorescence

XRF systems specifically designed for use on museum objects have been available for more than 40 years (Hall *et al.* 1973). They usually work in air (although some systems have been designed to be used in a helium atmosphere), and this limits the range of elements which can be detected – usually no element lighter than potassium (K) in the Periodic Table can be recorded. Nevertheless this often allows the heavier metallic elements present in a pigment to be identified. It must be understood, however, that the data contain no information on the minerals present – they only record the elements detected, and the molecular composition has to be deduced (or guessed) from knowledge of the elements observed. Portable, hand held instruments are also now available. In these, the X-ray beam has a much lower radiation intensity than those used in conventional systems, but are also likely to have much greater primary beam diameters, thereby limiting the spatial resolution of the analysis.

Laser ionisation (or laser-induced) breakdown spectroscopy (LIBS)/Laser-induced plasma spectroscopy (LIPS)

Although the LIBS equipment is able to be brought to the object for analysis *in situ*, the analysis actually requires the laser ablation of a sample from the surface of a manuscript.

Application of analytical techniques to manuscript research questions

The application of specific analytical techniques to manuscript research questions is discussed in greater detail in Part 3 of this volume. Broadly speaking, the techniques which are available for *in situ* analysis of manuscripts are more limited, both in terms of the range of equipment available, and in terms of the depth of information which can be provided. *In situ* methodologies allow investigation primarily of the following:

- surface analysis, particularly of pigments, inks and substrate materials
- visual investigation of alterations and additions, faded text and layering of decoration
- gross structural assessment for deterioration/ condition monitoring

However, even the adoption of a purely non-invasive *in situ* analytical approach can be extremely beneficial beyond the scope of monitoring and conservation functions, able to benefit curatorial research questions by allowing greater understanding and interpretation of manuscript collections. Manuscripts represent the largest repository of surviving medieval pictorial art: the Bodleian Library in Oxford alone contains 10,000 volumes of medieval European manuscripts. This archive offers not only the obvious window on medieval art and social history, but also an unparalleled and largely untapped resource for the history of an important medieval industry: the production of illuminated manuscripts, and the manufacture, trade and use of pigments.

The archaeological analysis methods described in the first part of this chapter open up avenues for a much larger range of scientific research, but inevitably sometimes require sampling. However, modern archaeological techniques, sensitive equipment and modern preparation protocols limit the size of the sample which is needed in order to achieve a useful result. The advantage of considering these techniques is that, where the information obtained by sample analysis would be of significant benefit, high quality results can be obtained. This opens up a much larger range of research avenues on library material, including the ability to date manuscripts by scientific means, and to provenance the materials used to create them using isotope analysis methods.

References

Chiari, G, and P. Sarrazin 2008 Portable non-invasive XRD/XRF instrument: a new way of looking at objects surface. Presented at *Art 2008: 9th International Conference on Non-destructive Testing of Art*. Jerusalem, Israel, 25-30 May 2008. Available online at *http://www.ndt.net/search/docs.php3?date=2008-09&issue=1&rppoffset=60* accessed 27.03.09

Derrick, M.R., D. Stulick and J.M. Landry 1999 *Infrared Spectroscopy in Conservation Science*. Scientific Tools for Conservation Series, Getty Conservation Institute, Los Angeles.

Eastaugh, N.J., V. Walsh, T. Chaplin and R. Siddall 2005 Pigment Compendium: Optical Microscopy of Historical Pigments. Elsevier, London

Fischer, C. and I. Kakoulli 2006 Multispectral and hyperspectral imaging technologies in conservation: current research and potential applications. *Reviews in Conservation* 7, 3-16

Giakoumaki, A., K. Melessanaki and D. Anglos 2007 Laser-induced breakdown spectroscopy (LIBS) in archaeological science- applications and prospects. *Analytical and Bioanalytical Chemistry* 387, 749-760

Gianoncelli, A., J. Castaing, L. Ortega, E. Dooryhée, J. Salomon, P. Walter, J.-L. Hodeau and P. Bordet 2008 A portable instrument for in situ determination of the chemical and phase compositions of cultural heritage objects. *X-ray Spectrometry* 37, 418-423

Hall, E.T., F. Schweizer and P.A. Toller 1973 X-ray fluorescence analysis of museum objects: a new instrument. *Archaeometry* 15 53-78.

Liang, H., K. Keita, B. Peric and T. Vajzovic 2008 Pigment identification with optical coherence tomography and multispectral imaging. In *Proc. OSAV 2008: The 2nd International Topical Meeting on Optical Sensing and Artificial Vision*. St Petersberg, Russia 12-15 May 2008, 33-42.

Mokretsova, I.P. 1997 Photographic methods for the examination of medieval manuscripts. In G.Fellows-Jensen and P. Springborg eds. *Care and Conservation of Manuscripts 3: Proceedings of the Third International Seminar held at the University of Copenhagen 14-15 October 1996*, 44-52

Pollard, A.M. and C. Heron 2008 *Archaeological Chemistry*. Royal Society of Chemistry: Cambridge (2nd revised edition).

Pollard, A.M., C. Batt, B. Stern and S.M.M. Young 2007 *Analytical Chemistry in Archaeology*. Cambridge University Press: Cambridge.

Chapter 4

Framing Analytical Research Questions

Mark Clarke

University of Amsterdam

Introduction

In addition to being vehicles for the transmission of texts and images, books are also archaeological artefacts, and one must constantly bear in mind this physicality. The benefits of an improved understanding of book materials to book conservation are manifold, evident and pressing, as outlined in Part I of the present volume. But an archaeological approach also benefits historians: chemical analysis has for example been shown capable of confirming provenance, distinguishing hands within a manuscript, and identifying altered appearance (thus helping to deduce original appearance), including alterations due to aging or to later deliberate alterations such as refurbishment, in the latter case by identifying intrusive anachronistic elements. When taken together these ultimately contribute to the larger context of, for example, the archaeology and history of manufacturing and exchange.

This is a golden age for the study of the physical properties of works of art in general and manuscripts in particular, with increasingly sensitive analytical instruments available, which combined with a renaissance in the philology of artists' recipe books has resulted in a greatly improved understanding of workshop methods and materials.

Nevertheless at present, considering the very large amount that has been written about the history of books, their manufacture and their decoration, there have been proportionally very few *analyses* published. The study of the materials used for making books (when compared to, say, the study of paintings on canvases, panels or walls) is in its infancy. To establish what was 'conventional' usage for different periods, regions, or ateliers, very much more work is needed to build up a substantial and statistically significant corpus of analyses, similar to that extant, for example, for easel paintings. However, in codicology, in conservation, and in 'technical art history' there are rarely natural structures in which research topics arise, such as there are in most other research fields, for example in an established research group headed by a professor who generates ideas and who encourages doctoral students to investigate them. More prejudicial still, unlike many fields in physical sciences and humanities, the interdisciplinary nature of the technical examination of books means that when someone *does* have a concrete question, it is rarely soluble with the techniques available in-house. On the contrary, more than in most disciplines, outside collaboration is almost invariably required. The framing of an answerable question therefore requires cross-disciplinary 'interpreters' who can explain the requirements and possibilities of their own specialisms to their opposite numbers.

Clearly analytical programmes must be collaborative, and the best analyses have been done by physicists and chemists working closely with conservators, librarians, and art historians. How are these collaborative analyses to begin? The present chapter suggests how achievable research questions may be framed, and how the results of these investigations may be disseminated in such a way as to inform wider questions than the immediate concerns that drove the initial research.

Choice of purpose

Research questions in the analysis of book materials are rarely driven purely by conservation questions, and more rarely still by purely art historical questions. In this, codicological analysis differs from analysis of paintings, where conservation and authenticity are the two principal drivers. In practice the analysis of book materials has, with a few notable exceptions, come as close to pure research as imaginable in that it has been driven almost entirely by curiosity. This is no bad thing. (Although each researcher must examine his own conscience as to what extent the reason presented to the *funder* is true: the often-touted putative 'conservation benefits' often seem to be lip service.) Nevertheless research questions do divide broadly into two overlapping areas, namely history and conservation.

Historical questions are attempts to ascertain as precisely as possible when an artefact was made, where, and by which individual or workshop, and to establish which parts of that artefact are original (i.e. were made together at the same time) and which parts were added later (restoration, forgery, or in the case of a book simply several un-related booklets bound together for convenience). But the *results* of historical questions need not be confined to individual books: the combination of results from many, many books can and should contribute to wider knowledge of developments in the history and technology of the book, the organisation of workshops, of trade and of exchange, and thus of the sociological changes that affected, and were affected by, changes in book technology.

Conservators, aware that every object is constantly degrading, seek to avoid further damage, retard or reverse degradation and damage, while at the same time preserving the archaeological material evidence embodied in the object. Conservation questions themselves thus may be divided in two. They either concern individual artefacts (condition and state of preservation, risk assessment for display or digitisation, characterisation of ink likely to degrade, assessment of suitable treatments), or they use examination of individual artefacts to answer more generally applicable questions (what can we do about ink corrosion, or pigment flaking, or red rot, or the brittleness of acid paper?).

Questions that address both historical and conservation questions simultaneously ask firstly how a book or decoration or illumination was executed (pricking, underdrawings, paint layers etc.) — all indicators of the conformity or independence of individuals with traditions and the relation of an artist to his materials — and ask secondly in what way the present appearance reflects the artefact as originally produced (discolouration, losses, repairs etc), perhaps with a view to returning the object to a more authentic or pristine state.

Choice of books to examine

Monuments are not where the majority of people live and work. Unfortunately the majority of analyses of the materials of books (especially the analyses of mediaeval manuscripts and incunabula) has been carried out on such 'monuments'; that is to say exceptional books, such as the most spectacularly decorated *x*, the earliest examples of *y*, and so forth. It is true that results from examining such books can be most interesting. But, while it is understandable that researchers will want to work on the remarkable rather than the quotidian, the consequence is that we remain largely ignorant about the latter. It is as though the history of architecture was written based entirely on examinations of Stonehenge, the Leaning Tower of Pisa, and the Eiffel Tower. Analysts of paintings (technically the closest comparable field to that of book analysis), in contrast, through years of routine examination and routine analysis of a tremendous variety of material (painted by masters and hacks alike), have built up a considerable knowledge of standard fabrication practices, and are thus in a position to appreciate exceptions to those standard practices, and so to derive useful conclusions about age, provenance, authorship, and degree of post-manufacture alteration. We remain remarkably ignorant about the materials of the conventional early book. And yet it is precisely an appreciation of what is work-a-day that increases appreciation of the exceptional efforts that produced non-standard 'master' works. All books, and especially all book decorations and materials, however low quality, deserve attention: indeed it is the simple material that forms the bulk of surviving material and will thus (i) most likely produce the most statistically significant evidence and indicators for dating and provenance, and (ii) present the greatest conservation burden (consider for example the example of nineteenth century acid paper brittleness).

Choice of analytical technique

How to know what technique to ask for? Available techniques, their strengths and weaknesses, and the types of question they can answer are addressed elsewhere in this volume. But, rather than formulating a research question and then commissioning the appropriate analysis, research questions in the analysis of book materials have often been formulated based firstly on what equipment is available. That is, questions are chosen to be appropriate to the equipment, rather than vice versa. This is not to be disdained. It seems to be putting the cart before the horse, but excellent results have nevertheless been achieved. This is as well since without considerable expenditure (certain large institutions have invested in analytical equipment precisely for book work, e.g. the British Library have a dedicated Raman spectrometer), this is unlikely to change.

There are always logistical problems getting books and instruments in the same room. Equipment can often not be moved, and books can be too fragile or valuable to be moved. It is on occasion possible to borrow instruments: for example, the Eu-ARTECH funded project 'MOLAB'[1] offers a mobile collection of portable equipment, suitable for *in-situ* non-destructive studies and diagnosis on artworks. Nevertheless it is to be hoped that curators will come to realise that the benefits of a well-directed programme of instrumental analysis are considerable, and the risk of moving books to laboratory facilities can be made minimal.

Sampling versus 'non-destructive' analysis

The main obstacle responsible for the study of the materials used for making books still *being* in its infancy has been the aspiration not to take samples for analysis. The consequence of this has been that for a long time the only analysis possible was visual examination: adequate for gross structures (sewing, quiring) but worse than useless (since it propagates misleading data) for pigments, adhesives and so forth. If readers of the present volume take away one idea, I hope that it will be that the identification of pigments by naked eye or by microscope is almost invariably incorrect, and that identifying parchment species by the same method is also as frequently incorrect too.

Recent advances in instrumentation have therefore facilitated reliable analysis because there are now numerous methods of analysis that do not require sampling. However there can be significant problems with using these:

- There are logistical problems bringing books and instruments together.
- Non-sampling methods cannot analyse all types of materials. Sadly most organic pigments cannot be analysed without samples: sad because these are the most vulnerable to fading or damage by inappropriate treatment, and sad because the relatively great variety in their use means that they have potentially the greatest use for identifying ateliers and localising places production; furthermore many modern printing inks are essentially organic dyes. Some publications claim that identification of pigments is possible with certain non-sampling techniques, but with very few exceptions their results are usually very inaccurate and often plain wrong. Organic pigment analysis — if it is to be accurate and reliable — requires samples. Very recent developments are starting to show hopeful results for some organic pigments without sampling (e.g. micro fluorescence) but these are still experimental. Should analysis wait until such techniques are more developed? No, it should not wait: partly because non-sampling techniques will never be able to detect certain pigments (safflower for example),[1] but mainly because the conservation questions are too urgent.
- While *in situ* non-sampling analysis seems on the face of it to be the ideal from a conservation perspective, but this is not always so. Most 'non-destructive' analysis techniques require the book to be held firmly in

---

[1] see http://www.eu-artech.org/

place. A conservator must always be present (this is not always done, and not always possible, but is essential — indeed, *in situ* analysis without a conservator present should never be done, ever). Sometimes the methods to clamp pages in place (such that the instrument may focus on them) are more damaging than sampling would have been.

- Layer structures are important in high-quality mediaeval decorated manuscripts and in modern coated papers. However, analysis without sampling will only detect either the top layer (in reflective or surface techniques, e.g. visible light spectroscopy or Raman spectroscopy) or may combine all the results from several or all of the layers (in penetrative techniques, such as certain X-ray techniques). Moreover, in western mediaeval manuscripts and in Islamic manuscripts of all periods, it seems that organic glazes (thin layers added on top of paint) were common, and about this we know almost nothing: it is perhaps the most urgent question today in conservation science since such organic glaze layers are highly vulnerable to cleaning, washing, and light-induced degradation.
- Many pigments were used mixed, and mixtures can be very difficult or impossible to understand without sampling. Where inorganic and organic pigments are mixed, it is impossible yet vital. A great weakness of much non-destructive examination has been that it detects the inorganic component, and concludes that this is the only pigment present, but it does not detect the organic component, or indeed — in the case of the addition of organic pigments and dyes (which mediaeval craft treatises and 'recipe books' tell us were indeed added) — even suspect it is there.

Sampling is routine around the world, in the best of museums and libraries, for paintings, antiquities, wall paintings, easel paintings, textiles, and archaeological finds; it is only rare for books. This is largely historical: until recently the required sample size was too large, because a sample that would leave a negligible lacuna in a canvas or wall painting, would leave a distractingly large one in objects so relatively small as a decorated initial, a miniature, or indeed a book. In practice, however, today's smaller samples (if taken by an experienced conservator, not by the analyst) are so small that they are only visible under a microscope, and are almost completely invisible to the naked eye, or even under a magnifying glass. The damage-to-knowledge ratio is very favourable. A well-planned set of samples can be used for years, for many instrumental analyses, including those not yet invented. Samples may be removed during conservation treatment and saved for later, until suitable analytical opportunities become available. Furthermore, they can be sent around to other laboratories, even abroad, without fear, rather than moving (and insuring, and protecting) the books themselves.

Note that the examination techniques used to reveal underdrawings and effaced or illegible writing do not require sampling. This is one of the most satisfying forms of technical examination, where a Visual Spectral Comparator (VSC) or similar[2] can, by the use of different light sources and filters, separate the text from a similar-coloured background (either faded text against the page colour, or unfaded text against a stain). A VSC is also used for making more apparent the almost imperceptible differences in ink of later alterations or additions (such is its use in forensic science for the examination of alteration or obliteration in questioned documents).

Putting it all together: framing questions

As noted above, questions divide broadly into history and conservation. In practice they further divide into questions about individual books, and general questions about many books. Until now individual books tended to be investigated from an historical perspective, whereas conservation questions tended to study a large number of books.

Example questions about individual books

To simply sit and identify, for example, all the pigments in a book, is no longer sufficient. While such routine analysis of course remains essential and must be done, (routine analysis often throws up unexpected and surprising information, notably intrusive and anachronistic elements) more sophisticated questions must be asked of the data so obtained.

- Dating. In our present state of knowledge the simplest and most obvious questions, such as 'when was this book made?', are the hardest to answer. The unavoidable imprecision of terminal dates for the introduction and deprecation of materials such as pigments (such dates being best expressed as a range of probabilities dependant on the rate and spread of adoption, and typically embrace several decades [Eastaugh, this volume, Chapter 5]), means that material analysis is unlikely to provide a more precise dating than would conventional palaeography.
- Intrusive elements. Instances where the imprecision of terminal dates is not a problem are those where the difference in date between the book and material identified on it is greater than the range of date-uncertainty. Put more simply: glaring anachronisms indicate later re-working of a book. Examples where analysis has been helpful include: the identification of nineteenth-century retouchings on fifteenth century manuscript decorations, and/or completely forged manuscript illuminations (in the first case mapped via multi-spectral imaging, then in both cases confirmed through an identification by Raman spectroscopy of post-mediaeval inventions such as Prussian blue and chrome yellow), and the identification of a mediaeval programme of renovation and improvement (identified by presence of ultramarine in a number of manuscripts two centuries too early to contain it).
- Localisation. An identification of unusual or rare materials will be helpful in narrower localisation (probably by identification of locally-sourced organic pigments,

---

[2] VSCs are essentially instruments which perform optical imaging using different wavelength of light to illuminate a manuscript page; methods of advanced optical imaging and reflectance spectroscopy are discussed further by Liang in Chapter 8 of this volume

or locally preferred species of animal used for parchment or leather).
- Manufacturing processes. It has been possible to separate elements of apparently homogeneously produced books by the analysis of materials. Examples of such successful analyses have included changes in paper within a twentieth century diary (indicating revisionist elements added later), and the consistent use of two different blue pigments on the same decorated manuscript which allowed a determination of how the work had been divided between two teams, each using one of the two pigments (several fifteenth century northern Netherlandish examples).
- Grouping. It is frequently attempted to group individual books to certain common locales of production (workshops or individuals) by means of stylistic and historical evidence. Analysis can of course help. If the materials are the same (the notable materials, that is, not the standard ones) in books that are supposed to originate in the same atelier, this can strengthen the connection, whereas inconsistency in material use will weaken it. Similarly analysis can be used to confirm a common origin of *disjecta membra*: for example DNA analysis of the membranes has been used to reunite fragments of the Dead Sea Scrolls.

Example questions about many books

It is a good idea to have a grand plan, then individual analyses can contribute to it. The 'master question' for *materials* is always: 'what was used where and when?'. The 'master question' for *techniques* is: 'how, where and when?'. Together this leads to a better understanding of workshop practices, and more sociological questions such as the demands and expectations of patrons and consumers, and so forth. This can only be answered by a considerable programme of coordinated analysis to determine statistically significant trends. Example questions that will be answerable might include: 'How do material changes permit new styles?' 'Does a technique change accompany a stylistic change?' 'Does a change in political allegiances or conquest of a new land introduce new materials?'.

Analysis of many books overcomes the uncertainty, imprecision and lack of reproducibility inherent in the examination of any individual archaeological artefact. For example, multiple analyses of similar types of object using one single analytical technique can produce data (for example spectra) which may be combined mathematically to produce statistically more valuable information, and indeed to reveal patterns and components not evident on simple inspection (this is the discipline of 'chemometrics').

Certain questions need specific programmes of research other than the 'master schemes' outlined above. An excellent example is the question 'Is the degradation in these books due to their manufacture or their storage environment, past and present?' One outstanding project to address this is the British Library 'Identical Books Project', where different libraries' copies of the same 400 printed books are analysed thoroughly for indicators of degradation: pH, colour, lignin content, sulphate content, bending brittleness etc. The study of environmental conditions can further be carried out by the use of surrogate book materials, that is, historically accurate reconstructions based on historical technical treatises and craftsmen's recipe books.

Interdisciplinary formulation

Analysts and art historians rarely appreciate each other's issues. Patience is needed, and a willingness to pay attention. The key to writing a proposal is an iterative consultation process.

Technical explanations benefit from being on a need-to-know basis, to avoid the rapid development of glazed facial expressions. An art historian, for example, does not need to be provided with excess technical information about the analytical mechanism employed by a particular analytical technique. Presentations of techniques by analysts to library professionals frequently lose the attention of their audience by including such detail. What the book historian, curator or conservator firstly needs to know is: 'can this technique answer my question and if not, which technique can you suggest?'. (To take trivial examples: carbon dating won't help date metal clasps, DNA analysis won't date anything, and X-Ray Fluorescence spectroscopy won't identify glues.) Secondly, 'will it damage my object?' (this is where an analyst might discuss the different instrumental settings which may be used to minimise damage, or present the case for sampling *versus* clamping a book in place). Decisions on the ratio of risk-of-damage to useful information can thus be arrived at iteratively.

Analysts are often surprisingly interested in the questions of art history and codicology, both historical questions and questions of the history of book technology (in particular many professional chemists have become very interested in historic dyes and pigments). Analysts will often benefit from a fairly full statement of a problem: they may then be able to suggest an individual technique, a combination of complementary techniques, or a statistical approach. Analysts (excluding those archaeometrists who are attached to libraries and museums) are not always interested in the *answers* to the book-research questions *per se*, but are commonly more interested in finding novel applications for their instruments, and in stretching the limits of what their instruments can do (the conservation preference for non-sampling or micro-sampling being a good example) — in other words, solid scientific progress that they can publish.

Meta-analysis

Common in medicine, practiced in archaeology, yet rare in conservation, 'meta-analysis' studies (or 'systematic reviews') critically examine the data of previously executed studies (typically publications) to answer new or larger questions. Such studies consider the validity of the methodology, the specificity and accuracy of analytical techniques used, and the actual results, so as to perform a 'meta-study' or 'virtual experiment' on a far larger range and number of subjects than would be possible for an individual team or project to do.[3] Given the expense, inconvenience and time consuming nature

---

[3] One such meta-study is Clarke (2001).

of analysis, such studies are invaluable, and more should be attempted in the field of book studies. Such studies will add a greater statistical validity to what, until now, has largely been an *ad hoc* series of analyses. Ideally, of course, all analysis worldwide would be coordinated, but this is unlikely to happen in the near future. Meta-analysis can alleviate some of the consequent lacks of this uncoordinated condition.

Timetabling and paying for analysis

Time and money for analysis is typically provided either by dedicated project funding or by making time in existing programmes, typically conservation programmes. Indeed, without specific project funding, the analytical burden typically falls on the conservation department of a library. It is thus subject to considerable pressure and limitation, but nevertheless the conservation environment is in many ways ideal for analysis: there is a conservator present to guard against hazardous procedures or inappropriate handling, and books and instruments can generally more easily be introduced to each other in a pre-conservation state, especially when the spine is broken (permitting flat opening) or better yet, when a book is pulled and disbound.[4] Micro-sampling should be carried out before interventive conservation treatments (especially before consolidation or aqueous treatments) to facilitate sample removal and to prevent contamination. Thus the opportunity for analysis (or at least sampling) should be seized at the moment of conservation intervention, and ideally routine simple analysis would be planned in to accompany all major interventions: even though this may be inconvenient, it will generally be a once-in-a-lifetime opportunity to apply otherwise physically or logistically impossible analytical techniques. How good it would be to see libraries prepared to supplement the budgets of conservation departments to incorporate such routine analysis.

As is true for any interdisciplinary research, funding for book analysis projects can be problematic to obtain, with each category of funding body (humanities or sciences) considering the project as belonging to the other, although this has become somewhat easier in the UK of late. The desire of funders and book holding institutions for high-profile newsworthy projects has doubtless contributed to research that has been skewed toward individual high-profile and newsworthy books. Strategies to overcome this will depend on the funder, but typically 'public access' is a common buzzword: this may be exploited by reference to the evident public interest in the making of artworks and historic objects, and in scientific 'detection'. Another strong persuader is the demonstration of successful precedents or pilot projects.

Collaboration is a strong asset, especially international. Offset against this is the high cost of travel: staff need accommodation, instruments may need a whole day of external technician time to install and re-calibrate them after a move, and insuring valuable books for a visit to a laboratory can be prohibitive, running to thousands of pounds per day for a single book.

Suggested priority questions

I would like to identify a few areas which I believe could usefully be prioritised.

The identification of inks and pigments *is* still a valid and useful area of research, but both the analysis itself and the questions asked of the results need to be more subtle and more comprehensive: rather than continue to be content with an identification of, for example, 'verdigris', we must investigate the composition, corrosive tendencies and relative stability of different forms of verdigris made according to different recipes.

The importance of organic pigments (especially in connection with glazes and organic additives to inorganic pigments) has been stressed already, and should receive more attention. The degree of visual alteration is as yet barely even suspected, let alone understood or quantified.

Recent advances in micro-sampling and immunological assays allow the analysis of binding media and adhesives with unprecedented precision. This is interesting for the history of technology (the sometimes doubted addition of ear-wax to glair, as described in mediaeval treatises, has only this year been experimentally identified, on Portuguese Romanesque manuscripts), but more so for informing conservation choices.

Proper analysis of parchment species is to be encouraged: a great many codicological conclusions have been published that are based on what I am confident will prove to be incorrect identifications (the visual differences are often mis-interpreted, and furthermore it is not commonly appreciated that the physiology of mediaeval goats and sheep were far more similar than today). The question of 'uterine vellum' versus the use of small animals would be one historic debate it would be well to resolve once and for all, and would provide useful localisation data.

The importance and consequences of layered paper and paint structures, and especially the issue of organic glaze layers, has been grossly under-appreciated.

Another area of growing importance is Islamic manuscripts. These have until now been comparatively ignored, but materials research has become urgent, as libraries with significant holdings are at present suddenly beginning large programmes of conservation and exhibition. Pigments are obviously a major subject for study, but also for example there are as yet only extremely imprecise ways to date Arab paper (a problem exacerbated by the different dates of adoption of similar paper furnish and structures around the Arab world).

Large-scale digitisation brings new questions: imaging technology is answering the question of how to photograph a book that does not open well (and even begins to image books that open not at all), but we should perhaps investigate what happens to the digitised book that will now be far less-frequently consulted: whether pages will become blocked or offset, whether a lack of regular airing will encourage mould growth, and so forth.

---

[4] This is also the perfect moment for digitisation.

Finally I would strongly suggest that far greater attention be given to common-or-garden, standard- or low-quality books, such that we may build up a better picture of common usage. The information that a certain unusual or imported material is found at a certain early date in a certain exceptional book from a certain location is not as helpful in formulating a chronology of materials and techniques as would be a good statistical overview of usage-frequency by date and region evaluated for *all* types of books.

Analysis can be seen as a super-documentation. Clearly not all features of all pages of all books will ever be analysed using all techniques. But (especially in the framework of meta-analysis) each analysis, however humble, contributes to the broader picture.

Applicability and audience of results

The applicability and audience of research *results* varies. A detailed examination of an individual object is of immediate concern to those responsible for its curation and conservation, while the more general questions are naturally more generally interesting and contribute more to the disciplines of 'technical art history' and the 'archaeology of the book'. One of the greatest challenges facing technical codicology is how to make results of specific examinations of individual books widely available in such a way that results may be combined to allow generalisations to be made. For example: an analysis of the pigments found on an individual manuscript is of concern to its conservator, but (unless that book be exceptional) only becomes of general use and interest when it is combined and compared with many others, such that one may discern whether it is typical or exceptional. (This is why the old model of awarding a doctorate for enumerating the pigments throughout a single magnificent illuminated manuscript should no longer be acceptable.) When an analysis has been done, every effort should be made to publish the results, in however abbreviated a form: for example as an appendix to a catalogue, or as an appendix to a yearbook, or on a webpage. This need not be an elaborate text, with a introduction, discussion and conclusions, but a simple, telegraphic even, statement of technique and results, perhaps in a simple table of results per manuscript: the purpose not being a formal academic paper but a simple dissemination of data with which future syntheses may be built.

Conclusions

Analysis is most successful when it complements traditional codicology, or when it answers a specific conservation question. The amount of analytical work done has increased recently, as increasingly sensitive and unambiguous techniques have been developed. Nevertheless it is still true that not nearly enough is known about the materials of books. Regardless of any academic interest, to know what conservation treatments will be safe and suitable, we must make such analysis a priority. The biggest area of ignorance, and that with the biggest possible impact on conservation and display, is the question of organic colours. If certain organic pigments are discovered to be present, display conditions and display policies (especially regarding light levels) will have to be completely re-thought. At present we simply do not know. Until now the majority of books have never been displayed for any length of time. If we start new programmes of displaying books now, we may destroy pigments (and thus colours) that have survived for centuries, and we may destroy them in only a few weeks of display. Where wet treatments are needed, such as de-acidification, consolidation, or the application of insecticides, or where there is a demand to reduce climate control costs (e.g. by relaxing currently stringent guidelines on acceptable levels and fluctuations in relative humidity), we have insufficient idea how many books will react, as we do not know what is present. Finally, of course, there is the pure scientific advantage of such research: whether this is an appropriate use of resources for any individual or institution cannot possibly addressed here, but in this author's opinion this is the type of research that collections should be encouraged and helped to do.

Framing a research question is comparatively easy: framing one that can be answered with the resources available (or indeed, at all) is less easy. Clearly collaboration is essential, not just in executing analysis but in formulating questions. The present relative scarcity of book analysis, perceived and genuine, leads on occasion to negative comment (typically by art historians) as to the worth of analysis. This attitude has two manifestations: (i) 'if nobody does it, how can it be useful?' (a childish but surprisingly commonly encountered attitude) (ii) 'if there is so little comparative data, what use is the analysis of my few objects of interest?' (a fair point, but a situation that will only improve with further analysis). Each clearly leads to vicious circle of non-analysis. But the pioneering has been done: what is needed now are those far-sighted (and altruistic) enough to become early adopters and to make analysis mainstream and inevitable.

How is this to happen? It is a good idea to have a grand plan, then individual contributions can build to it. While not every feature of every books will ever be fully analysed, whatever analysis *can* be done contributes to the overview. Analysis can be seen as a super-documentation: ideally a way needs to be devised to build in to routine examinations some forms of routine, rapid protocols of simple and inexpensive analysis.

Until now much materials research into books has been *ad hoc*, and has depended on whatever equipment or books could conveniently be brought together. While this has produced some fascinating and useful results, it is not enough: systematic, coordinated, and programmes of analysis must be devised, and their results must be well disseminated.

References

Clarke, M. 2001 The analysis of medieval European manuscripts. *Reviews in Conservation* **2**, 3-17

Chapter 5

Defining Methodological Problems: A Case Study on Paint Analysis and the Technological Study of Manuscripts

Nicholas Eastaugh

The Pigmentum Project, University of Oxford
Art Access and Research Ltd., London

Introduction

Manuscripts[1] present a broad set of challenges for paint analysis, frequently bounded by understandable limitations on access and sampling. Yet at the same time the scope for discovering new knowledge on the basis of the clear characterisation of the pigments and binding materials ought to none-the-less encourage us to actively develop new avenues of research. Discussion of such avenues might, for present purposes, be divided into three areas: a) how can we best define the topics we want to study and select the most appropriate material for that; b) are the analytical tools we currently use best suited for the kinds of questions we are really wanting to ask; c) how can we best use and most insightfully interpret the data we are acquiring? This document will specifically explore the first two of these; the last is left open for discussion around specific research problems.

A. Defining topics

What do we want to know?

There are a number of classic areas where paint analysis is used to inform us. Of these, the documentation of artefacts, exploring aspects of condition and conservation, and answering questions of attribution and authenticity, have hitherto formed the core subjects of study. Increasingly, however, interest has also grown in what we can learn about what we might call the 'socio-economic context of production'; that is, what implications the presence of certain materials and techniques have for the wider framework of how these objects were made, the sources of materials used and their trade, specialisation in manufacture, and so forth.

Looking at the published studies of manuscript analysis it is difficult to avoid the conclusion that much is the result of serendipitous, *ad hoc* analysis of single, unrelated, or very small groups of objects. Presumably the rationale has been similar to that of comparable analysis projects in the easel paintings field: to highlight an important artist or work in focus; as an adjunct to an exhibition; to support conservation treatment. Without underplaying the worth of these studies, shouldn't we at the same time also be seeing a bigger picture? How can we ensure that the analysis carried out on one artefact is comparable to that on another? Wouldn't this then help us to make meta-studies, where data can be consolidated and explored in new ways, opening up different directions of study? Three specific (but not exhaustive) examples may help here:

Condition and conservation

Understanding the material structure of an object is taken as a prerequisite in contemporary conservation practice. The impact of conservation decisions on artefacts is not however always so apparent. There are also numerous examples of poorly-understood mechanisms of deterioration that prevent us from making informed strategic decisions. To address such issues it is imperative that we comprehend as much as we can about the chemistry of the materials: not just a specific pigment, say, but the group of compounds to which it belongs. Even seemingly simple compounds can hide surprisingly complex colour generation mechanisms, or less than benign interactions with binding media, substrates, environments and treatments.

Attribution and authenticity

Studies of materials and techniques are often co-cited in cases of attribution and authenticity along with other forms of scholarship such as stylistic analysis. Clearly, from the frequency of these appeals, knowledge of how something was created and what with has an important role to play, one that is seemingly increasing. The alliance though is often an uneasy one and synthesis, or decision-making in the face of disparate evidence, can be difficult to achieve. Coherent and robust ways of handling such situations must be developed. The topic is a large one and substantially falls outside the scope of this discussion paper; the narrower question of dating of objects on the other hand can be briefly mentioned.

Discussion of dating techniques for BookNET has been covered in another paper,[2] but we might add to that that studies of materials and techniques potentially provides us with a different set of methodologies. Perhaps most familiar is the idea that we can supposedly identify anachronistic or anatopistic (out of place) materials within an object that then allows us to reject its authenticity. A well-known example might be the so-called 'Vinland Map' and the contentious identification of a titanium-based pigment, one that also neatly illustrates that these studies can be less than straightforward in practice. However, the central point to be raised here is the use of 'terminal' dates, points around which a material, or a process, or a technique, was used/not used. This idea does

---

[1] 'Manuscripts' is used here loosely and as a matter of convenience since similar questions to those discussed exist of course for illustrated books, maps, works of art on paper such as watercolours and so forth.

[2] See Chapter 12 of this volume

not stand scrutiny though, mainly because there is no clean, sharp transition from non-use to use and generally the take-up of materials and techniques instead seem to follow classic diffusive patterns. If we are prepared to suspend terminal dates as a methodology we can in fact substitute far more informative approaches based on likelihood, borrowing on ideas much developed by the radiocarbon and allied communities. Essentially we can construct probability 'models' that indicate the likelihood that an object originates from a specific time and place.

A further consequence of these lines of thinking is that we should be looking at the information more richly; that the analysis process can provide more information than merely pigment identification. Often, significant differences between artists working in a narrow milieu resides in the choices made of available pigments, the particular mixtures used, specific techniques employed, their combinations and suchlike. These are features that can be systematically examined, recorded, interpreted; it is up to us as a community to find effective ways of doing so.

The social and economic history of materials and techniques

The BookNET Research Cluster is expressly committed to 'technological' study; is this going to mean more than that we analyse manuscripts as physical objects? Are we actually going to explore the area of technology and culture, the relationship between producers and their socio-economic context? If so, then we need to address the specific needs of this community by developing approaches that allow sophisticated study of broader or tangential questions. For instance, rather than framing questions around specific objects or object groups, what can we do to explore diffusion of ideas and *material*? As a case example, a remarkably under-used approach is to study what we might call the 'epidemiology' of materials and techniques. This involves systematic historical mapping of examples of well-defined concepts, such as a way of working, or a substance, such as a particular pigment (or characteristic mixture or juxtaposition). Numerous examples exist including some that would be simple to study, such as the introduction of 'Indian yellow' into miniature painting. However, this requires us to look at objects more as collective conveyors of data, less as supreme individual instances of a specific class of object.

B. Tools and techniques

The ways in which we carry out analysis on objects might initially seem a straightforward matter of choice for the individual analyst given the particular set of constraints, such as available instrumentation, sampling issues (including invasive/non-invasive and ease of access to the manuscript page(s)), time and cost, skill-set and so forth. However for us to make the most out of such analysis as a community we need to be sure that studies are conducted in consistent ways that can be compared, that sufficient regard is given to what sort of data can be acquired through the various means we use, including individual limitations, and how we can best share and exploit this knowledge.

Tools

An unfortunate degree of focus seems to go into the specific analytical tools to be used, either the exploitation of new ones, or the application of nearly-new ones to different problems. It is undoubtedly important that we have a tool-kit appropriate to the task, but we need to be very clear about what these are and whether they actually give us what we need, either alone or in combination. It could be argued that a surprising amount (to some) of submitted and published pigment analysis gives quite trivial results that, while technically novel (say, an object that has not been analysed before, or use of an unusual technique that duplicates other, more common, forms of analysis), does little or nothing to extend the field and our knowledge of manuscripts. This 'so what?' situation is often seemingly a consequence of the researchers being unaware of what is known about particular pigments and the kinds of features that can actually be determined to give truly useful information. There is also a 'community separation' phenomenon, where specific techniques are championed, rather than careful study made of the problems to be answered and approaches selected to best achieve answers. In the area just mentioned of socio-economic studies, the systematic, routine application of extant methods would go far to providing the information that is essential to such research. At the same time, the development of improved forms of existing tools – such as greatly increased sensitivity, or satisfying analytical gaps (such as good, non-invasive stratigraphical methods) – is both needed and can be readily explored in consultation with experienced practitioners.

Protocols

Stepping from the tools, the need to carry out the analyses in an informed way with due awareness of the limitations of each has to be underlined. A perennial problem is the invasive *vs.* non-invasive[3] debate and the basic question – do we take physical samples from an object – hides a remarkably complex set of issues. The argument for non-invasive analysis is beguilingly simple to express: that the analytical process should have no lasting physical impact on the object, changing nothing measurable afterwards. It might also appear that we have such tools available already in techniques like XRF and Raman. The truth is slightly different, with equipment limitations placing constraints on the size and format of the objects which can be studied, the form of the analysing beam (spatial resolution, intensity/sensitivity) varying with different types of instrument, degree of detail (spatial, chemical, morphological) achievable, portability and so forth. More important perhaps though is that it is still difficult to achieve certain forms of investigation without invasion – particle morphology and layer structures spring to mind. Furthermore, techniques commonly called 'non-invasive' still interact with objects to some extent and *may* induce temporary or permanent alteration as part of the analysis process, if only through handling. Briefly put then, analysis can be seen as a series of compromises between the richness of data acquired

---

[3] A brief definition for those unused to the terminology: 'non-destructive' analysis is where you end up with the same sample after the procedure, even if you have had to physically remove it for the analytical process; 'non-invasive' analysis is where no sample is taken, the process carried out *in situ*.

and the degree of invasiveness required to obtain it. For these various reasons it would be helpful to be able to apply some kind of cost-benefit analysis whereby different strategies could be evaluated, and thereby enable the informed selection of analytical instrumentation which could be employed by an end-user with greater confidence both in the achievable results and the safety of the objects being analysed.

Analytical reference standards

All analysts are familiar with the need for good instrumental reference standards. However, it is unclear whether the reference standards which are currently used in the paint and pigments field represent reliable or appropriate ones. Material used in reference collections appears to be generally formed on the basis of convenience and little has apparently been done to generate coherent collections characterised using multi-analytic procedures. A couple of simple examples: currently the number of 'standard' pigments that have been analysed by Raman spectroscopy is trivial when compared to the size of the database available for XRD studies; while extensive FTIR databases exist, where they cover pigments this has largely been with reference to modern commercial pigments. Although an unglamorous area (including for funding bodies), we are truly reliant on the reference standards we use having sufficiently broad coverage and accurate representation. One attempt to address this has been the Pigmentum Project collection of historical pigments, now running in excess of 2000 specimens, which has strict criteria on inclusion and characterisation.[4] So far it has been possible to analyse the collection almost in its entirety using polarised light microscopy (PLM), XRD and FTIR. More selective analysis has been conducted with SEM-EDX and Raman (~40% in the latter case), as well as Liquid Chromatography- Mass Spectrometry (LC-MS) studies of the dye-based pigments. This will hopefully soon be extended to include full XRF and Raman coverage (although funding is desperately needed to finish this and provide long-term access). There remains a need to integrate this information more fully, so that the data which is available from the XRD studies of different pigments can be used to inform the nomenclature and organisation of FTIR and Raman reference tables to provide more specific categorisation of pigments on manuscripts, which cannot themselves be analysed in depth using multiple techniques.

Inter-laboratory reliability

It is clear from reviewing the literature that little inter-laboratory comparison takes place. Widely used and normally expected in other fields, there has been a noticeable lack of such standards-supporting ventures in our own. Exceptions are the archaeometric fields of radiocarbon and dendrochronology, and more recently certain programmes for binding media analysis under the EU LabS-Tech and ARTECH initiatives.[5] However, if we are going to ensure that the work we do is consistent and reliable, then we should be looking at checking that comparable results come out of different laboratories.

Standard reporting methodologies and data sharing

For obvious reasons the normal medium of communication for results is through the academic paper, or narrow informal exchange between individual researchers, or networks such as BookNET. Hidden, however, are consistent ways of storing and sharing information, especially data generated from studies. One of the major barriers to the development of materials and techniques studies is actually access to results, either because when studies are published only sufficient data to justify the conclusions are given (an exemplar spectrum for example), or because they are presented in formats that are difficult to harmonise.

To overcome these kinds of problems there is a pressing need to share data, as opposed to just interpretations based on it, in ways that it can be readily accessed and consolidated. (Currently important data is being lost: we are aware for example of some major studies where the original data is largely inaccessible and only a couple of short publications based on the findings remain.) This of course necessarily implies that there has to be a suitable infrastructure available that can be widely accessed, such as an online database.

Finally, a plea: the terminology used to describe pigments (and to a lesser extent binding media) is very lax, such that it is often difficult or impossible to understand what exactly is being referred to. We need to agree what we mean. A proposal in the form of a systematic pigment taxonomy was made as part of the *Pigment Compendium* project (Eastaugh *et al.* 2002 and Eastaugh *et al.* 2004), but this is relatively complex to use and there are often situations in which we cannot be as precise as is ideally the case. Consequently we need something like a hierarchical taxonomy that describes not only the pigment, but also the level of understanding we have about it. For example, it is not uncommon to use the term 'lead white'; the basic (and basest) meaning is 'a white pigment that contains lead', but there is often an inference that it is 'lead carbonate hydroxide'. In fact this is a sizeable group of compounds, even when we don't include the lead sulfates and phosphates that might also reasonably be called 'lead white'. A structure where we can move from, say, 'Lead-based whites group' to 'Lead carbonates group' to 'Lead carbonate' would overcome such difficulties. Similar situations pertain with such seemingly common terms as 'vermilion', which is often used as a shorthand for any red mercury(II) sulfide compound whether it is the mineral cinnabar or synthetically produced by either of the two common routes, and 'yellow ochre', a catch-all phrase for a hugely variable material with a number of components present.

Conclusions

Paint analysis and the technological study of manuscripts and other similar printed and painted objects provide a unique set of challenges. In comparison to some allied fields there is much groundwork yet to be established, notably in establishing a common set of approaches to questions and a valid toolset with which to go about answering these. Some quite profound issues face us, such as how to derive rich, meaningful data from these often fragile objects. Such challenges are however frequently at the core of good research.

---

[4] http://pigmentum.org
[5] http://www.chm.unipg.it/chimgen/LabS-TECH ; http://www.eu-artech.org/ (both accessed 13.05.10)

References

Eastaugh, N., Walsh, V., Siddall, R., Chaplin, T., and Herman, H. 2002 Towards a taxonomy of pigments. *Art 2002. 7th International Conference on Non-destructive Testing and Microanalysis for the Diagnostics and Conservation of the Cultural and Environmental Heritage.* University of Antwerp 2-6 June 2002

Eastaugh, N., Walsh, V., Chaplin, T. and Siddall, R. 2004 *The Pigment Compendium. A Dictionary of Historical Pigments.* Elsevier, Oxford

Part Three:
Analytical Solutions to Manuscript Research Questions

Chapter 6

Paper Degradation and Conservation: Overview of Recent Research (2000-2010)

Matija Strlič

Centre for Sustainable Heritage, The Bartlett School of Graduate Studies, University College London

Introduction

During the last decade there have been a number of step changes in archival and library heritage research, many of which took place in international collaborative projects. The research encompassed domains of fundamental science of paper degradation, but also developments of new characterisation and conservation techniques, tools, and services. New knowledge of paper and ink oxidation led to development of antioxidant-based deacidification solutions. New techniques of cleaning historic paper using lasers have been developed and evaluated. New micro- and non-destructive techniques were developed for chemical and mechanical properties of interest in conservation and condition assessment of historic paper objects. Mass deacidification and other mass preservation strategies have been evaluated, and new techniques for identification and characterisation of inks and pigments have been applied.

This paper attempts to outline this explosion of new knowledge, however, it is by no means comprehensive. Detailed reviews of the literature were published in two books (Strlič & Kolar 2005; Kolar & Strlič 2006) and further reviews of current research are available in the preprints of "Durability of Paper and Writing" conferences (Kolar et al. 2004; Strlič & Kolar 2008) and of the "Advances in Paper Conservation Research" conference (Horie 2009).

Key research into paper degradation mechanisms

Hydrolysis and oxidation of cellulose

Building on the solid knowledge of acid-catalysed cellulose hydrolysis,[1] the interest of the paper conservation research community turned to oxidation in the early 1990s. The process of 'autoxidation'[2] is now known to lead to degradation of papers with neutral and mildly alkaline pH, and various ways of slowing down this process were discussed (Kolar et al. 1998). However, the interplay of endogenous (originating in paper itself) and exogenous (environmental) factors affecting the stability of paper is complex (Figure 1).

During the oxidation reactions, some of the excess energy is released in the form of light (chemiluminescence). As part of the PAPYLUM collaborative project, 2001-2005,[3] a new

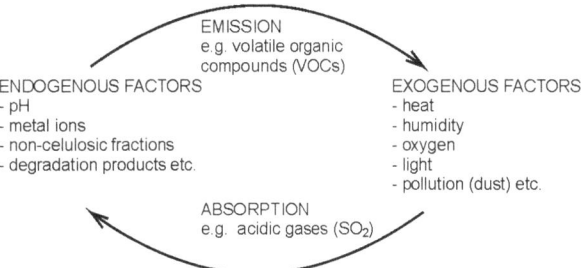

Figure 1: Factors affecting the stability of paper (Strlič & Kolar 2005).

treatment	factor of stabilisation
Ca(HCO$_3$)$_2$	2.5
Ca(HCO$_3$)$_2$ + KI	58
Ca(HCO$_3$)$_2$ + KBr	4.5
Ca(HCO$_3$)$_2$ + KSCN	13
Mg(HCO$_3$)$_2$	4.5
Mg(HCO$_3$)$_2$ + KI	8
Mg(HCO$_3$)$_2$ + KBr	7.5
Mg(HCO$_3$)$_2$ + KSCN	12

Figure 2: Factors of stabilisation of a historic paper using a variety of treatments, compared to no treatment (factor of stabilisation = 1, Strlič & Kolar 2005).

instrument was developed to enable researchers to measure this light and understand the autoxidation processes better. This is particularly relevant for rag papers and for paper after deacidification. In the course of the project, various aqueous (water-based) deacidification techniques were assessed, and the beneficial effect of some antioxidants was evaluated in terms of how many times paper lifetime is prolonged (Figure 2).

Oxidation and hydrolysis of cellulose can occur simultaneously, and the 'mixed-control concept' was introduced to describe the concurrent degradation processes (Barański et al. 2006). In paper, hydrolysis is controlled by acidity, and oxidation is controlled by the partial pressure of oxygen. A recent study using Fourier Transform InfraRed (FTIR) spectroscopy described the possibilities to discriminate between the two possible degradation pathways using *in situ* measurement methods and various types of spectral analysis (Łojewska et al. 2005). These concepts may be of particular value in

---

[1] 'hydrolysis' is the term used to describe the acid-catalysed chemical process of cellulose breakdown.
[2] 'autoxidation' describes oxidative processes leading to cellulose degradation under the influence of atmospheric oxygen.
[3] Papylum webpage, http://www.science4heritage.org/papylum/

studies of paper degradation in hypoxic or anoxic conditions, where oxygen is either present in a very low concentration or absent, respectively. Changes in the morphology of cellulose fibres were followed during accelerated ageing (Piantanida *et al.* 2005) using Atomic Force Microscopy (AFM). After topographic image analysis and correlation with chemical analysis, it was concluded that degradation of fibres into fibril bunches occurs non-homogeneously across the paper surface. This phenomenon was associated with oxidation processes.

Metal-mediated paper degradation

Transition metals are often found in association with manuscripts, in the form of iron gall inks and pigments such as copper-based greens, and these compounds have been noted to significantly affect the condition of the paper substrate. Much research has therefore been devoted to understanding transition metal-mediated degradation of cellulose and paper. In a recent publication, analogies between the catalytic role of the metals in solution and in cellulosic systems at mildly alkaline conditions were described (Šelih *et al.* 2007). To tackle the problem of ink corrosion, new non-aqueous stabilisation methods were developed during the INKCOR collaborative project, 2002-2005.[4] One hundred historic objects were characterised and the main reasons for ink corrosion were detailed, among which ink acidity, and not iron content, was found to be the most prominent cause of degradation.

The research on ink corrosion led to significant advances in the development of new conservation treatments for transition metal-catalysed degradation based on antioxidants, and a patent application was filed on the use of antioxidants for stabilisation of heritage materials. Imidazolium-based antioxidants were developed and tested, effective not only in iron-mediated corrosion, but also in copper-mediated corrosion (Ceres *et al.* 2008; Kolar *et al.* 2008). This is a significant advantage, as phytate-based treatments are ineffective for copper-containing compounds. The phytate treatment, which is perhaps the only treatment for ink corrosion targeted at iron inactivation in general use at present (Neevel, 1995), was optimised and a new procedure was proposed using magnesium phytate, thus avoiding the use of ammonia in the preparation of the treatment solution and ensuring effective chelation of iron (Kolar *et al.* 2007). Copper corrosion of paper remains of high interest and further research has been performed to understand the processes and possibilities of inhibition, particularly using size exclusion chromatography and determination of functional groups introduced during degradation (Henniges *et al.* 2006; Henniges *et al.* 2007).

Analysis of degradation products

In recent years, the interest in volatile organic compounds emitted from paper has increased considerably, partly due to concerns about indoor pollution (Figure 3). Studies of volatile organic compounds emitted by paper during degradation have produced valuable information on the reactions which have taken place (Strlič *et al.* 2009a). Using multivariate analysis of volatile degradation products emitted from papers of various

Figure 3: The volatiles emitted by degrading paper have recently been shown to contain useful information on stability and composition of the object, in the project Paper VOC (Strlič *et al.* 2009a).

compositions, it was possible to identify degradation markers for individual components of paper, such as rosin or lignin. This approach has the potential to be developed into a non-destructive characterisation technique for valuable heritage objects as in principle no sampling of the object is necessary. This is one of the key research questions in the new Heritage Smells! project (2010-2013), funded by the UK AHRC/EPSRC Science and Heritage Programme.[5]

Using Solid Phase MicroExtraction (SPME) in conjunction with Gas Chromatography-Mass Spectrometry (GC/MS) numerous volatiles emitted by paper have been identified (Lattuati-Derieux *et al.* 2004; Lattuati-Derieux *et al.* 2006; Gibson & Robertson 2009) and it was later shown that emission of furfural (a particular cellulose degradation compound) depends on the acidity of paper and could thus be used as a quantitative marker in its assessment (Strlič *et al.* 2007). However, it is only by applying multivariate data analysis to gas chromatographic data, that the technique reveals exciting new potentials in terms of identification and even quantification of paper properties.

Development of interventive conservation methods

Laser cleaning

In the past decade, two international projects focused on development and understanding of laser cleaning of paper and other organic materials. In the framework of the EUREKA LACLEPA project, 1999-2001,[6] various types of laser were tested and researched. A new laser cleaning workstation was developed, making use of a Nd:YAG[7] laser working at 1064 nm and 532 nm, and interactions between laser light and cellulose were intensively researched in order to understand the reasons why laser cleaning of paper has often been found to cause yellowing. While the interactions between laser light and clean paper were minimal, it was noted that soiled paper

---

[4] Inkcor webpage, http://www.infosrvr.nuk.uni-lj.si/jana/Inkcor/

[5] Heritage Smells! webpage, http://www.ucl.ac.uk/sustainableheritage/heritagesmells.htm
[6] LACLEPA webpage, http://www.infosrvr.nuk.uni-lj.si/jana/EUREKA/LACLEPA.html
[7] Nd:YAG laser: Neodymium-doped yttrium aluminium garnet based laser (Nd:$Y_3Al_5O_{12}$)

Figure 4: Testing of new conservation treatments for any adverse side effects is crucial. Photo from the final Inkcor[4] workshop, 2005.

yellowed considerably during the cleaning process. Further analysis suggested that this was caused by thermal degradation reactions taking place as a result of interactions between the soiling particles and the substrate. It was concluded that due to the induced yellowing, laser cleaning of paper may not be the method of choice for large surface areas, but may be a tool used for localised applications, particularly where the material was fragile or damaged (Strlič et al. 2005). The subsequent CRAFT project PARELA, 2001-2003[8] focussed on further development of the laser workstation and integration of scanning and laser cleaning in the same device. Various techniques were used for evaluation of the degradation (see Rudolph et al. 2004), and encouraging results were obtained with removal of undesired inks, stains and similar high precision cleaning tasks.

Polymer grafting

The PAPERTECH collaborative project, 2004-2007[9] focussed on the development of various conservation techniques, including cleaning, use of adhesives, consolidants, acrylic polymer grafting, and the effect of the application of these methods on durability of not only paper but also parchment. In a number of recent publications, the process of grafting acrylic polymers onto paper was described and the end-product characterised (Princi et al. 2006; Princi et al. 2008). It is hoped that by the process of grafting, brittle and degraded paper

---

[8] PARELA webpage, http://www.art-innovation.nl/index/PaReLa
[9] PAPERTECH webpage, http://www.phantasya.it/papertech/

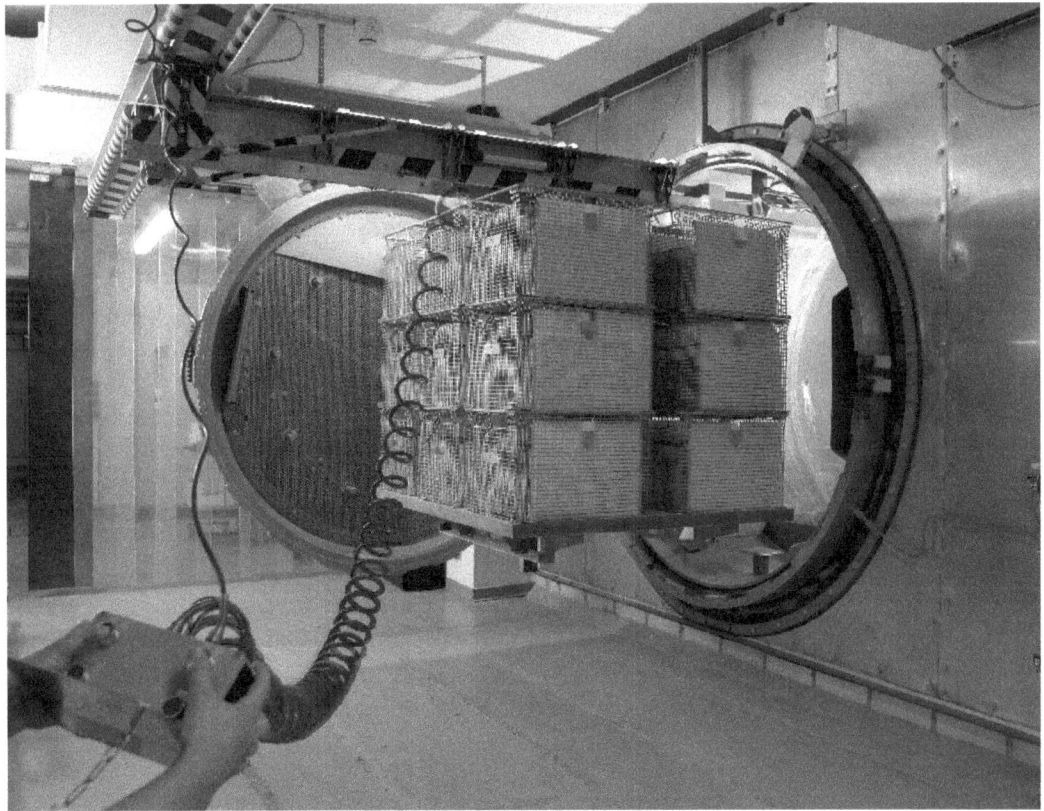

Figure 5: Mass deacidification at the Zentrum für Bucherhaltung (ZFB), Leipzig. Photo: ZFB.

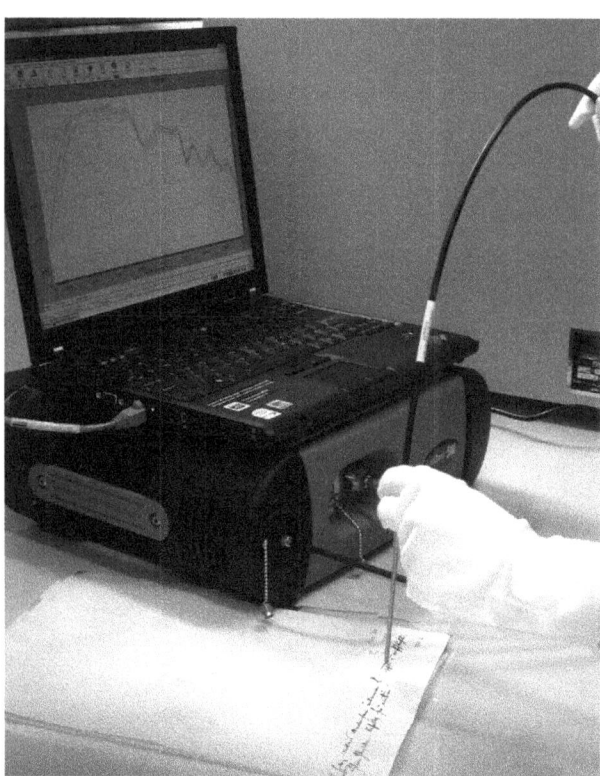

Figure 6: Examination of historic paper and iron gall ink using portable fibre-optics near infrared spectroscopy. Photo: L. Cséfalvayová.

could be reinforced. During the process, paper objects need to be irradiated with ultraviolet light to form radical species in the substrate, following which the grafting reaction takes place. The whole process needs to be carried out.

Evaluation of mass preservation options

The PAPERTREAT collaborative project, 2005-2008,[10] addressed the urgent need for evaluation of various mass preservation options, including mass deacidification. The mass deacidification techniques included BookKeeper, CSC, Neschen, and PaperSave (Figure 5). The efficiency and homogeneity of deacidification was evaluated and a catalogue of side effects was built and evaluated. The emissions of remaining solvents and other volatile organic compounds were evaluated along with possible adverse health effects.

The interesting series of contributions "Mass-deacidification of paper and books", appearing in various journals, started with an outline of the various processes (Cheradame et al. 2003) and then introduced a new method based on aminosilanes (Ipert et al. 2005). The procedure is valuable, as it not only leads to deacidification of the object, but also to its mechanical reinforcement. Various newer aminosilane formulations were tested recently (Ipert et al. 2006).

Development of new characterisation tools

Tools for cellulose and paper characterisation

In the course of most collaborative projects, new tools had to be developed as many cellulose and paper characterisation methods are several decades old and not useful for historic objects. Two international projects were almost entirely focussed on development of new instruments for paper characterisation (Strlič & Kolar 2008b). A chemiluminometer was built during the PAPYLUM project[3], and this has now been marketed by the Polymer Institute of the Slovak Academy of Sciences.[11] It has subsequently been used for parchment (Strlič et al. 2009b), and also for analysis of historic plastic materials during the POPART collaborative project, 2008-2012.[12] Infrared spectroscopy remains a very interesting technique of analysis and various novel approaches to paper characterisation and data analysis have been published in the last decade. FTIR spectra of cellulose were recently interpreted using quantum chemical modelling (Łojewski et al. in press), and *in situ* methods for studies of paper degradation have also been developed (Łojewska et al. 2005a).

Using the comparatively understudied Near Infrared (NIR) spectroscopy (Figure 6), a novel and entirely non-destructive paper characterisation and condition surveying methodology was developed during the SURVENIR collaborative project, 2005-2008.[13] By building a large database of historic samples and characterising them in detail, an incredible resource was built and is now available for further studies. This database was used for chemometric calibration of a purpose-built NIR spectrometer, now successfully marketed by Lichtblau e.K..[14] Using the technique, even non-destructive dating of paper and parchment is now possible (Trafela et al. 2007; Možir et al. in press). In UV-VIS-NIR imaging (365-1100 nm), quantitative analysis of spectra was recently attempted and mapping of different inks was made possible using multivariate analysis (Klein et al. 2008). Using cameras with extended wavelength regions (up to 2500 nm), it should be possible to extract quantitative chemical information from NIR images (Cséfalvayová et al. 2009).

Using fibre-optics NIR spectroscopy and multivariate analysis of data, spectra of iron gall inks were correlated with chemical properties of the inks. This is crucial for the evaluation of ink stability, pH and for assessing the degree of polymerisation of cellulose (Strlič et al. 2010a). Following the analyses of both ink and paper, it was possible to evaluate the time necessary for ink lines to degrade to the extent where their safe handling would be endangered, and classification of objects was proposed. The NIR characterisation technique has subsequently been applied to other materials such as historic plastic materials, parchment, films, photographs and has proven to be an extremely valuable recent development in heritage preservation (Wouters, 2008). In 2008, a COST D42 workgroup meeting was dedicated to the technique and abstracts are available, providing a

---

[10] PAPERTREAT webpage, http://www.infosrvr.nuk.uni-lj.si/jana/papertreat/

[11] Lumipol webpage, http://www.lumipol.com/?page=products 14.
[12] POPART webpage, http://popart.mnhn.fr/
[13] SURVENIR webpage, http://www.science4heritage.org/survenir/
[14] Lichtblau e.K. webpage, http://www.lichtblau-germany.com/

Figure 7: Understanding the degradation of paper in microenvironments in large collections is still an issue – the accumulation of indoor-generated pollutants, the influence of variations in temperature and RH, and the cross-infection between objects in close vicinity are intensively researched areas. Photo from the State National Archives, Dubrovnik.

convenient overview of the current research efforts.[15] As part of the POPART project, further applications for historic plastic objects are in development, to be marketed by Morana RTD d.o.o..[16]

Tools for ink and pigment characterisation

In ink and pigment analysis, decisive steps forward have been taken. In the Inkcor project[4], Proton Induced X-Ray Emission (PIXE) (Budnar *et al.* 2006), and Scanning Electron Microscopy with X-ray microanalysis (SEM-EDS) were used extensively. PIXE has also been used for elemental mapping in iron gall inks (Remazeilles *et al.* 2001). Following the earlier efforts with Laser Ablation - Inductively Coupled Plasma/Mass Spectrometry (LA-ICP/MS) (Wagner & Bulska, 2004), the technique was used in studies of metal migration (Strlič *et al.* 2008) and quantitative approaches to metal analysis in inks have been developed.

Among the new methods recently applied to ink and pigment analysis are also Laser Induced Breakdown Spectroscopy (LIBS) and Laser Induced Fluorescence (LIF) spectroscopy (Oujja *et al.* 2005). The techniques are interesting, as they are micro-destructive (LIBS) or possibly non-destructive (LIF) and are available as portable tools. Raman spectroscopy remains to be a very powerful tool used for both ink characterisation (Lee *et al.* 2008) and characterisation of pigments on paper (Eremin *et al.* 2008; Murcia-Mascarós, 2008). More recently, visually similar types of ink were systematically analysed using this technique, principally iron gall ink and logwood ink, which are difficult to distinguish using other techniques (Bicchieri *et al.* 2008).

Spectroscopic methods based on synchrotron radiation are increasingly used, e.g. X-Ray Absorption Spectroscopy (XAS), providing very interesting insight on speciation of iron in iron gall ink (Arčon *et al.* 2007), and even maps of Fe(II)/Fe(III) were produced, showing the distribution of the catalytically more active Fe(II) in iron gall ink (Kanngießer *et al.* 2004; Proost *et al.* 2004).

Development of preventive conservation strategies

The storage environment

Much of the previously-cited literature deals with degradation of paper-based collections which is caused by their environment, in particular temperature and relative humidity. A collection of further literature is frequently updated on the webpage of the "Indoor Air Quality" group.[17] It is generally understood that increased relative humidity and increased temperature lead to faster degradation of paper, although acidic and alkaline papers respond very differently (Strlič & Kolar 2005). Modelling software is available commercially (Climate Notebook[18]) for evaluation of the effect of the indoor climate on paper and other types of collections. Freely available software to model pollution in indoor environments is also available, as a result of the IMPACT collaborative project, 2000-2004.[19] However, it is still not clear to what extent fluctuations in relative humidity or temperature affect paper degradation, although many reports provide evidence that cycling conditions lead to faster degradation of paper. The mechanisms for this remain unknown (Bogaard & Whitmore 2002; Bigourdan & Reilly 2002). It is also generally accepted that cycling humidity

---

[15] "NIR/Chemometrics for Cultural heritage" workshop abstracts: http://www.science4heritage.org/COSTD42/Final%20programme%20D42%20workshop.pdf
[16] Morana RTD d.o.o. webpage, http://www.morana-rtd.com/
[17] Indoor Air Quality Group website, http://iaq.dk/biblio/biblio.htm
[18] Climate Notebook webpage: http://www.climatenotebook.org/
[19] Impact project webpage: http://www.ucl.ac.uk/sustainableheritage/impact/

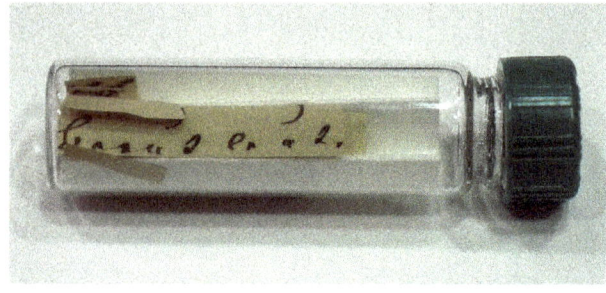

Figure 8: Using closed-vessel degradation experiments, it is possible to study the effect of one material on another. Here: an experiment showing the negative effect of paper containing iron gall ink on the degradation of another paper in its close vicinity
(Strlič *et al.* 2010 b).

causes faster degradation of ink-containing paper, and cycling conditions are often applied during accelerated degradation of iron gall ink containing paper (Kolar & Strlič 2006).

Pollution is another aspect which has received increased interest recently, and a review of its effects on libraries and archives was published by Tétreault (2003). In a recent comparison of various European archives and libraries, pollution levels (both outdoor and indoor generated pollutants) were compared and it was ascertained that indoor generated pollutants (such as volatile organic compounds) are found in much higher concentrations than traffic generated ones (Fenech *et al.* 2010). It was also shown that the composition of the indoor atmosphere in libraries and archives strongly depends on the type of materials stored, which is in line with studies published elsewhere (Strlič *et al.* 2009a). Acetic acid found in high concentrations in microenvironments (such as where library materials have been stored in enclosed boxes) could have particularly negative effects – especially on colour photographs (Fenech *et al.* in print), and while the influence of acetic acid on paper was recently discussed as a being controversial (Tétreault, 2010), more systematic research is needed to understand its effects, particularly in conjunction with temperature and relative humidity. Research into anoxic (or hypoxic) storage of paper also intensified recently. Although much of this is focussed on stability of pigments and dyes (which are not part of this overview) removal of oxygen does retard oxidative processes of paper degradation. This topic was recently reviewed (Thomas *et al.* submitted).

Studies of cross-infection, i.e. emission of volatile degradation products from a material (including paper itself) and their absorption into paper, are becoming of increased interest (Figure 8). The emission rates of various volatile degradation products of paper have been determined (Ramalho *et al.* 2009). In the Dutch-Slovenian PaperVOC[20] project focussing on the aspects of indoor-generated pollution, it has recently been shown that cellulose degraded together with groundwood-containing paper decays at a 100% faster rate than on its own (Strlič *et al.* 2010c). It is therefore possible that paper degradation depends strongly on its microenvironment. This is a problem which would benefit from more systematic research and is related to degradation of paper in closed books. A new test procedure was recently developed to allow for the assessment of storage materials and environmental modification strategies in view of the preservation effect they offer (Strlič *et al.* 2010c).

Collection modelling

Condition assessment of objects is a difficult topic, which has been shown to be fairly subjective (Taylor & Stevenson, 1999). Careful evaluation is needed to increase the reliability of data interpretation (Taylor & Watkinson, 2007), and aspects of lifetime modelling could potentially be integrated into a single collection model. This should allow for synergistic effects between temperature, relative humidity and pollutants to be evaluated. Aspects of building modelling, which have already been used for modelling library and archival environments (Taylor *et al.* 2005; Chang & Falk 2009), could also be integrated. In a current project at the National Archives, Kew, comprehensive modelling of the repository environment is taking place with the aim of optimising environmental management practices (Hong *et al.* 2010).

A holistic collection model would enable the appraisal of long-term priorities in terms of collection and environmental management, taking into account climate change scenarios. To do this, long-term forecasting of the outdoor climate (including pollution) needs to be integrated with models of material change under various indoor environmental conditions. This is a key research question addressed in the Collections Demography project (2010-2013), funded by the UK AHRC/EPSRC Science and Heritage Programme.[21]

Networking and capacity building activities

The 5th EU Framework Programme MIP thematic network, 2003-2006,[22] was a strong capacity-building initiative, capitalising on international and national collaborative projects. Within the network, paper and ink degradation and characterisation were discussed; however, it also contributed to dissemination of knowledge of conservation and standardisation. The Mellon-funded Identical Books project[23] significantly increased the research capacity among legal deposit libraries in the UK (Horie 2009). The COST D42 ENVIART action, 2006-2010[24] represents a further successful networking activity, in the frame of which the three working groups addressed various issues of interactions between historic objects and materials and the indoor environment. Library and archival materials feature very strongly in this project and numerous short scientific missions were funded on this topic. The ENVIART project is of further importance as it provides a platform for discussion of the current standardisation efforts in the frame of CEN Technical Committee 346, where

---

[20] PaperVOC project website: http://www.science4heritage.org/papervoc/

[21] Collections Demography webpage, http://www.ucl.ac.uk/sustainableheritage/collectionsdemography.htm
[22] MIP webpage, http://www.miponline.org
[23] Identical Books project webpage: http://www.library.jhu.edu/departments/preservation/hcs/index.html
[24] ENVIART webpage, http://www.echn.net/enviart/

standards related to cultural heritage, including archival and library collections, are discussed.

There are also substantial current research initiatives. Some of the Mellon-funded Post-Doctoral fellowships at the John Hopkins University are focussed on paper heritage. Two collaborative research projects funded by the UK AHRC/EPSRC Science and Heritage Programme, both starting in 2010, will entirely or partially focus on archival and library heritage, thus enabling further growth in the field and contributing to both the development of new tools (Heritage Smells![5]) and to holistic understanding of archival and library collections (Collections Demography)[21].

Conclusions and future directions

During the past decade of intensive and fruitful research into library and archival heritage a vibrant research community has grown and collaborated on many international projects. New knowledge has been accumulated in understanding paper degradation, development of conservation treatments, appraisal of mass preservation options, characterisation of paper and media on paper, and understanding of how the environment affects paper and collections. There was also significant cross-fertilisation with other areas of scientific endeavour, and heritage science often contributed new and significant knowledge on material characterisation and behaviour. Reports on success stories were published in influential science magazines and media, thus putting paper heritage science into the focus of the scientific community[25][26] which is important for the heritage scientific domain.

The key areas of research are slowly distilled into practice: treatments for iron gall ink and deacidification treatments have been optimised, mass preservation options appraised, dating tools and portable characterisation tools based on NIR spectroscopy are becoming available on the market, and best practices and guidelines are being developed by international standardisation bodies. This demonstrates the significance of the research for the wider end-user community.

Areas of further interest are:

- Development of damage functions taking into account various environmental parameters simultaneously
- Understanding of degradation of paper in microenvironments, e.g. in enclosures.
- Understanding of books as composite objects, and of collections as ensembles of objects.
- Understanding of the relationship between loss in value and degradation under different contexts of use.
- Development of damage function- and risk-based specifications for environmental conditions for storage and display.
- Development of management and decision-making models for the long term sustainable stewardship of collections.
- Development of the underpinning basic scientific knowledge.

All of the above should be framed by wider environmental, societal and strategic issues. For this, the input of heritage institutions is essential, because the translation of research into practice would lead to faster adoption of research results in collection management. Throughout the past decade, heritage institutions have been intensively involved in research projects, which helped in focussing the development and in faster dissemination and impact. There are also significant on-going and recently started large and international projects, which is highly promising.

References

Arčon, I., Kolar, J., Kodre, A., Hanžel, D. and Strlič, M. 2007 XANES analysis of Fe valence in iron gall inks. *X-Ray Spectrometry* **36**, 199-205.

Barański, A., Łagan, J.M. and Łojewski, T. 2006 The concept of mixed-control mechanisms and its applicability to paper degradation studies. *e-Preservation Science* **3**, 1-4.

Bicchieri, M., Monti, M. Piantanida, G. and Sodo, A. 2008 All that is iron-ink is not always iron-gall!, *Journal of Raman Spectroscopy* **39**, 1074-1078

Bigourdan, J-L. and Reilly J.M. 2002 Effects of Fluctuating Environments on Paper Materials—Stability and Practical Significance for Preservation. *La Conservation à l'Ère du Numérique, Actes des Quatrièmes Journées Internationales d'Études de l'ARSAG, Paris, May 27-30, 2002*, 180-192.

Bogaard, J. and Whitmore, P.M. 2002 Explorations of the role of humidity fluctuations in the deterioration of paper. In V. Daniels, A. Donnithorne, P. Smith (Eds.) *Works of Art on Paper Books, Documents and Photographs*, 11-15. International Institute for Conservation, Baltimore.

Budnar, M., Uršič, M., Simčič, J., Pelicon, P., Kolar, J., Šelih, V.S. and Strlič, M. 2006: Analysis of iron gall inks by PIXE. *Nuclear Instruments & Methods in Physics Research Section B-Beam Interactions With Materials and Atoms* **243**, 407–416.

Ceres, G., Mirruzzo, V., Strlič, M., Kolar, J. and Conte, V. 2008 Imidazolium based Ionic liquids in efficient treatments of iron gall inked papers. *ChemSusChem* (Chemistry and Sustainability) **1**, 921-926.

Cheradame, H., Ipert, S. and Rousset, E. 2003 Mass-deacidification of paper and books I: study of the limitations of the gas phase processes. *Restaurator* **24** 227-239

Chang, J.D. and Falk, B. 2009 Experimental and Computer Simulation Approach to Investigating the Environmental Performance of a Rare Books Archive. *e-Preservation Science* **6**, 180-185.

Cséfalvayová, L., Karjalajnen, H. and Strlič, M. 2009 NIR imaging of historic plastic materials. *COST D42 workshop "Modelling of the historic environment and of materials", Sibiu, Romania, September 21-22, 2009.*

---

[25] http://www.nature.com/news/2005/050905/full/news050905-7.html
[26] http://www.sciencemag.org/content/vol326/issue5957/r-samples.dtl

Eremin, K., Stenger, J., Huang, J.-F., Aspuru-Guzik, A., Betley, T., Vogt, L., Kassal, I., Speakman, S. and Khandekar, N. 2008 Examination of pigments on Thai manuscripts: the first identification of copper citrate. *Journal of Raman Spectroscopy* **39**, 1057-1065

Fenech, A., Strlič, M., Kralj Cigić, I., Levart, A., Gibson, L., de Bruin, G., Ntanos, K., Kolar, J. and Cassar, M. 2010 Volatile Aldehydes in Libraries and Archives. *Atmospheric Environment* **44**, 2067-2073

Fenech, A., Strlič, M., Degano, I. and Cassar, M. 2010 Stability of Chromogenic Colour Prints in Polluted Indoor Environments. *Polymer Degradation and Stability*, in print.

Gibson, L.T. and Robertson, C. 2009 Analysing smelly old books. In *Advances in Paper Conservation Research Conference, March 23-24, 2009, British Library, London*, 40-42.

Henniges, U., Banik, G., and Potthast, A. 2006 Comparison of Aqueous and Non-Aqueous Treatments of Cellulose to Reduce Copper-Catalyzed Oxidation Processes. *Macromolecular Symposia* **232**, 129-136

Henniges, U., Bürger, U., Banik, G., Rosenau, T., and Potthast, A. 2007 Copper Corrosion: Comparison between Naturally Aged Papers and Artificially Aged Model Papers. *Macromolecular Symposia* **244**, 194-203

Horie, C.V. (Ed.) 2009 *Advances in Paper Conservation Research*. British Library, London.

Hong, S.H., Ntanos, K., Strlič, M., Ridley, I., Bell, N. and Cassar, M. 2010 *Monitoring and Modelling the Storage Environment at The National Archives, Kew, UK*. Conference: Indoor Air Quality in Museums and Archives, Chalon-sur-Saone, April 21-23, 2010.

Ipert, S., Rousset, E. and Cheradame, H. 2005 Mass Deacidification of Papers and Books III: Study of a Paper Strengthening and Deacidification Process with Amino Alkyl Alkoxy Silanes. *Restaurator* **26**, 250-264

Ipert, S., Dupont, A.-L., Lavédrine, B., Bégin, P., Rousset, E. and Cheradame, H. 2006 Mass deacidification of papers and books. IV – A study of papers treated with aminoalkylalkoxysilanes and their resistance to ageing. *Polymer Degradation and Stability* **91**, 3448-3455

Kanngießer, B., Hahn, O., Wilke, M., Nekat, B., Malzer, W. and Erko, A. 2004 Investigation of oxidation and migration processes of inorganic compounds in ink-corroded manuscripts. *Spectrochimica Acta B* **59** 1511-1516

Klein, M.E., Aalderink, B. J., Padoan, R., de Bruin, G. and Steemers, T. A. 2008 Quantitative Hyperspectral Reflectance Imaging. *Sensors* **8**, 5576-5618

Kolar, J., Strlič, M., Novak, G. and Pihlar, B. 1998 Aging and Stabilization of Alkaline Paper. *Journal of Pulp Paper Science* **24**, 89-94

Kolar, J., Strlič, M. and Havermans, J. B. G. A. (Eds.) 2004 *Durability of paper and writing 1: book of abstracts*. 1st International Symposium and Workshops, Ljubljana, Slovenia, November 16-19, 2004, http://www.science4heritage.org/Zbornik.pdf

Kolar, J. and Strlič, M. (Eds.) 2006 *Iron Gall Inks: On Manufacture, Characterisation, Degradation and Stabilisation*. National and University Library, Ljubljana, Slovenia.

Kolar, J., Možir, A., Strlič, M., de Bruin, G. and Pihlar, B. 2007 Stabilisation of Iron Gall Ink: Aqueous Treatment with Magnesium Phytate. *e-Preservation Science* **4**, 19-24

Kolar, J., Mozir, A. Balazic, A., Strlič, M., Ceres, G., Conte, V., Mirruzzo, V., Steemers, T, and de Bruin, G. 2008 New antioxidants for treatment of transition metal containing inks and pigments. *Restaurator* **29**, 184-198

Lattuati-Derieux, A., Bonnassies-Termes, S. and Lavédrine, B. 2004 Identification of volatile organic compounds emitted by a naturally aged book using solid-phase microextraction/gas chromatography/mass spectrometry. *Journal of Chromatography A* **1026**, 9-18

Lattuati-Derieux, A., Bonnassies-Termes, S. and Lavédrine, B. 2006 Characterisation of Compounds Emitted During Natural and Artificial Ageing of a Book. Use of Headspace-Solid-Phase Microextraction/Gas Chromatography/Mass Spectrometry. *Journal of Cultural Heritage* **7**, 123-133

Lee, A.S., Otieno-Alego, V. and Creagh, D. C. 2008 Identification of iron-gall inks with near-infrared Raman microspectroscopy. *Journal of Raman Spectroscopy* **39**, 1079-1084

Łojewska, J., Miśkowiec, P., Łojewski, T. and Proniewicz, L.M. 2005a Cellulose oxidative and hydrolytic degradation: In situ FTIR approach. *Polymer Degradation and Stability* **88**, 512-520

Łojewska, J., Lubańska, A., Łojewski, T., Miśkowiec, P. and Proniewicz, L. M. 2005b Kinetic approach to degradation of paper: in situ FTIR transmission studies on hydrolysis and oxidation. *e-Preservation Science* **2**, 1-12

Łojewski, T., Miśkowiec, P., Missori, M., Lubańska, A., Proniewicz, L. M. and Łojewska, J. (in press). FTIR and UV/VIS as methods for evaluation of oxidative degradation of model paper. DFT approach for carbonyl vibrations. *Carbohydrate Polymers*

Možir, A., Strlič, M., Trafela, T., Kralj Cigić, I., Kolar, J., Deselnicu, V. and de Bruin, G. (in press) On Oxidative Degradation of Parchment and Its Non-destructive Characterisation and Dating. *Applied Physics A*, forthcoming.

Murcia-Mascarós, S. and García-Ramos, J. V. 2008 Raman Spectroscopy – Principles and Some Case Studies. In M. Schreiner, M. Strlič, R. Salimbeni (eds.) *Use of Lasers in Conservation and Conservation Science*, Chapter 4.1. COST office: http://alpha1.infim.ro/cost/pagini/handbook/index.htm

Neevel, J. 1995 Phytate: a potential conservation agent for the treatment of ink corrosion caused by irongall inks. *Restaurator* **16**, 143-160

Oujja, M., Vila, A., Rebollar, E., García, J. F. and Castillejo, M. 2005 Identification of inks and structural characterization of contemporary artistic prints by laser-induced breakdown spectroscopy. *Spectrochimica Acta B* **60**, 1140-1148

Piantanida, G., Bicchieri, M. and Coluzza, C. 2005 Atomic force microscopy characterization of the ageing of pure cellulose paper. *Polymer* **46**, 12313-12321

Princi, E., Vicini, S., Pedemonte, E., Gentile, G., Cocca, M. and Martuscelli, E. 2006 Synthesis and mechanical characterisation of cellulose based textiles grafted with acrylic monomers. *European Polymer Journal* **42**, 51-60

Princi, E. and Vicini, S. 2008 Graft polymerisation of ethyl acrylate/methyl methacrylate copolymers: A tool for the consolidation of paper-based materials. *European Polymer Journal* **44**, 2392-2403

Proost, K., Janssens, K.,Wagner, B., Bulska, E. and Schreiner, M. 2004 Determination of localized Fe^{2+}/Fe^{3+} ratios in inks of historic documents by means of µ-XANES. *Nuclear Instruments and Methods in Physics B* **213**, 723-728

Ramalho, O., Dupont, A.-L., Egasse, C. and Lattuati-Derieux, A. 2009 Emission Rates of Volatile Organic Compounds from Paper. *e-Preservation Science* **6**, 53-59

Remazeilles, C., Quillet, V., Calligaro, T., Dran, J. C., Pichon, L. and Salomon, J. 2001 PIXE elemental mapping on original manuscripts with an external microbeam. Application to manuscripts damaged by iron-gall ink corrosion. *Nuclear Instruments and Methods in Physics B* **181**, 681-687

Rudolph, P., Ligterink, F.J., Pedersoli Jr,. J.L., van Bommel, M., Bos, J., Aziz, H. A., Havermans, J.B.G.A., Scholten, H., Schipper, D. and Kautek, W 2004 Characterization of laser-treated paper. *Applied Physics A* **79**, 181-186

Šelih, V.S. Strlič, M., Kolar, J and Pihlar, B. 2007 The role of transition metals in oxidative degradation of cellulose. *Polymer Degradation and Stability* **92**, 1476-1481

Strlič, M. and Kolar, J. (eds.) 2005 *Ageing and Stabilisation of Paper*. National and University Library, Ljubljana, Slovenia

Strlič, M., Šelih, V. S., Kolar, J., Kočar, D., Pihlar, B., Ostrowski, R., Marczak, J., Strzelec, M., Marincek, M., Vuorinen, T. and Johansson, L. S. 2005 Optimisation and on-line acoustic monitoring of laser cleaning of paper. *Applied Physics A* **81**, 943-951

Strlič, M., Kralj Cigić, I., Kolar, J., de Bruin, G. and Pihlar, B. 2007 Non-Destructive Evaluation of Historical Paper Based on pH Estimation from VOC Emissions. *Sensors* **7**, 3136-3145

Strlič, M. and Kolar, J. (eds.) 2008a *Durability of paper and writing 2: book of abstracts*. 2nd International Symposium and Workshops, Ljubljana, Slovenia, July 5-7, 2008, http://www.science4heritage.org/DPW2/DPW2 book.pdf.

Strlič, M. and Kolar, J. 2008b Recent developments in non- and micro-destructive analysis of historical paper. In M. P. Colombini, L. Tassi (eds) *New Trends in Analytical, Environmental and Cultural Heritage Chemistry*, 477-491. Kerala: Transworld Research Network

Strlič, M., Šelih, V. S. and Kolar J. 2008 Analytical Methods Based on Laser Ablation Sampling. In M. Schreiner, M. Strlič, R. Salimbeni (eds.) *Use of Lasers in Conservation and Conservation Science*, Chapter 4.5. COST office: http://alpha1.infim.ro/cost/pagini/handbook/index.htm

Strlič, M., Thomas, J., Trafela, T., Cséfalvayová, L., Kralj Cigić, I., Kolar, J. and Cassar, M. 2009a Material Degradomics: on the Smell of Old Books. *Analytical Chemistry* **81**, 8617-8622

Strlič, M., Kralj Cigić, I. Rabin, I., Kolar, J., Pihlar, B. and Cassar, M. 2009b Autoxidation of Lipids in Parchment. *Polymer Degradation and Stability* **94**, 886-890

Strlič, M., Cséfalvayová, L., Kolar, J., Menart, E., Kosek, J., Barry, C. Higgitt, C. and Cassar, M. 2010a Non-destructive characterisation of iron gall ink drawings: not such a galling problem anymore. *Talanta* **81**, 412-417

Strlič, M., Menart, E., Kralj Cigić, I., de Bruin, G., Kolar, J. and Cassar, M. 2010b Emission of volatiles and reactive oxygen species during degradation of iron gall ink. *Polymer Degradation and Stability* **95**, 66-71

Strlič, M., Kralj Cigić, I., Možir, A., Thickett, D., de Bruin, G., Kolar, J. and Cassar, M. 2010c Test for Compatibility with Organic Heritage Materials – A Proposed Procedure. *e-Preservation Science* **7**, 78-86

Taylor, J. and Stevenson, S. 1999 Investigating subjectivity within collection condition surveys. *Museum Management and Curatorship* **18**, 19-42

Taylor, J., Blades, N., Cassar, M. and Ridley, I. 2005 Reviewing past environments in a historic house library using building simulation. In I. Verger (ed.) *ICOM - Committee for Conservation 14th Triennial Meeting, The Hague*, 708-715. James and James, London

Taylor, J. and Watkinson, D. 2007 Indexing Reliability for Condition Survey Data. *The Conservator* **30**, 49-62

Tétreault, J. 2003 *Airborne Pollutants in Museums, Galleries and Archives: Risk Assessment, Control Strategies and Preservation Management*. Canadian Conservation Institute, Ottawa

Tétreault, J. 2010 *Carbonyl vapors and their impact on paper degradation*. Conference: Indoor Air Quality in Museums and Archives, Chalon-sur-Saone, April 21-23, 2010

Thomas, J., Townsend, J., Strlič, M. and Hackney, S. (submitted) A Review of Anoxia as Applied to Works of Art on Paper. *Reviews in Conservation*

Trafela, T., Strlič, M., Kolar, J., Lichtblau, D. A., Anders, M., Pucko Mencigar, D. and Pihlar B. 2007 Non-destructive analysis and dating of historical paper based on IR spectroscopy and chemometric data evaluation. *Analytical Chemistry* **79**, 6319-6323

Wagner, B. and Bulska, E. 2004 On the use of laser ablation inductively coupled plasma mass spectrometry for the investigation of the written heritage. *Journal of Analytical Atomic Spectrometry* **19**, 1325-1329

Wouters, J. 2008 Coming soon to a library near you? *Science* **322**, 1196-1198

Chapter 7

Investigating the Structural Integrity of Historical Documents using X-ray Diffraction Techniques

Kate Thomas, Lee Gonzales & Tim Wess

School of Optometry and Vision Science, Cardiff University

Introduction

Until the digital era, the writings of historical documents, books and manuscripts have provided us with a wealth of knowledge. In addition to the written word, the writing surface not only provides information about the cultural context, but its integrity is essential to the survival of the object. Writing materials have varied greatly over the years with the two most common media being parchment and paper. Although the origins of parchment and paper differ greatly (consisting of animal hide and plant fibres respectively), they have one major factor in common: they both degrade with time. As technology allows us to become more adept at identifying degradation, science begins to play a crucial part in the long-term survival of these documents.

New and already established technologies allow us to help inform conservators from a firm science based approach, and many technologies have been used and proposed over recent years for the examination and extraction of data from historical documents. One technique that has significantly aided the evaluation of the chemical structure and organisation of historical writing materials is X-ray diffraction. Since 1895 when W. C. Röntgen discovered X-rays and their ability to be scattered by matter, X-ray diffraction has become an essential technique to study the structure of matter at a molecular and atomic level.

Our studies on parchment, paper and leather are capable of determining:

- Their structural nano-architecture
- Chemical composition
- Physical and mechanical properties

Other features of the technique include small samples sizes (sub micron is possible) and non-destructive analysis. Therefore, a complement of research techniques that are allied to and cut across X-ray diffraction analysis can give a detailed analysis of the reactive history of writing media. This paper gives a broad overview of the factors affecting the survival of parchment and paper media, and discusses the application of X-ray diffraction analysis to investigate historical documents. The technique of X-ray diffraction is discussed in greater detail in the technical appendix at the end of the chapter.

Structure of parchment and paper

Parchment and leather

The process of writing on prepared animal skin has been used for many centuries and is of fundamental significance as it documents much of our written history. Parchment is a proteinaceous collagen-based writing material that is made from processed, untanned animal skins, mainly calf, sheep or goat (Larsen, 2002; Reed, 1973). Leather is produced by tanning animal hides and skins. Microscopically, collagen based tissues are hierarchically arranged, with a structural relationship between the different hierarchical levels (Maxwell et al. 2006). A more in-depth look at the structure of collagen and subsequently parchment is given in the technical appendix at the end of this chapter.

Paper and papyrus

The major structural component found in paper, wood and textiles is cellulose. Cellulose is a polysaccharide (carbohydrate) material, and the most abundant naturally occurring organic substance. It is organised in crystalline domains called microfibrils (Emons and Mulder, 2000) where the diameter of the microfibrils varies between 2nm and 25nm. The arrangement of molecules in cellulose is sufficiently ordered for cellulose to give an X-ray diffraction pattern. Cellulose has been shown to be arranged in a spiral arrangement which provides the properties of stiffness and extensibility. Papyrus is a paper-like material produced from the pith of the papyrus plant which was believed to be first used in ancient Egypt. In dry climates, like that of Egypt, papyrus is fairly resistant, but in European countries papyrus appears to be more susceptible to degradation. Papyrus is extremely sensitive to environmental conditions, in particular exposure to light, mechanical handling and relative humidity. In addition, the analysis of paper, cellulose and papyrus is often interested in measuring the pH, which is an essential parameter that has a large impact on its durability.

Degradation of parchment and paper

Over time, historical documents made from both parchment and paper will degrade. This can be further accelerated by a range of factors, including temperature, relative humidity, mechanical damage, radiation damage and bacterial/fungal growth (Kennedy *et al.* 2004b). This range of factors has been shown to cause irreversible damage to the structural integrity of historical documents. The effect of these factors is outlined in further detail below.

Temperature

Parchment is extremely sensitive to fluctuations in temperature, especially in the presence of elevated relative humidity (RH).[1] The response of parchment heated under dry conditions is less severe; Reed (1973) found that when parchment was heated in the absence of moisture, degradation was less drastic and that the parchment was able to withstand temperatures of 100°C with no change in colour, dimension or shape of the parchment sample. Parchment heated in the presence of moisture was found to accelerate degradation, and the parchment was gelatinised.

Relative humidity (RH)

High humidity conditions trigger micro-biological growth on the surface of parchment, while low humidity conditions cause the collagen fibres to shrink and harden (Hansen *et al.* 1992). Storage recommendations for parchment seem to vary greatly, with a number of different research reports suggesting a variety of ranges. One study advises a humidity range from 50% RH to 65% RH (Hansen *et al.* 1992), while others suggest a value between 45%RH and 60%RH (Kite and Thomson, 2006). Peters (1996) suggested that it is preferable to maintain a consistent relative humidity value in a range as low as possible under ambient conditions. Hansen *et. al.* (1992) studied the effects of relative humidity of the physical properties of modern vellum.[2] They found that variations in RH caused the parchment to swell and shrink, producing internal strain which eventually resulted in irreversible damage. It was noted that an RH lower than 25% increases the stress induced into the parchment while humidities above 40% RH increase the process of gelatinasation and allow biological growth.

Mechanical damage

The most common damage to parchment and paper is mechanical damage, which is most often seen as tears on edges and folds as a result of frequent handling. Damage caused by everyday use is mainly cosmetic and does not result in changes in the structure of the material. However, mechanical damage in the form of tears and breakage can also result from excessive dryness, while excessive dampness can cause deformations and warping.

Radiation damage

The ultraviolet (UV) radiation in daylight and artificial light plays an important role in parchment and paper degradation. Parchment is affected by photochemical reactions in which hydrogen peroxide is formed. The parchment is broken down and gelatinised in the process (Reed, 1973). This causes the parchment to become brittle, fragile and liable to split. Paper is also found to degrade under radiation damage, where a discolouring is often seen in paper that has been stored under bright light.

Bacterial/fungal growth

Temperature and relative humidity play a significant role in the degradation of both parchment and paper. The ideal conditions for deterioration by bacteria or fungi is a combination of a high level of relative humidity (70%-100%RH) with a high temperature (>22°C) (Reed, 1973).

Application of X-ray diffraction to manuscript research questions

There are several possible manuscript research questions which X-ray diffraction analysis can help to investigate, including:

- What is the mechanism of deterioration?
- What is the best way of storing historical documents?
- How can we detect deterioration without damaging documents?
- If it is too damaged to unroll or repair can we still read it?

A series of studies have been carried out using X-ray diffraction as a valuable scientific technique on a number of historical documents. Four such studies are summarised below.

Dead Sea Scrolls

The Dead Sea Scrolls comprise over 800 Biblical documents written between 200BC and 68AD, which are of great historical and religious interest. Degradation of these important documents is a serious factor placing them at risk; therefore there is a need to preserve them. The technique microfocus X-ray diffraction was implemented to assess the variations in a cross section of parchment from surface-to-

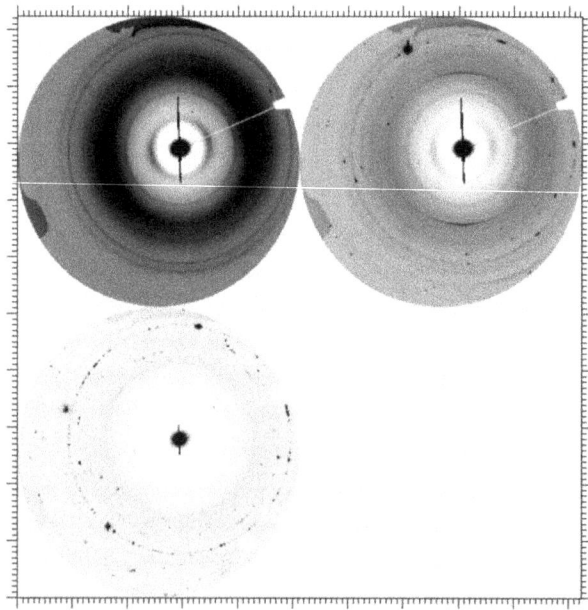

Figure 1: Microfocus X-ray diffraction images taken from Dead Sea Scroll sample showing presence of mineral.

---

[1] Relative humidity (RH) is a term which describes the relationship between the moisture content of the air and the temperature, since warm air can hold more moisture than cold air. It is expressed as a percentage which relates to the maximum amount of water that the air can hold at a given temperature; therefore an RH of 100% means that the air surrounding an object is saturated with moisture. To decrease the RH, either the air temperature must be increased or water removed from the air.

[2] Vellum is parchment made from the skin of young or unborn calves

surface. Microfocus X-ray diffraction images taken from Dead Sea Scroll sample showing presence of mineral are shown in Figure 1. Using this technique it was found that parchment containing mineral deposits has a greater intact collagen substructure content, suggesting a relationship between mineral content and parchment integrity. This was further investigated using an X-ray diffraction thermal experiment where it was found that in Dead Sea Scroll samples containing mineral, the collagen structure is rigid and unchanged even upon heating to 120°C. Using attenuated total reflectance-Fourier transform infrared spectroscopy it was further found that those samples with mineral deposits exhibit intact collagen structure on the surface and those without mineral have extensively degraded collagen on the surface. In this study, it is hypothesised that the mineral plays an inherent role in the stability of the collagen lattice in the Dead Sea Scrolls. This permits the parchments to withstand environmental changes more effectively- thereby, reducing the harmful effects of elevated temperatures and humidities. Our results provide evidence that CO_3^{2-} and SO_4^{2-} bind at a molecular level within the collagen matrix, restricting movement of the lattice and providing a platform of mineral growth at the surface of the parchment.

Domesday Book

The Domesday Book was a land survey commissioned by William the Conqueror in 1086 and is a valuable part of English history and heritage. Information collected on the land and resources available at this time and was recorded onto parchment and compiled into two volumes: 'Great Domesday' and 'Little Domesday'. The writing itself provides a wealth of knowledge on medieval England but the parchment it is written on can also supply us with vitally important information.

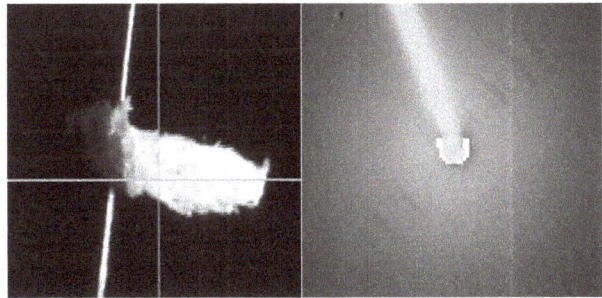

Figure 2: Image of Domesday sample mounted on a capillary in the X-ray beam (on left). X-ray diffraction image taken from Domesday sample (on right).

Microfocus X-ray diffraction was able to be conducted on Domesday Book samples due to the extremely small X-ray beam (a few microns). The samples in this case were sourced as scrapings from the surface of the parchment and were sub-millimeter in size and approximately 50 micron in thickness. Analysis of these historically significant samples using X-ray diffraction has given a clearer picture of the condition of the Domesday Book and allowed greater understanding of the degradation mechanisms in parchment.

Leather bookbindings project

Samples were sourced from a major investigation started in the 1930s to determine the causes of leather deterioration and to determine how the long term durability of leather is affected by the treatments and tannins used. The significant part of this study is that each of the samples were cut in two, and stored

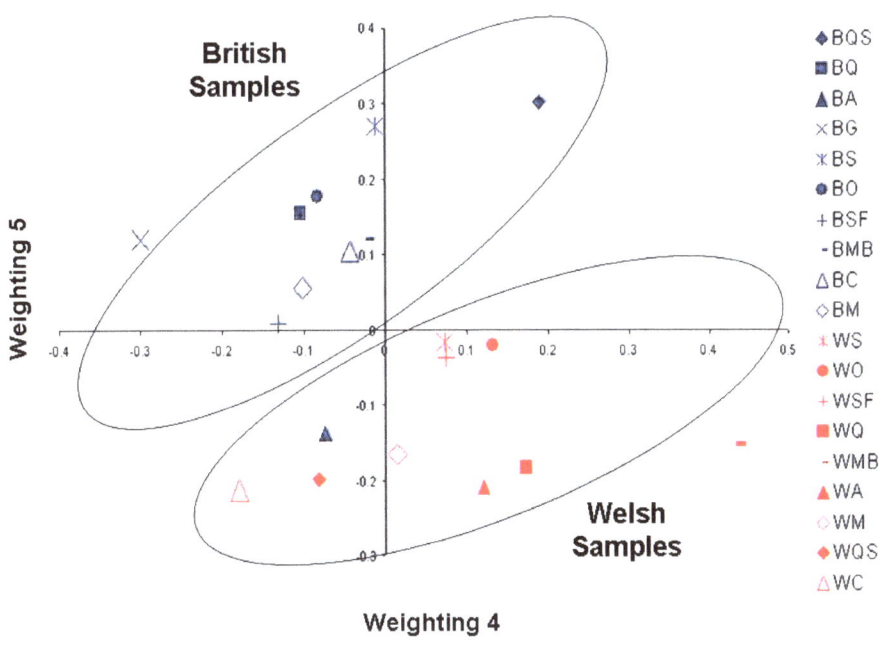

Figure 3: Using the mathematical technique of principal Component Analysis it is possible to separate the samples by location at which they were stored; the British Library, London (blue data points) and the National Library of Wales, Aberystwyth (red data points).

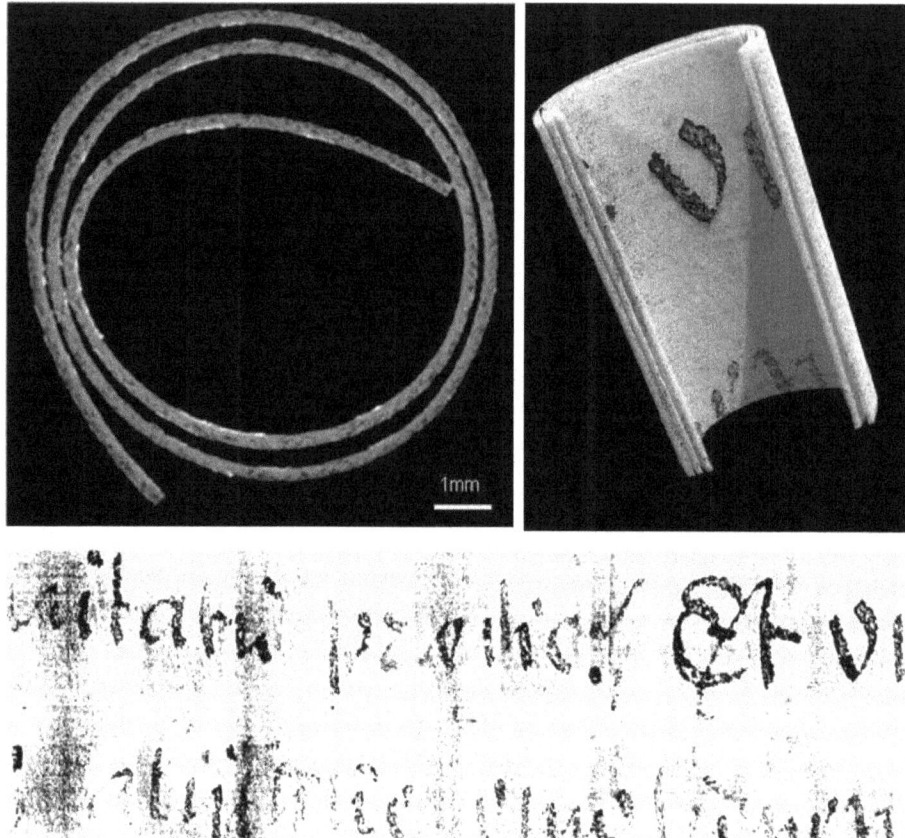

Figure 4: Feasibility study on small 17th century parchment. A small cut sample from a historical parchment was rolled and scanned with the high definition XMT scanner at Queen Mary, University of London (QMUL).
Upper left: Cross-sectional tomographic slice with contrast enhanced to show ink on the surface of the parchment. Upper right: Volume rendered cutaway view with pseudo-colouring (related to the X-ray linear attenuation coefficient), revealing text (see www.microtomography.org/images/scroll.wmv for movie). Bottom: Virtual unrolling of the microtomography data performed at Cardiff using a relatively simple algorithm applicable to such a small, well formed scroll.

for more than 50 years in two different locations. Locations were the British Library in London and the National Library of Wales in Aberystwyth. The objective of this study was to examine the effects of air quality on collagen based tissue samples. The aim was to determine if there were differences between two sets of identical samples purely based on the effects of storage location. The use of the mathematical principle Principal Component Analysis (PCA) as a tool to identify small but significant changes, which would normally have been disregarded, has been fundamental to this investigation. It is likely that these minute changes would occur at various hierarchical levels of the collagen structure. PCA has been shown to distinguish mathematically the differences between the samples due to varying locations of storage.

X-ray tomography of parchment scrolls

The purpose of this project is to develop a facility using high definition X-ray microtomography (XMT) in conjunction with advanced image processing algorithms to enable the reading of such fragile historic documents without the need to physically unravel them, thus providing valuable information to a wide range of scholarly disciplines. The technique can also be applied to some of the many documents damaged by fire, whose content has yet to be determined. The project develops novel data collection methods in conjunction with computational strategies to reveal text to conservators, historians, palaeographers, social scientists and thence the public.

Conclusions

X-ray diffraction has been carried out on a large collection of materials including parchment, leather, paper and papyrus. In addition to evaluating the structure of these materials, X-ray diffraction has been utilised to assess the effect of degradation by a number of external factors, including temperature, relative humidity, mechanical damage, radiation damage and bacterial/fungal growth.

Technical Appendix

Collagen structure (including leather and parchment)

Collagen based tissues such as skin and its by-product parchment are hierarchically arranged where a structural

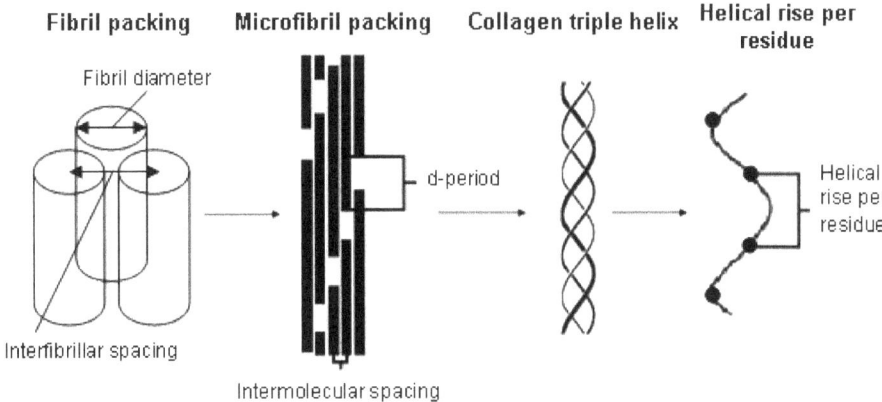

Figure 5: Illustration of the collagen hierarchy. From left to right, fibril packing, microfibril packing, collagen triple helix and helical rise per residue. Diagram is not to scale.

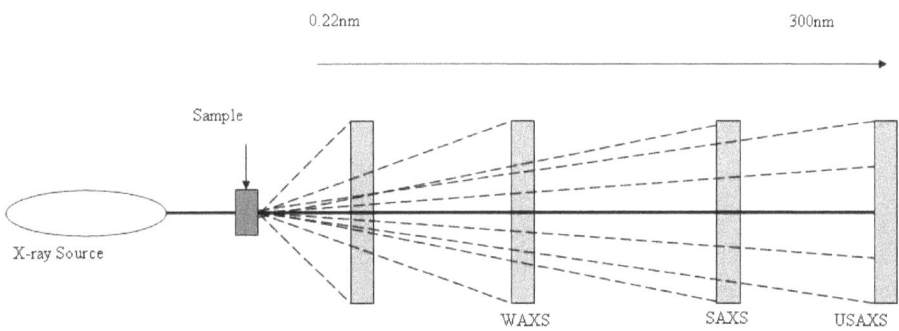

Figure 6: Illustration of sample to detector distances (camera lengths). The main beam is scattered following interaction with the sample. Depending on the position of the detector different length scales can be investigated. Short sample to detector distances means X-rays scattered at wide-angles can be collected pertaining to structures in the region of a few nanometers. Longer sample to detector distances allows the collection of X-rays scattered at small-angles which provides structural information at length scales of a few hundred nanometers. Diagram is not to scale and is adapted from Maxwell *et al.* 2006.

relationship is observed between the different hierarchical levels (Maxwell *et al.* 2006). Parchment is comprised predominately of type I collagen fibres orientated randomly and distributed as a feltwork (Kennedy *et al.* 2002). Type I collagen, the main constituent of skin, is comprised of three α-chains (α1, α2, α1) that are helically wound into a triple helix and contain approximately 1000 amino acids per polypeptide chain. These three α-chains contain the Gly-X-Y repeating sequence where X is often proline or hydroxyproline (Traub, 1978). Collagen molecules are approximately 300nm in length and are staggered axially relative to their neighbouring molecules by d (fundamental axial periodicity), where d ~ 65nm in skin and d ~ 67nm in tendon (Brodsky *et al.* 1980; Stinson and Sweeny, 1980; Menon, 2002). This stagger results in a gap and an overlap region between adjacent molecules. The collagen hierarchy is illustrated in Figure 5 where the fibril packing, microfibril packing, collagen triple helix and helical rise per residue are shown.

In order to investigate these different length scales of collagen, X-ray diffraction can be utilised. By using a series of different camera lengths, shown in Figure 6, information is obtained regarding the structural features in the region of 0.22nm up to 300nm.

X-ray diffraction and scattering

All matter scatters X-rays. Diffraction is a specific type of scattering that leads to large scale interference effects, where incoming X-rays are scattered by atoms in all directions. The majority of X-rays scattered by matter will interfere destructively, however, in some directions, the scattered X-rays will be in phase; therefore, reinforcing each other and forming diffracted beams (Cullity, 1978). It is the constructive interference that creates the observed diffraction pattern (example diffraction patterns are demonstrated in Figure 7). The ordering of the material leads to the inference of whether diffraction or scattering occurs. Scattering occurs when the electron density changes within the sample, these fluctuations can then be analysed to provide structural information. The intensity of the scattering corresponds to the number of atoms present and their relative location.

The distance between the detector and the sample provides information at different structural levels in collagen (see Figure

6). Sample to detector lengths frequently used to investigate collagen structure are Small-angle X-ray Scattering (SAXS) and Wide-angle X-ray Scattering (WAXS).

Small-angle X-ray Scattering (SAXS)

Scattering by X-rays at small angles (<6°) gives information regarding the long-range order of structures (Glatter and Kratky, 1982). Collagen fibrils from skin and subsequently parchment exhibit a fundamental axial periodicity in the region of 65.5nm which is observable within the capacity of SAXS (Brodsky *et al.* 1980). The fundamental axial periodicity is the result of regular fluctuations in the electron density of collagen in the axial direction (Hodge and Petruska, 1963). Small angle X-ray diffraction has been used to compile a detailed explanation of how degradation affects the structural integrity of historical parchment (Kennedy *et al.* 2003). It has also facilitated a greater understanding of how factors like UV, hydration, relative humidity misuse and the presence of lipids affects the structure of parchment and causes irreversible damage (Wess and Orgel, 2000; Ghioni *et al.* 2005; Kennedy *et al.* 2004b; Maxwell *et al.* 2006). Leather is produced from the tanning of animal hides and skins. The leather industry is a vast area with many products ranging from clothing to book bindings being made from leather. Understanding the structure of leather is considered important in trying to produce better quality leather and aid preservation of leather products. SAXS experiments have been carried out on leather to investigate the effects of biaxial stretching on the fibre orientation (Sturrock *et al.* 2004) and the production process of leather and parchment (Maxwell *et al.* 2006).

Wide-angle X-ray Scattering (WAXS)

Scattering at wide-angles provides information on structural features sub-nanometers in size. Two features detected in collagen by wide-angle are the intermolecular spacing and the helical rise per residue. The key features in collagen at wide-angles are the reflections seen at 0.29nm and 1.2nm (Meek and Quantock, 2001; Sionkowska *et al.* 2004). The reflection seen at approximately 0.29nm relates to the helical rise per residue, which is the distance between the amino acid residues along the collagen triple helices. The intermolecular lateral packing corresponds to the distance between one collagen molecule and its nearest neighbour, which is observed at approximately 1.2nm.

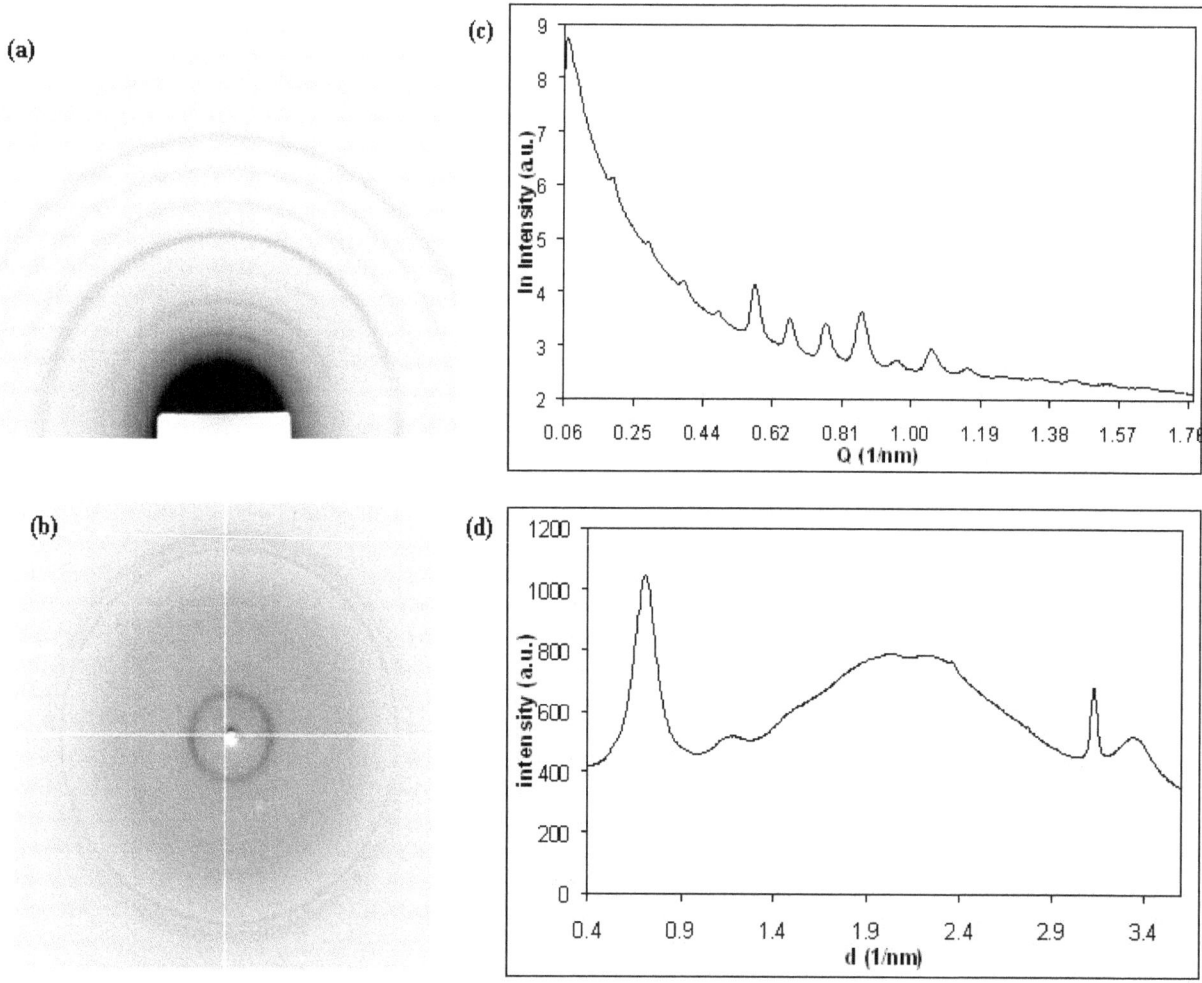

Figure 7: Two X-ray diffraction patterns taken from collagen at (a) small angles and (b) wide angles. The corresponding linear traces calculated from the two-dimensional X-ray diffraction patterns is shown in (c) and (d) for small angle and wide angle respectively.

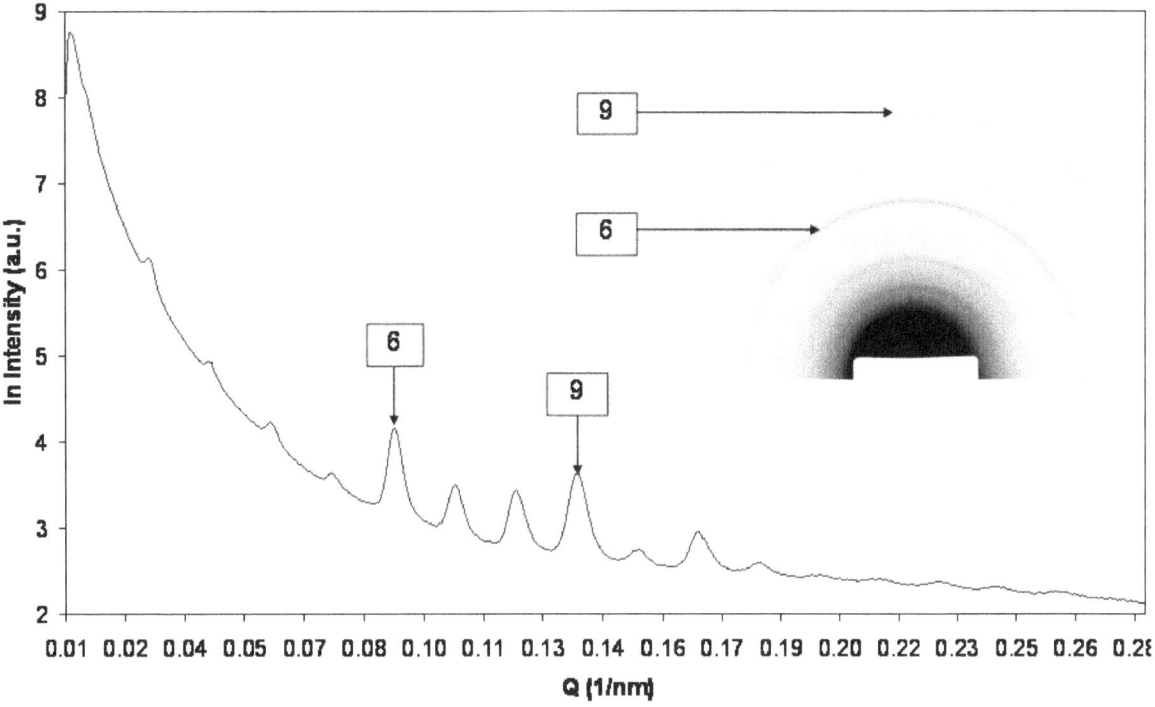

Figure 8: Demonstrates the conversion of a two-dimensional X-ray diffraction image (inset) to a linear profile, generated using FibreFix software (Rajkumar *et al.* 2005). The pattern collected is taken from modern parchment where the 6th and 9th orders of collagen diffraction are highlighted on both the image and linear plot.

X-ray scattering of parchment provides the user with the ability to assess the structural integrity of the collagen structure and evaluate the condition of the parchment. Two dimensional diffraction patterns are converted into linear traces as shown in Figure 7 in order to analyse the data.

Data correction

X-ray scattering patterns are usually accompanied by other scattered radiation, background radiation which is not due to the interaction with the sample. Before data analysis it is important to subtract this background radiation from the original data to obtain correct intensity values and a clearer scattering image. This is achieved by repeating the same experimental conditions and recording the image of an empty cell without the specimen present. This background image can then be subtracted from the collected data to remove many artefacts introduced to the original image. Once corrected for the background radiation and artefacts the data can be analysed.

Data reduction and analysis

The main aim of data analysis is to extract information from the scattering data that relates to physical parameters within the sample. Data can be reduced by the conversion of the scattering images into polar plots. For collagen the scattering is isotropic therefore an integration is taken over the whole angular distribution of the detector. Once the two-dimensional data is reduced to a polar plot it is possible to create a one-dimensional linear intensity profile from the scattering data. The conversion of Cartesian co-ordinates to polar co-ordinates allows the intensity distribution of the scattering to be plotted against angular position allowing the estimation of structural parameters. Various computer programmes are currently available for data reduction and processing. These change on an almost a year by year basis and are frequently updated to account for new modalities of software analysis. The most useful and commonly used are Fit2D (Hammersley, 1997) and FibreFix (Rajkumar *et al.* 2005). Figure 8 demonstrates the conversion of a two-dimensional X-ray diffraction pattern to a linear trace.

References

Brodsky, B., Eikenberry, E. F. and Cassidy, K. 1980 An unusual collagen periodicity in skin. *Biochimica et Biophysica Acta (BBA) - Protein Structure* **621**, 162-166.

Cullity, B. D. 1978 *Elements of X-ray diffraction* (2nd edition). Addison-Wesley, Massachusetts.

Emons, A. M. C. and Mulder, B. M. 2000 How the deposition of cellulose microfibrils builds cell wall architecture. *Trends in Plant Science* **5**, 35-40.

Ghioni, C., Hiller, J. C., Kennedy, C. J., Aliev, A. E., Odlyha, M., Boulton, M. and Wess, T. J. 2005 Evidence of a distinct lipid fraction in historical parchments: a potential role in degradation? *Journal of Lipid Research* **46**, 2726-2734

Glatter, O. and Kratky, O. 1982 *Small Angle X-ray Scattering*. Academic Press, London.

Hammersley, A. P. 1997 *FIT2D: An Introduction and Overview.* ESRF Internal Report. Publication no. ESRF97HA02T. Grenoble, France.

Hansen, E. F., Lee, S. N. and Sobel, H. 1992 The Effects of Relative Humidity on Some Physical Properties of Modern Vellum: Implications for the Optimum Relative Humidity for the Display and Storage of Parchment. *Journal of the American Institute of Conservation* **31**, 325-342.

Hodge, A. J. and Petruska, J. A. 1963 Recent studies with the electron microscope on ordered aggregates of the tropocollagen molecule. In G. N. Ramachandran (ed.) *Aspects of Protein Structure,* 289-300. Academic Press, New York.

Kennedy, C. J., Hiller, J., Odlyha, M., Nielsen, K., Drakopoulos, M. and Wess, T. J. 2002 Degradation in Historical Parchments Structural, Biochemical and Thermal Studies. *Papier Restaurierung* **3**, 23-30.

Kennedy, C. J., Hiller, J. C., Lammie, D., Drakopoulos, M., Vest, M., Cooper, M., Adderley, W. P. and Wess, T. J. 2004a Microfocus X-Ray Diffraction of Historical Parchment Reveals Variations in Structural Features through Parchment Cross Sections. *Nano Letters* **4**, 1373-1380.

Kennedy, C. J., Nielsen, K., Ramsay, L. and Wess, T. J. 2003 Analysis of collagen structure in parchment by Small angle X-ray diffraction. *Fibre Diffraction Review* **11**, 117-118.

Kennedy, C. J., Vest, M., Cooper, M. and Wess, T. J. 2004b Laser cleaning of parchment: structural, thermal and biochemical studies into the effect of wavelength and fluence. *Applied Surface Science* **227**, 151-163.

Kite, M. and Thomson, R. 2006 *Conservation of Leather and related materials.* Elsevier, London.

Larsen, R. 2002 *Microanalysis of Parchment.* Archetype, London.

Maxwell, C. A., Wess, T. J. and Kennedy, C. J. 2006 X-ray diffraction study into the Effects of Liming on the Structure of Collagen. *Biomacromolecules* **7**, 2321-2326

Meek, K. M. and Quantock, A. J. 2001 The Use of X-ray Scattering Techniques to Determine Corneal Ultrastructure. *Progress in Retinal and Eye Research* **20**, 95-137.

Menon, G. K. 2002 New insights into skin structure: scratching the surface. *Advanced Drug Delivery Reviews* **54**, S3-S17.

Peters, D. 1996 Our environment ruined? Environmental control reconsidered as a strategy for conservation. *Journal of Conservation and Museum Studies* **1**, available at http://www.ucl.ac.uk/~ycrnw3c/JCMS/issue1/peters.html (accessed 14.5.10)

Rajkumar, G., Al-Khayat, H. A., Eakins, F., He, A., Knupp, C. & Squire, J. M. 2005 FibreFix - A New Integrated CCP13 Software Package. *Fibre Diffraction Review* **13**, 11-18

Reed, R. 1973 *Ancient Skins, Parchment and Leathers* (International series of monographs on science in archaeology). Academic Press, U.S.

Sionkowska, A., Wisniewski, M., Skopinska, J., Kennedy, C. J. & Wess, T. J. 2004 Molecular interactions in collagen and chitosan blends. *Biomaterials* **25**, 795-801.

Stinson, R. H. and Sweeny, P. R. 1980 Skin collagen has an unusual d-spacing. *Biochimica et Biophysica Acta* **621**, 158-161.

Sturrock, E. J., Boote, C., Attenburrow, G. E. and Meek, K. M. 2004 The effects of the biaxial stretching of leather on fibre orientation and tensile modulus. *Journal of Materials Science* **39**, 2481-2486.

Traub, W. 1978 Molecular assembly in collagen. *FEBS Letters* (Federation of European Biomedical Societies) **92**, 114-120.

Wess, T. J. and Orgel, J. P. 2000 Changes in collagen structure: drying, dehydrothermal treatment and relation to long term deterioration. *Thermochimica Acta* **365**, 119-128.

Chapter 8

Advanced Optical Imaging Methods for Investigating Manuscripts

Haida Liang

School of Science and Technology, Nottingham Trent University

Introduction

This paper gives an overview of advanced optical imaging methods relevant to the study of manuscripts. While some of the methods covered are well established, others are very much in active development. 'Optical' in this context is loosely defined to cover the near ultraviolet, visible and the near infrared part of the electromagnetic spectrum. Optical imaging methods are in general non-destructive and can be applied *in situ*. They are non-invasive if care is taken to ensure a safe dosage of illumination during the imaging process. The examples given in this paper are biased towards work that the author has been involved in. This is by no means a comprehensive review. The aim of the paper is to illustrate how advanced optical imaging techniques can assist in the investigation of manuscripts.

Simple optical techniques are in use routinely by historians, curators and conservators in examining manuscripts. These include examination with a magnifying glass, a microscope and examination under UV light. For example, microscopic examination can reveal the individual paint particles on the surface of a miniature which can aid the identification of a paint mixture. Low powered UV light (black light or Wood lamp) can be used to detect faded writing and reveal the presence of organic material through UV fluorescence. UV light incident on a material can induce fluorescence emission in the visible and hence be observable by eye. Visual observation using raking light (that is light applied at grazing incidence on the manuscript surface) is an effective method of revealing surface texture, e.g. indentation from writings on a previous page that is now missing.

Application of optical imaging methods to the examination of cultural heritage has a long history. Instead of visual observation, high resolution macro-photography has been used to reveal details. Infrared photography was used to examine paintings as early as in the 1930s (Lyon, 1934). By the 1950s, it was a well-established routine technique used in museums. In the 1960s, infrared imaging using a vidicon detector termed 'infrared reflectography', which is sensitive to longer infrared wavelengths (up to 2 μm) than infrared photography (~900nm), was invented to provide better penetration of paint layers and clearer underdrawing images (van Asperen de Boer, 1969).

In the following sections, we will concentrate on two types of advanced imaging techniques: spectral imaging and optical coherence tomography, which is used for non-invasive imaging of subsurface layers.

Spectral imaging: multispectral and hyperspectral imaging

A classic fibre optic UV-VIS spectrometer records the spectral reflectance of a single point (e.g. Bacci, 1995). Multispectral and hyperspectral imaging are examples of spectral imaging where images of an object are obtained in a series of spectral windows such that spectra at millions of spatial points are collected simultaneously (see Figure 1). The distinction between multispectral and hyperspectral imaging is rather blurred and very much discipline dependent. In general, hyperspectral imaging consists of more finely divided spectral channels (or windows) than multispectral imaging. For example, images taken in the visible spectral range at six evenly divided spectral channels (rather than three in the case of a colour image) would be called multispectral imaging rather than hyperspectral imaging. Multispectral imaging can sometimes refer to a set of images (usually scaled to the same size) taken at vastly different parts of the electromagnetic spectrum, e.g. three visible images in red, blue and green, an infrared image and an X-ray image of an object. For the rest of the paper, we will refer to multispectral and hyperspectral imaging together as spectral imaging.

Spectral imaging was first developed in remote sensing and astronomy. Since the early 1990s, it has found increasing applications in heritage science. In the case of paintings, multispectral imaging was first developed to increase the colour fidelity of the images for conservation monitoring. A number of European Union projects have been dedicated to the design and implementation of high colour and spectral fidelity, high resolution scanning systems for the recording of museum paintings and other objects (e.g. Burmester *et al.* 1992; Saunders & Cupitt 1993; Lahanier *et al.* 2002; Liang *et al.* 2005). Spectral imaging enables rendering of colour accurate images of objects under any lighting conditions, unlike a normal tri-colour image which can only capture an accurate colour image under the specific illumination used at the time. Nowadays spectral imaging systems are capable of recovering the spectral reflectance per pixel of a painting with accuracy comparable to a fibre optics spectrometer for the purpose of colour rendering and pigment identification. Spectral imaging can also be used for qualitative inter-band comparison for detection of damage, past intervention, the presence of preparatory drawings and faded writing. This is particularly effective when comparing the UV and NIR images with those of the visible wavelength single band images or colour images. Since the eye is not sensitive to the UV and near infrared, these bands are most likely to reveal extra information.

Spectral imaging devices can be portable or fixed in a studio. For small objects such as manuscripts, it is convenient to use portable devices. For large maps and drawings in the collection of libraries, the problems with capturing large objects at high resolution is similar to those encountered in scanning large paintings. Traditionally, large paintings are scanned in studios using fixed scanners, however, the size of the studio ultimately limits the maximum size of painting that can be scanned. For example, the Vasari scanner at the National Gallery can scan paintings to a maximum size of 1 m x 1 m. A recently developed spectral imaging system PRISMS (Portable Remote Imaging System for Multispectral Scanning) for *in situ* scanning of large paintings such as wall paintings, has the flexibility of imaging paintings or other objects of any size at sub-millimetre resolution (Liang *et al.* 2007, 2008).

Classic multispectral imaging systems use interference filters of intermediate bandwidth (e.g. around 40-50nm) since the spectral reflectance of pigments are fairly smooth and devoid of sharp peaks. Recently, hyperspectral imaging using tunable filters such as Liquid Crystal Tunable Filters (LCTF) and Acousto-Optics Tunable filters (AOTF) have been developed for heritage applications in the 400 nm - 700 nm range (Hardeberg *et al.* 2002; Balas *et al.* 2003; Berns *et al.* 2005), the 650 nm - 1040 nm range (Mansfield *et al.* 2002) and in the 900-1700nm (Liang *et al.* 2010). The advantage of these tunable filter devices is ease of control, flexibility in the choice of filters and fast response (ms or ns). The disadvantage is the lower efficiency since both kinds of tunable filters are polarisation sensitive which means only half of the reflected light is recorded.

A review aimed at the conservation community is given in Fischer and Kakoulli (2006) and a more current review on the technology and applications to heritage science (Liang, 2011). Figure 1 shows an example of a spectral imaging setup for examining manuscripts.

In principle, with a single spectral imaging scan, one can obtain the spectral reflectance spectrum of any region in the image, derive the colour image for any given type of illumination (e.g. Tungsten or daylight), and extract the infrared images at the appropriate spectral bands equivalent to infrared photography or infrared reflectography. Therefore, all the common imaging needs such as colour, infrared and false colour infrared images can be obtained with one set of calibrated spectral imaging data. With the appropriate UV light source and filters, the same spectral imaging device can also be used for UV fluorescence imaging.

Calibration of spectral images is crucial to obtaining quantitative scientific information. Usual calibration involves corrections for the thermal noise of the digital camera (dark correction), corrections for the inhomogeneity of the illumination and the pixel-to-pixel gain variation of the digital camera (flatfield correction), and finally corrections for the

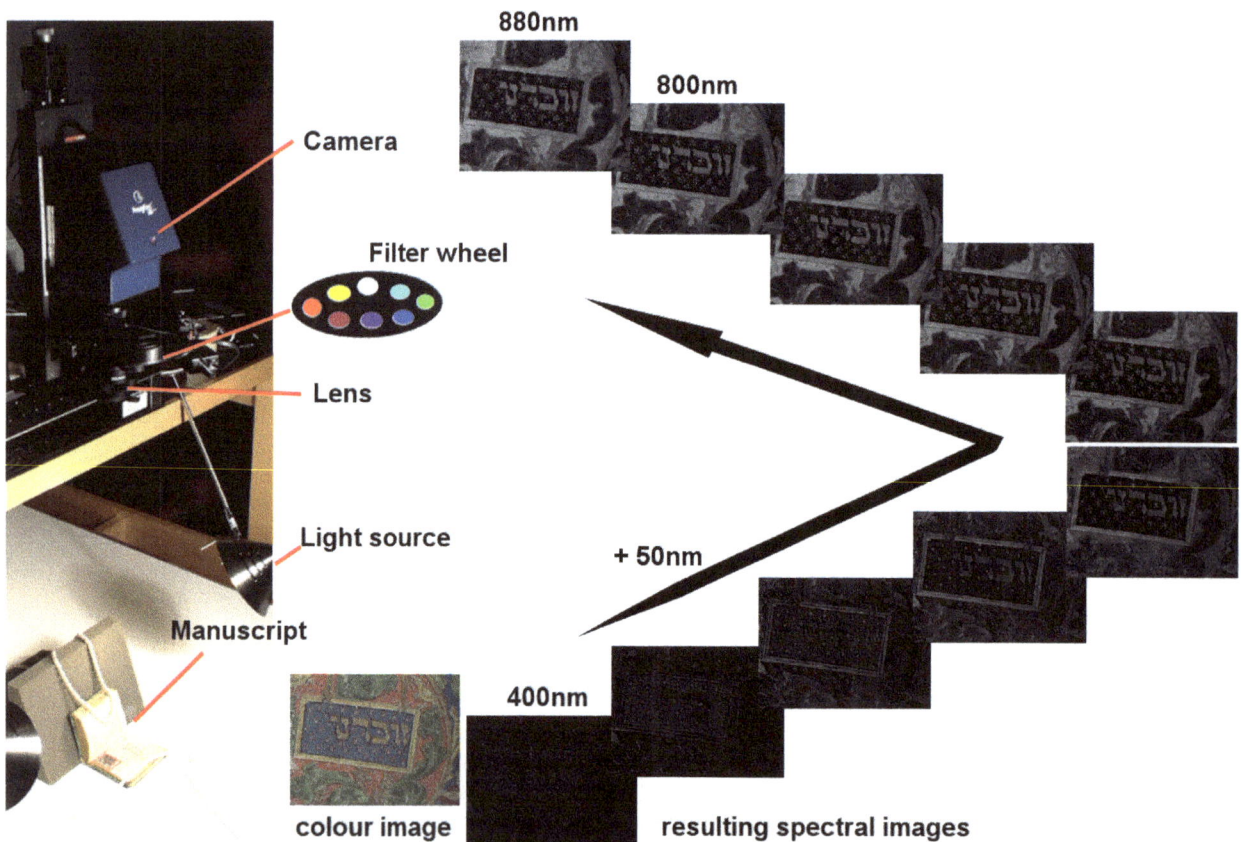

Figure 1. Left: A multipsectral imaging system (modified PRISMS) imaging a manuscript at the Bodleian Library, University of Oxford. Right: the colour image and the series of monochrome images at wavelengths between 400nm and 880nm from which the colour image was derived (courtesy of the Bodleian Libraries, University of Oxford).

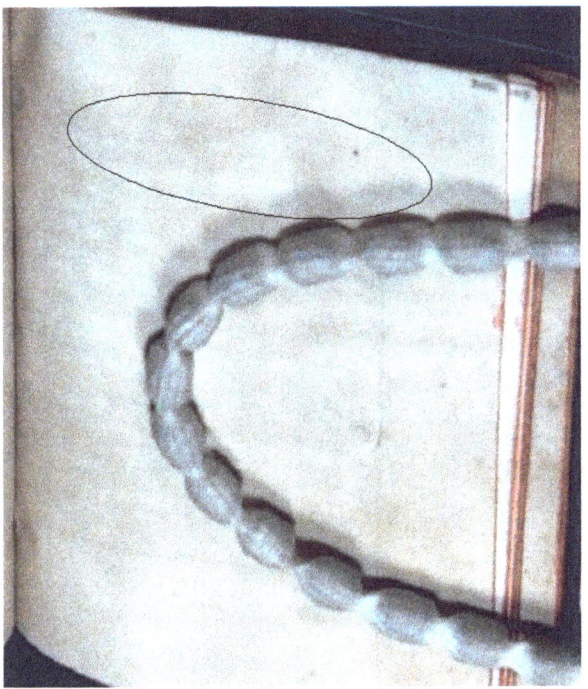
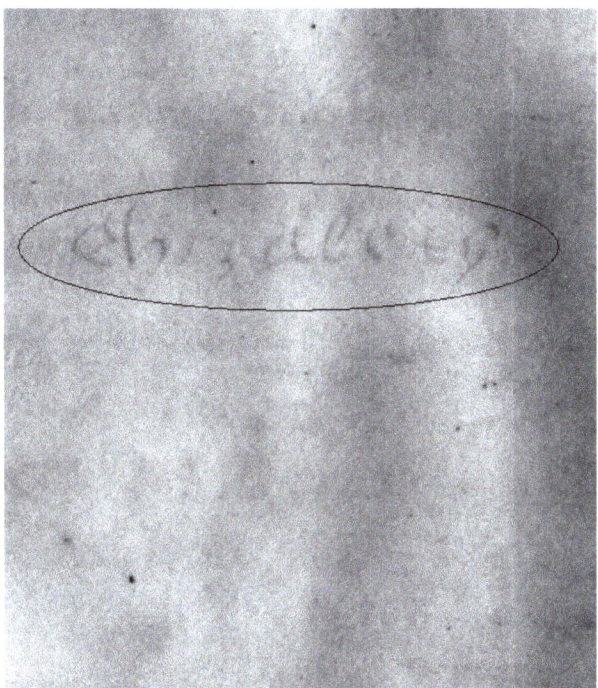

Figure 2. (a) Normal colour image of folio 202r of MS Lat. Liturg. g.1. from the Bodleian Library collection (courtesy of the Bodleian Libraries, University of Oxford.); (b) near infrared image (880nm spectral band) taken with a modified PRISMS of the corresponding area (circled in black) in the colour image on the left.

difference in throughput between the spectral bands (spectral correction). For dark correction, dark frames are taken with the lens cap on, at the same exposure time as the image to be corrected. Flatfield frames can be taken with a matt white or grey card at the same position as the target to be imaged through the same filter. An image of the target is calibrated by subtracting the dark frame and dividing by the normalised (i.e. divide the frame by the average pixel intensity) dark corrected flatfield frame. Spectral calibration is achieved by imaging a spectral standard (e.g. a Labsphere Spectralon white standard) through all the filter channels. For some systems it may be necessary to align and register the frames of various spectral bands. The software for both the hardware control and post-processing of the data is crucial for the effective use of a spectral imaging system. An open source image processing software VIPS/nip designed for heritage science applications has been used for the processing of spectral images given in this paper (Cupitt and Martinez, 1996).

Applications of spectral imaging

To illustrate the various applications of spectral imaging, examples and case studies will be given in the following sections. The spectral imaging instrument used in the following examples is a modified version of PRISMS, which is an in-house built instrument (Liang *et al.* 2008). PRISMS was originally designed for imaging large paintings from a distance using a telescope. It was adapted for imaging manuscripts by replacing the telescope with an appropriate lens and the whole imaging system attached to a motorised X-Y micrometer stage (Figure 1). PRISMS uses interference filters for the spectral range of 400nm to 880nm with central wavelengths at 400, 450, 500, 550, 600, 650, 700, 750, 800 and 880nm. Each filter has a spectral bandwidth of 40nm except for the one at 880nm which has a 70nm bandwidth. The eye is not sensitive to light beyond 800nm. For the short wave infrared region between 900nm and 1700nm, PRISMS using an acousto-optic tunable filter (AOTF) where the central wavelength can be arbitrarily chosen between 900 and 1700nm and the bandwidth can vary between 10nm and 150nm.

Revealing faded writing

If the writing on a manuscript is invisible to the eye, it means that the ink is transparent at the visible wavelength or that the reflectance of the ink in the visible is similar to that of the substrate. The optical property of the ink may have very different characteristics outside of the visible range, hence near infrared or UV imaging can often reveal hidden or faded writing. Figure 2 shows an example of faded writing where it was barely visible by the naked eye but the signature of the owner of the manuscript showed up clearly in the 880nm near infrared spectral window.

Identifying preparatory drawings

Identification of preparatory drawings is important to our understanding of the production of illuminated manuscripts. Figure 3 illustrates an example of an image in the near infrared band of a spectral image cube (i.e. images of the same area in a series of spectral bands) showing clearly that the preparatory drawing of some of the pictorial features was different from the painted version (right hand side of Figure 3b). One way

Figure 3. a) An image from the 600nm spectral band of part of folio 83r of MS Opp. 776 from the Bodleian Library collection; b) 880nm image of the same region in a); c) a mosaic of three adjacent images of folio 83r at 880nm and d) colour image of the same region in c) derived from the mosaiced spectral imaging cubes obtained with a modified PRISMS. Courtesy of the Bodleian Libraries, University of Oxford.

to overcome the trade off between the resolution and field of view of an image is to mosaic a few overlapping high resolution images to create a larger image. For example, the images in Figure 3c and d were created by mosaicing three separate images using the VIPS/nip software[1]. The mosaiced image in Fig. 3c shows that there were preparatory drawings showing the plan for the position of the text and the miniature.

Pigment and ink identification

Inks or paints that look alike in colour may not be the same material. Spectral imaging and their derived spectral reflectance are better at distinguishing between materials than colour information alone. Figure 4 illustrates an example from a Bodleian Library map where the blue pigment used on the mountain tops had the same visible colour but very different reflectance image in the near infrared.

---

[1] http://www.vips.ecs.soton.ac.uk/

 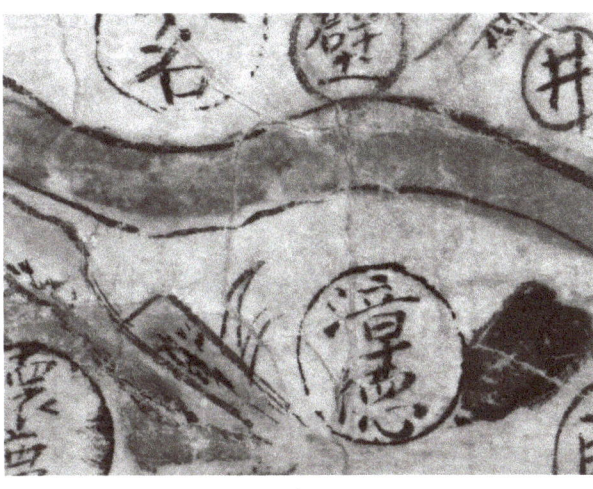

a b

Figure 4. (a) colour image derived from multispectral images obtained with a modified PRISMS of a detail of the 'Selden Map' (Bodleian Library MS Selden Supra 105); (b) a near infrared image at 880nm of the same area showing that the blue mountain tops were painted with different materials. Courtesy of the Bodleian Libraries, University of Oxford.

A simple comparison of spectral reflectance obtained from spectral images can give an indication of whether the material used on different parts of a manuscript are the same or not. Figure 5 shows spectra obtained from the manuscript page shown in Figure 3. This shows that the blue pigment used to write the text in Figure 3d is the same as the darker blue in the garment of the right figure in the miniature.

The spectrum of an unknown pigment or ink can be compared with the spectrum of known pigments or inks from a reference library for identification. The positions of spectral features such as peaks and troughs are indicative of the pigment type. However, the amplitude of the spectral reflectance depends on the pigment to medium ratio. In the ideal case, the effect of concentration is just a constant shift in y-axis of the spectrum when spectral reflectance is expressed in terms of $-\log(K/S)$ where K/S is the ratio of absorption to scattering coefficient calculated from the spectral reflectance using Kubelka-Munk theory (Kubelka and Munk 1931). Hence it is customary to plot spectral reflectance in terms of $-\log(K/S)$ for the purpose of pigment identification. Figure 6 shows that the bright blue hat of the left figure in the miniature in Figure 3d has a similar spectrum to that of natural azurite in linseed oil.

In the case of mixtures of pigments, it is still possible to identify the pigments using Kubelka-Munk theory, which works very well for paints that are neither high in absorption nor very transparent (Liang *et al.* 2008). Figure 7 gives an example where the measured spectrum of the mixture of a red earth pigment and azurite corresponds well with the predicted spectrum from Kubelka-Munk theory. This method was used to identify the purple paint in the miniature of Figure 3d, with a mixture of azurite and vermilion both of which were identified in other areas of the miniature or text.

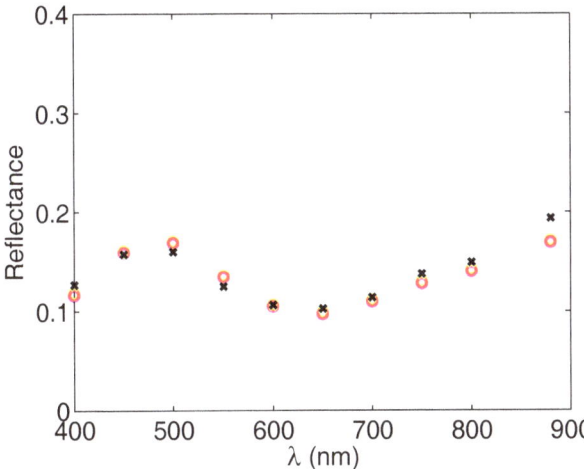 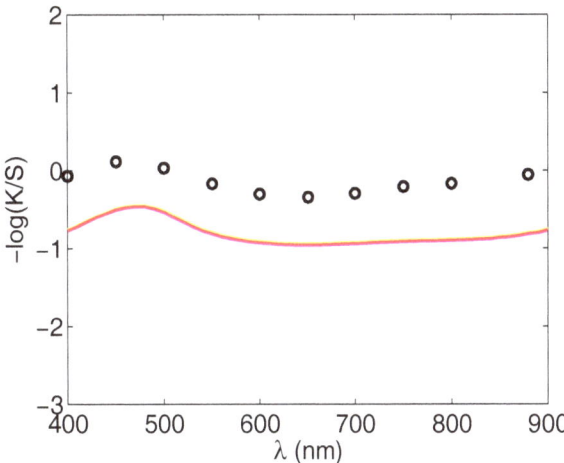

Figure 5. Spectral reflectance obtained from multispectral images taken with a modified PRISMS of the blue text (red circle) and the darker blue in the garment of the right figure (cross) in the miniature on folio 83r of Bodleian Library MS Opp. 776 (see Figure 3d).

Figure 6. Spectrum of the bright blue hat of the left figure in Figure 3d obtained with a modified PRISMS (black circle) is identified with a spectrum of natural azurite in linseed oil from a reference spectral library (solid red curve).

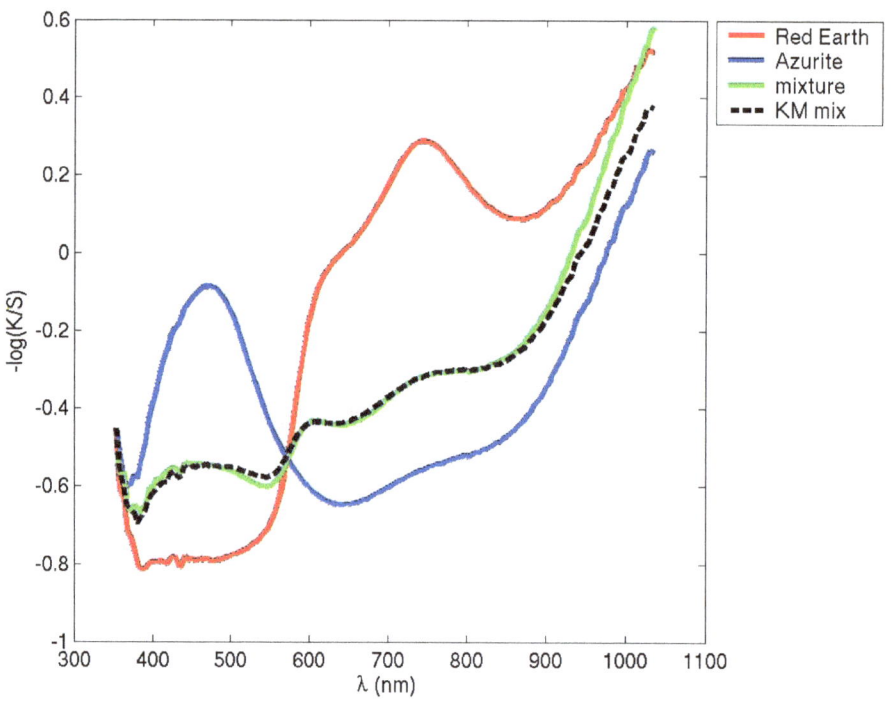

Figure 7. Measured spectrum of a mixture of two known pigments (red earth in solid red and azurite in solid blue) shown in solid green compared with the predicted spectrum of the mixture using Kubelka-Munk theory shown in dashed black.

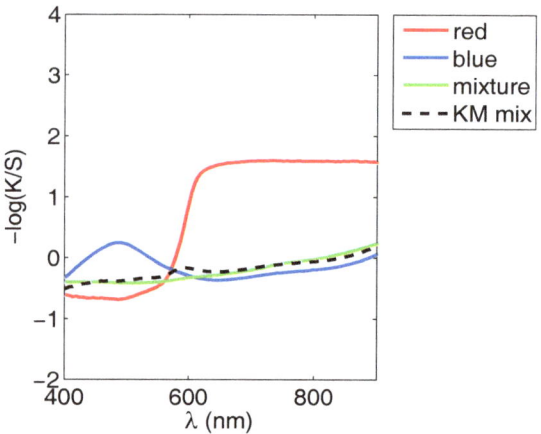

Figure 8. Model spectrum of mixture of natural azurite mixed with lead white (solid blue) with vermilion (solid red) in dashed black compared with the spectrum of the purple in the miniature below the figures in Figure 3d (solid green).

Monitoring degradation

Long term monitoring of the degradation of a material is possible through measuring the spectral and colour difference over time. For such monitoring, precision calibration is necessary to observe the minute difference over time.

While spectral imaging is known in the heritage conservation and curatorial community, its application has not been fully exploited partly because of the cost of the equipment and lack of in-house technical expertise. However, the cost of a multispectral imaging system need not be more than that of an average microscope and with increasing hyperspectral imaging systems developed commercially for terrestrial use they will become more user-friendly.

Optical coherence tomography

Optical coherence tomography (OCT) is a high-resolution, fast, 3D scanning Michelson interferometer which can be used for depth analysis and layer investigation to show the structure of an object made of multiple layers. A near infrared source is generally used for illumination of both the reference mirror and the object. The back scattered light from both the reference and object arms are brought together at the detector which records the interference between the back scattered light from the two paths (see Figure 9 for illustration). Interference fringes of maximum contrast occur when the optical path of the backscattered light from within the object equals that from the reference mirror, thus enabling depth determination. An equivalent explanation is that it measures the echo time of back scattered light from a certain depth within a sample. The image intensity corresponds to the strength of the backscattered light from the internal structure of the object. The interfaces between layers of strong mismatch in refractive index reflect the highest fraction of the incident light. For layered material, this enables the interfaces to be clearly delineated, and for inhomogeneous layers, scattering centres such as large pigment particles can sometimes be seen. OCT scanning is non-invasive, non-contact and often performed at a safe distance of ~1cm. OCT collects either cross section images or *en face* images at various depth, and a series of these can be combined to give 3D information of the surface and subsurface structure. The depth resolution depends on the spectral bandwidth of the illuminating source and the resolution in the other two axes is determined by the numerical aperture of the objective lens. The depth range depends on both the type of OCT and the scattering properties of the material.

OCT was first invented in the early 1990s for the *in vivo* examination of the eye. Considerable effort has been invested in the last twenty years on improving the resolution and speed of OCT for clinical and biomedical applications. OCT is becoming established as a routine instrument for ophthalmology. The application of OCT to conservation and archaeology is relatively recent (Yang *et al*. 2004; Targowski *et al*. 2004; Liang *et al*. 2004). Details of the various OCT applications to heritage science can be found in recent reviews (Targowski *et al*. 2006; Liang *et al*. 2008) and a list of articles on the subject can be found on http://oct4art.eu/. This is an emerging field of research and has potential to become one of the routine methods of examination in heritage science. Here we focus on the potential application of OCT to the study of manuscripts.

Examples shown in this paper are obtained with a Thorlabs SROCT adapted by the author's research group at Nottingham Trent University. The OCT operates at a wavelength of 930nm, an axial resolution of 6μm, a transverse resolution of 9μm and a depth range of 1.6mm. The instrument is small and portable, capable of automatically scanning a 15cm x 15cm area and operating at a safe distance of around 1.5 cm from the object surface.

OCT applications

Imaging paint layers

OCT has been successfully applied to the examination of paint layer structures non-invasively (Liang *et al*. 2005; Spring *et al*. 2008). Figure 10c shows an OCT cross-section image of a varnish layer followed by a translucent paint layer in parts of the cross-section corresponding to the brown paint of the capital letter in the book depicted in the painting. Unlike paintings where it is possible to take small samples for analysis to find out the layer structure of the paint, it is generally not possible to take samples from illuminated manuscripts. OCT imaging may be the only possible way of obtaining information on the paint layer structure. The degree of scattering or absorption of the layers can help in identifying the material. The example shown in Figure 10 is that of an easel painting rather than an illuminated manuscript, however, the paint used on illuminated manuscripts are often similar to easel paintings.

Imaging of preparatory drawings

OCT is suitable for high resolution and high dynamic range imaging of preparatory drawings beneath the paint layers. Since OCT collects 3D subsurface volume images, it can distinguish

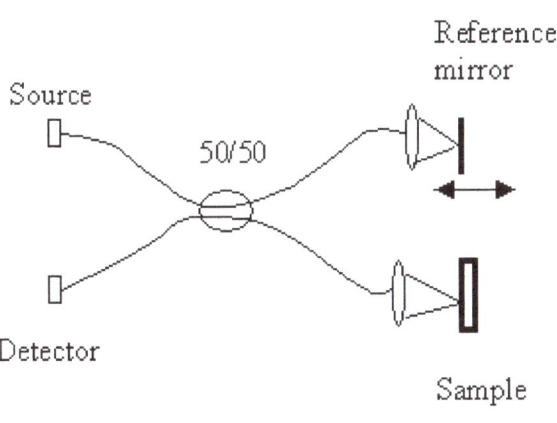

a

b

Figure 9. a) Schematic diagram illustrating the principle of OCT: light from the source is guided by an optical fibre and split into two paths using a 50/50 fibre couple, one towards the reference mirror and the other towards the sample; the back scattered light from the two paths are brought together and recorded by the detector; b) an OCT probe scanning the leather cover of the Fadden More bog bible.

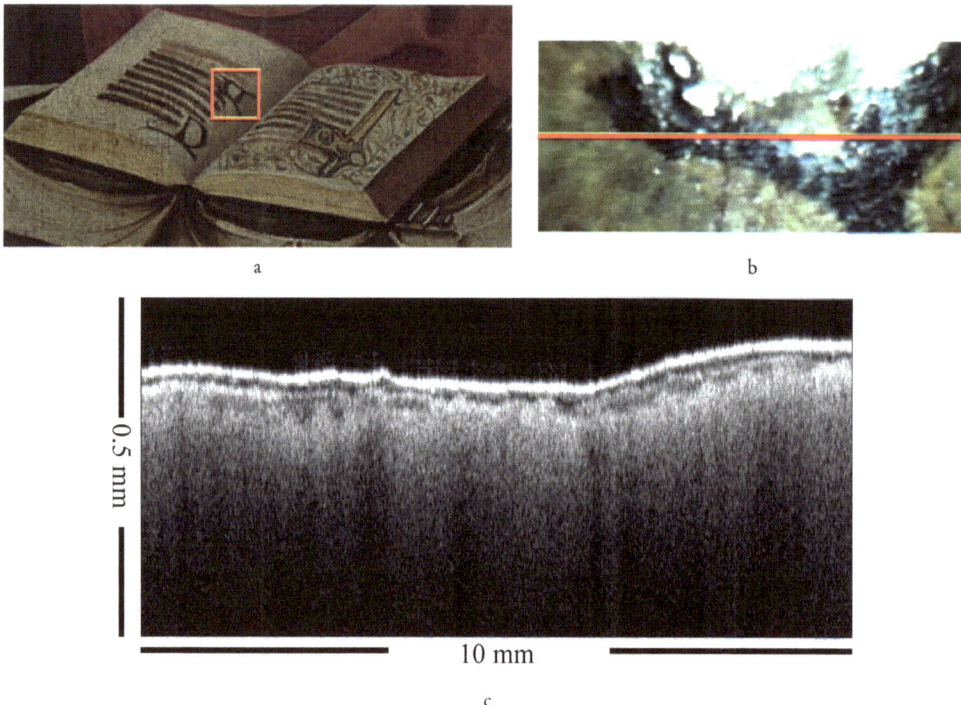

Figure 10. a) A region of the painting The Magdalen by an anonymous Netherlandish artist (National Gallery, London N00719 © The National Gallery, London), the red box indicates the area scanned with OCT; b) detail capture by the monitoring camera attached to the OCT showing the scanned area; c) OCT cross-section image taken from the position indicated by the red line in b). The image is 0.5mm in depth and 10mm across the surface of the paint, the top bright interface is the air/varnish interface, the dark brown paint of the letter shows up as an extra paint layer.

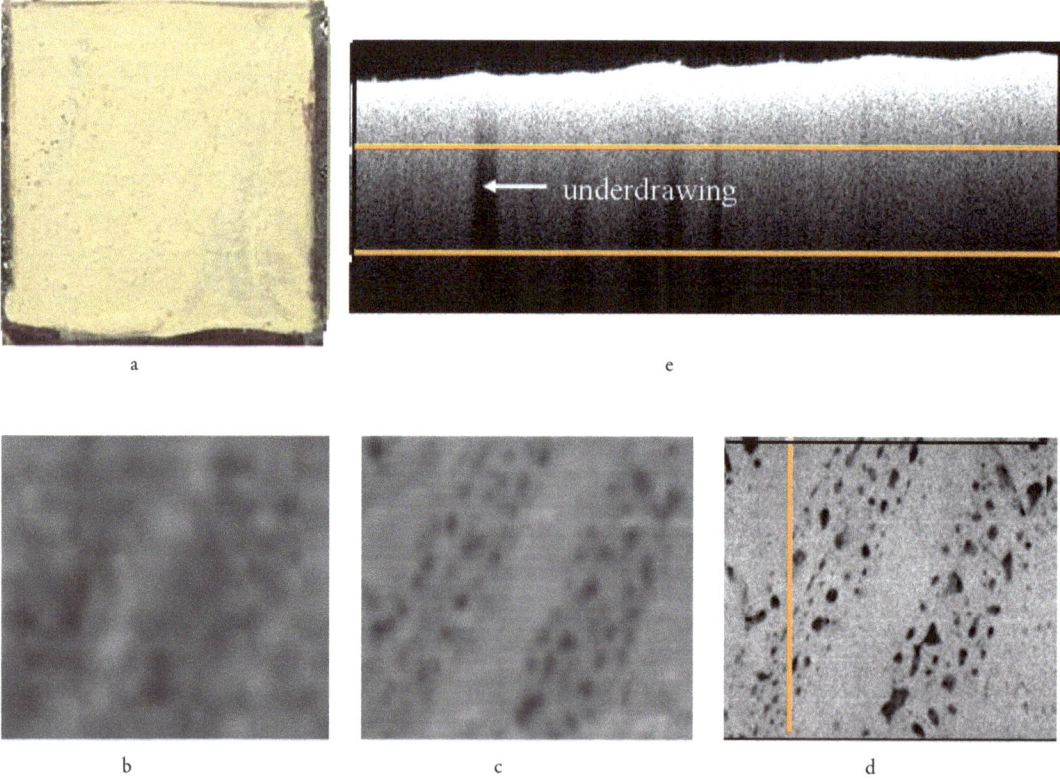

Figure 11. Near infrared images of a painted patch of two layers of lead-tin yellow over under-drawing made with bone black in gum executed with a quill pen; a) colour image; b) near infrared vidicon image; c) digital near infrared image from an InGaAs camera sensitive to the spectral range between 900 and 1700nm; d) 930 nm OCT image, averaging the *en face* images between the horizontal lines in (e), where the under-drawing information is located; e) OCT cross-section image of a scan marked with a line in images (a) and (d).

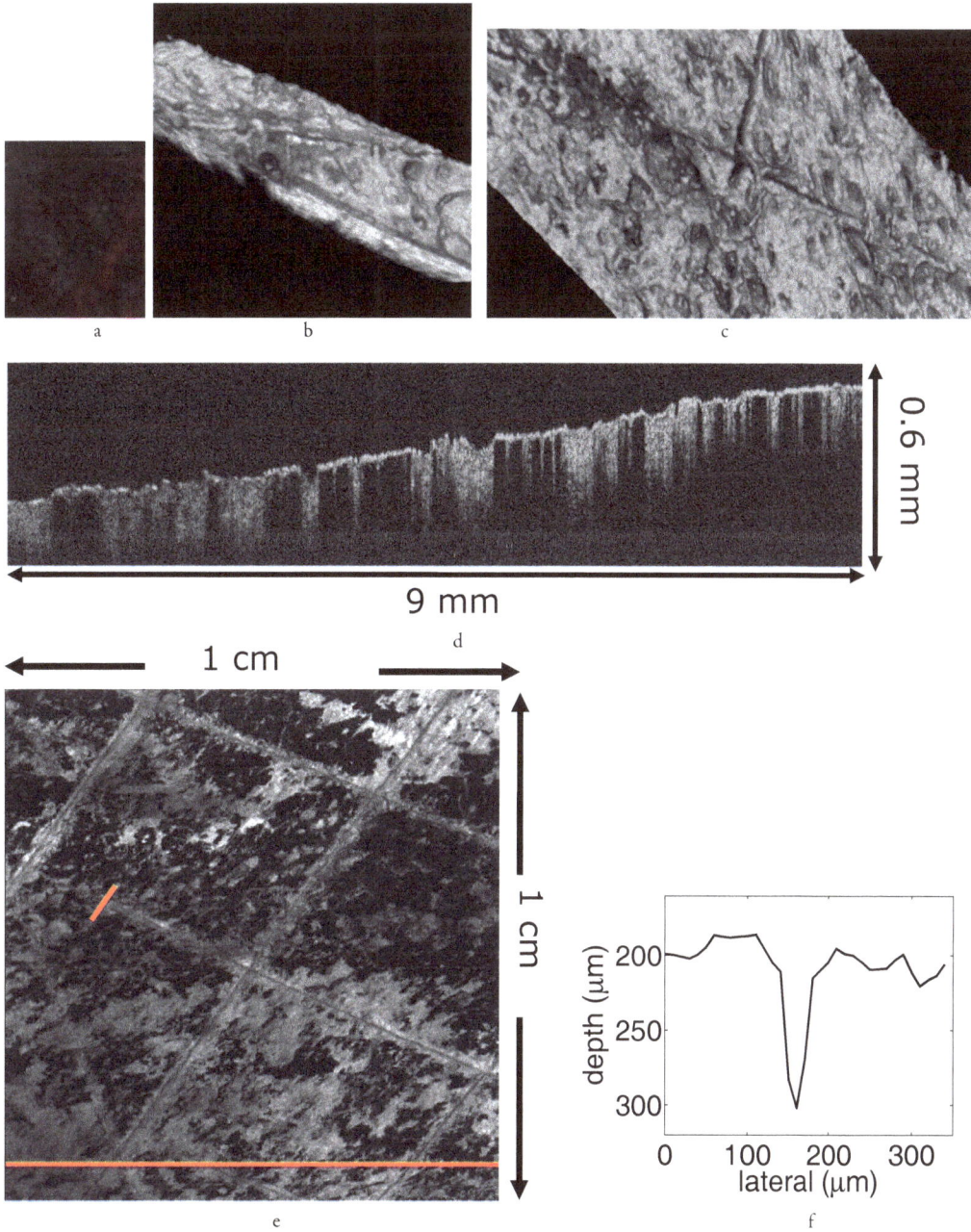

Figure 12. (a) A detail of the leather cover of the Fadden More bog bible showing very faint marks (courtesy of National Museum of Ireland); b) a 3D rendering of a small volume of the OCT image cube showing follicles and cuts into the leather; c) a zoomed in 3D view of another small area of the leather cover giving a magnified view of the cuts into the leather; d) an OCT cross-section image of the region around the red line in e) showing surface cuts, follicles and areas with surface paint (regions where it is dark beneath the surface); f) profile of the leather surface showing one of the cuts in the leather at the position of the short red line segment in e).

between paint layers and drawing layers. It is the ability to extract only the layers with under-drawing information that enables it to provide the best dynamic range images of under-drawings compared to direct imaging methods described earlier. The high resolution of OCT makes it best suited to imaging fine features of under-drawings. The OCT image of under-drawings in Figure 11d is extracted from the 3D volume image and it shows the fine details of the under-drawing. It is possible to determine that the drawing material was liquid based, and from the droplet shape the direction of the stroke can be deduced.

OCT imaging of leather & parchment

OCT has been used in biomedical applications to examine human skin and it was found that in some cases it was possible to detect the birefringence of the skin which in turn allows measurement of the orientation of the collagen. Gora *et al.* (2006) used a polarisation sensitive OCT to examine parchment and found that the birefringence decreased somewhat as the parchment aged. OCT imaging of paper was used to estimate the filler content of paper (Alarousu *et al.* 2005).

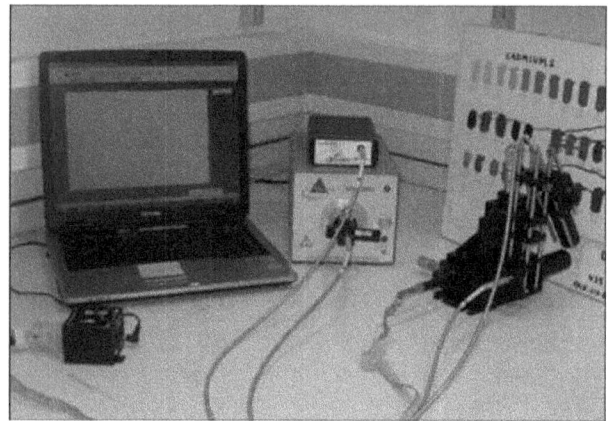

Figure 13. A microfading spectrometer (microfadometer) fading a sample of paint (Lerwill *et al.* 2008).

A case study is presented here of an OCT examination of the leather cover of the Fadden More bog bible in the collection of the National Museum of Ireland. Carvings into the leather cover were found by visual examination but it was faint and difficult to see (Figure 12a). A 3D rendering of a small piece of the OCT scanned leather cover shows both the details of the cut into the leather and the follicles (Figure 12b,c). The shape of the follicles and their inclination can help identify the type of skin used to make the leather. Averaging a number of slices parallel to the surface gives a clear image of the surface features and the carving patterns (Figure 12e). The dark patches correspond to regions that were painted with a material (or the degraded material) that strongly absorbs light at 930nm (the operating wavelength of the OCT). The cross-section image obtained from the OCT show the cross-section of the follicles and the carvings (Figure 12d). Figure 12f shows the surface profile of the leather near a carved feature extracted from an OCT cross-section image using a surface fitting algorithm. The cuts appear to be as deep as 100 microns and about 50 microns wide at the surface which gives information on the tool used for the carving.

In summary, OCT provides a non-invasive method of probing the depth structure of materials which could be used to examine paint layers on miniatures, to obtain high resolution surface profiles for the identification of tool marks, to image the 3D structures of follicles in skins and to obtain depth resolved high resolution image of preparatory drawings. In addition, absorption and scattering properties of the material could be used as an aid for material identification.

Determining light-fastness for display strategy

It is worth mentioning another optical technique, microfading spectrometry (or microfadometer), which is not an imaging technique and is not non-invasive but micro-destructive (Whitmore *et al.* 1999; Lerwill *et al.* 2008). Given the vulnerability of manuscripts to light, there is always a trade off between optimum light level for display and light induced degradation. A microfadometer illuminates a tiny spot of ~0.2-0.4 mm in diameter with a high intensity lamp for *in situ* accelerated light aging, which is monitored by a fibre optic spectrometer. The time required to fade a spot to a colour difference of a few ΔE gives an indication of the light-fastness of the material[2]. Since the faded spot is so tiny, a small colour difference in such a spot is not noticeable with the naked eye. Such *in situ* microfading can be used to inform the long term display strategy of manuscripts. For example, it may be better to display certain pages in a manuscript rather than another with more vulnerable pigments. Figure 13 shows a portable microfadometer fading a paint sample, and Figure 14 shows the result of fading blue wool standards over 15 minutes.

---

[2] ΔE, or Delta-E, is a measure of colour difference

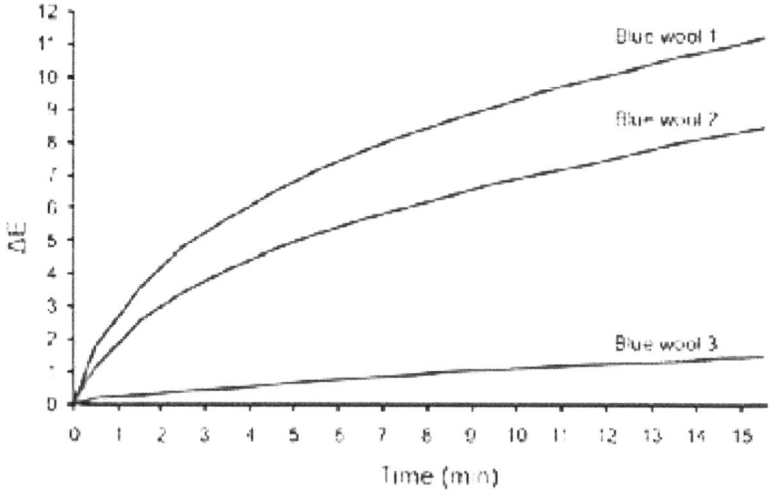

Figure 14. Colour difference as a function of time for the fading of blue wool 1, 2 and 3 using the microfadometer shown in Figure 13.

Conclusions

Advanced optical imaging techniques such as spectral imaging and optical coherence tomography are capable of providing information on spectral reflectance and other optical properties of material. These are useful for material identification and monitoring of degradation, revealing hidden writing and preparatory drawings, and giving depth resolved 3D images of subsurface layers and microstructure of paint and substrates such as leathers and parchment. The non-invasive nature of these optical imaging methods makes them powerful tools for scientific examination of manuscripts.

Acknowledgements

I would like to acknowledge contribution from current and former research students and fellows at Nottingham Trent University: Simon Godber, Kafing Keita, Rebecca Lange, Samuel Lawman, Andrew Lerwill, Borislava Peric and Tom Vajzovic. I would like to thank my collaborators: Marika Spring and other colleagues of the National Gallery, colleagues of the Bodleian Library, National Museum of Ireland, Tate, Gooch & Housego plc., and finally Sarah Neate for initiating the collaboration with the Bodleian.

Funding from the Leverhulme Trust, National Museum of Ireland, Engineering & Physical Sciences Research Council (EPSRC), Arts and Humanities Research Council (AHRC) and the Science & Heritage Programme are gratefully acknowledged.

References

Alarousu, E., Krehut, L., Prykari, T., and Myllyla, R. 2005 Study on the use of optical coherence tomography in measurements of paper properties. *Measurement Science and Technology* **16**, 1131-1137

Bacci, M. 1995 Fibre optics applications to works of art. *Sensors and Actuators* **B29**, 190-196

Balas, C., Papadakis, V., Papadakis, N., Vazgiouraki, A. and Themelis, G. 2003 A Novel hyper-spectral imaging apparatus for the non-destructive analysis of objects of artistic and historic value. *Journal of Cultural Heritage* **4** (1), 330.

Baronti, S., Casini, A., Lotti, F. and Porcinai, S. 1998 Multispectral imaging system for the mapping of pigments in works of art by use of principal-component analysis. *Applied Optics* **37**, 1299.

Berns, R., Taplin, L., Imai, F., Day, E., Day, D. 2005 A comparison of small-aperture and image-based spectrophotometry of paintings. *Studies in Conservation* **50**, 253.

Burmester, A., Cupitt, J., Derrien, H., Dessipris, N., Hamber, A., Martinez, K., Muller, M. and Saunders, D. 1992 The Examination of Paintings by Digital Image Analysis. In *3rd International Conference on Non Destructive Testing, Microanalytical Methods and Environmental Evaluation for Study and Conservation of Works of Art*, Rome, 210-124.

Cupitt, J. and Martinez, K. 1996 VIPS: An Image Processing System for Large Images. *Proceedings of the SPIE* **1663**, 19.

Delaney, J., Walmsley, E., Berrie, B. and Fletcher, C. 2005 Multispectral imaging of paintings in the infrared to detect and map blue pigments. In *Sackler NAS Colloquium – Scientific Examination of Art: Modern Techniques in Conservation and Analysis*, 120-136. Proceedings of the National Academy of Sciences of the United States of America (PNAS).

Fischer, C. and Kakoulli, I. 2006 Multispectral and hyperspectral imaging technologies in conservation: current research and potential applications. *Reviews in Conservation* **7**, 3-16

Góra, M., Pircher, M., Götzinger, E., Bajraszewski, T., Strlic, M., Kolar, J., Hitzenberger, C. and Targowski, P. 2006 Optical Coherence Tomography for Examination of Parchment Degradation. *Laser Chemistry*, **2006**, Article ID 68679, 6 pages, doi:10.1155/2006/68679.

Hardeberg, J., Schmitt, F. and Brettel, H. 2002 Multispectral color image capture using a liquid crystal tunable filter. *Journal of Optical Engineering* **41**, 2532

Kubelka, P. and Munk, F. 1931 Ein Beitrag zur Optik der Farbanstriche. *Z. technische Physik* **12**, 593.

Lahanier, C., Alquié, G., Cotte, P., Christofides, C., Deyne, C. de., Pillay, R., Saunders, D and Schmitt, F. 2002 CRISATEL: A High Definition and Spectral Digitisation of Paintings with Simulation of Varnish Removal. ICOM Committee for Conservation. *ICOM Committee for Conservation 13th Triennial Meeting*, Rio de Janeiro, Brazil, 295-300.

Lerwill, A., Townsend, J., Liang, H., Thomas, J. and Hackney, S. 2008 Portable Microfading Spectrometer for Versatile Light Fastness Testing. *E-Preservation Science* **5**, 17-28.

Liang, H., Saunders, D. and Cupitt, J. 2005 A new multispectral imaging system for examining paintings. *Journal of Imaging Science and Technology* **49**, 551-562

Liang, H., Keita, K. and Vajzovic, T. 2007 PRISMS: A portable multispectral imaging system for remote in situ examination of wall paintings. *O3A: Optics for Arts, Architecture, and Archaeology, Proceedings of the SPIE* **6618**, 661815

Liang, H., Keita, K., Peric, B. and Vajzovic, T. 2008 Pigment identification with optical coherence tomography and multispectral imaging. *Proc. OSAV 2008: The 2nd International Topical Meeting on Optical Sensing and Artificial Vision*. St Petersberg, Russia 12-15 May 2008, 33-42.

Liang, H., Keita, K., Vajzovic, T. and Zhang, Q. 2008 PRISMS: remote high resolution in situ multispectral imaging of wall paintings. *International Council of Museums, Committee for Conservation (ICOM-CC) Triennial Conference*, Delhi, Vol. I, 353-358

Liang, H., Keita, K., Pannell, C. and Ward, J. 2010 A SWIR Hyperspectral System for Art History and Art Conservation. *IX Congreso National del Color*, Alicante June 2010, 189-192.

Liang, H, 2011, Advances in Multispectral and Hyperspectral Imaging in Archaeology and Art Conservation, *Applied*

Physics A - Special Issue on Optical Technologies in Art and Archaeology.

Lyon, R.A. 1934 Infra-red radiations aid examination of paintings. *Technical Studies in the field of the Fine Arts* **II**, 4, *203-212*

Mansfield, J., Attas, M., Majzels, C., Collins, C., Cloutis, E. and Mantsch H. 2002 Near Infrared Spectroscopic Reflectance Imaging: A New Tool in Art Conservation. *Vibrational Spectroscopy* **28**, 59-66.

Ribes, A., Brettel, H., Schmitt, F., Liang, H., Cupitt, J. and Saunders, D. 2003 Color and spectral imaging with the CRISATEL Acquisition System *Proceedings of PICS 2003: an International Technical Conference on the Science and Systems of Digital Photography, including the Fifth International Symposium on Multispectral Color Science.* Rochester, NY, May 2003, 215-219.

Saunders, D. and Cupitt, J. 1993 Image processing at the National Gallery: The VASARI project. *National Gallery Technical Bulletin* **14**, 72-85

van Asperen de Boer, J. 1969 Reflectography of paintings using an infra-red vidicon television system. *Studies in Conservation* **14**, 96-118

Whitmore, P., Pan, X. and Baillie, C. 1999 Predicting the fading of objects: Identification of fugitive colorants through direct nondestructive lightfastness measurements. *Journal of the American Institute of Conservation* **38**, 395-409.

Chapter 9

Analysis of Pigments on Manuscripts by Raman Spectroscopy: Advantages and Limitations

Lucia Burgio

Victoria and Albert Museum, London

Introduction

The analysis and characterisation of pigments and dyes on manuscripts is of major significance in the cultural heritage world, as it can assist with the dating and authentication of the artwork, as well as inform its conservation and increase our knowledge about the society that produced it. A wide variety of analytical techniques has traditionally been employed in the identification of pigments on art objects; examples include polarised light microscopy (PLM), scanning electron microscopy (SEM) and energy-dispersive X-ray analysis (EDX), X-ray diffraction (XRD), X-ray fluorescence (XRF), Fourier-transform infrared spectroscopy (FTIR), UV-vis absorption and fluorescence spectrophotometry, gas or liquid chromatography coupled to mass spectrometric detection, laser-induced breakdown spectroscopy and finally particle induced X-ray/g-ray emission (PIXE/PIGE). Valuable analytical results have been obtained with the above techniques; however, quite often it is necessary to employ more than one method in order to achieve unambiguous results. Some of the techniques mentioned above are destructive and/or may require sampling, which affects the integrity of the manuscript under analysis.

A little over two decades ago Raman spectroscopy experienced a renaissance as scientists all over the world began using it for the analysis of pigments and dyes on art objects in general and manuscripts in particular (Guineau 1984, 35; Guineau 1989, 38; Davey *et al.* 1994, 53; Coupry *et al.* 1994, 89; Clark 1995, 187; Clark *et al.* 1997, 91; Burgio *et al.* 1997a, 79; Burgio *et al.* 1997b, 1; Clark and Gibbs 1997, 1003). The addition of an optical microscope to a conventional Raman spectrometer allowed high sensitivity and spatial resolution to be achieved non-destructively; the technique is reasonably free of interference from surrounding materials, especially if a confocal setup is used, and the analysis can be performed in situ, avoiding sampling and consequently the possibility of damage to the object under examination. Even more recently, remote Raman microscopy (employing probes attached to the spectrometer by fibre optics) or free space, open architecture configurations (using horizontal objectives attached directly to the main microscope head, or microscopes mounted on a gantry) have expanded the applicability of Raman spectroscopy by overcoming the size restrictions of a conventional microscope.

This chapter intends to explain to an audience not familiar with this powerful method why Raman microscopy is one of the currently favoured techniques for the analysis of manuscripts and related artefacts, and will expand on its advantages and limitations. The various types of experimental set-ups will also be discussed, and a brief theoretical background will be provided. Finally, a few case studies will be examined and the application of Raman spectroscopy to the investigation of fakes and forgeries will also be discussed.

Why Raman microscopy?

The analysis of pigments and dyes on manuscripts is of major significance for museum and cultural heritage institutions. The materials present on a manuscript can help in the dating and authentication of the work, as well as provide information on its geographical provenance or any trade routes involving artists' materials. From a conservation point of view, the knowledge of the exact chemical nature of materials on manuscripts and of their degradation products is also critical in order to select the conservation method to be employed. Inappropriate conservation and consolidation procedures may cause undesired chemical reactions on the works of art, and in the long term may have unexpected and undesirable effects. Moreover, if light-sensitive pigments are identified on a work of art, strict display conditions have to be employed in order to choose the correct lighting level and to avoid fading. Even if a manuscript does not present any sign of degradation, knowing the materials used to decorate it can help to maintain it in its best condition and preserve it for future generations.

When dealing with valuable historical objects such as manuscripts, non-destructive, non-intrusive techniques are usually preferred. Raman microscopy fits these requirements: if used properly, it is a non-destructive technique, and it can be used *in situ*, i.e. on the artefact itself, without any need for sampling. It is also highly specific, as it provides a unique fingerprint for most materials analysed. It is very fast, usually providing an identifiable spectrum within a few seconds or minutes. A wide variety of materials that might be used on manuscripts can be analysed, including inorganic and organic pigments, dyes, gemstones and minerals. Last but not least, its high spatial resolution allows the analysis of complex mixtures. More details on these characteristics are given below after the discussion about the theoretical background of the Raman effect.

Theoretical background

In a conventional Raman microscope configuration, the object under observation is positioned on the microscope stage, and a microscopic grain of pigment on its surface is brought into focus using one of the microscope's objectives. The same

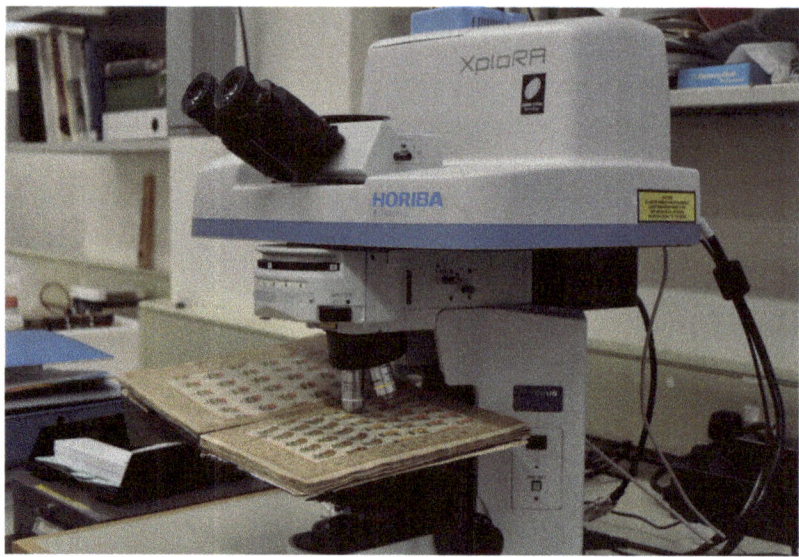

Figure 1: A conventional Raman microscope configuration (the Horiba XploRA at the V&A) where the manuscript is positioned on the microscope stage.

Figure 2: Greg Smith at the British Library, London, analysing one of the Gutenberg Bibles with a Renishaw remote probe on loan from University College London. The manuscript is arranged on a specially designed cradle. Image courtesy of Greg D. Smith.

grain of pigment is then irradiated through the microscope's objective with the Raman laser, a monochromatic beam of light of wavenumber v_0. A small proportion of this light is scattered, both elastically and inelastically: elastically scattered photons have the same energy as those of the incident radiation, whilst inelastically scattered photons are characterised by a loss or gain in energy relative to that of the incident radiation. Raman spectroscopy involves the analysis of the energy of these scattered photons. The line in the resulting Raman spectrum corresponding to elastically scattered radiation is called the Rayleigh line, whilst the other lines are called Stokes or anti-Stokes lines or bands, if their frequency is lower or higher, respectively, than that of the incident light (Ferraro *et al.* 2003). It is the latter ones that contain information on the structure of the sample under analysis. In the work reported here, the shift in frequency, v_i, from that of the incident radiation, v_0, usually corresponds to one of the vibrational modes of the molecule. A vibrational Raman spectrum is therefore unique for each compound and so can be used as a means of identification.

Equipment configuration

Until recently, the conventional configuration for the Raman analysis of a manuscript saw the manuscript or folio being positioned on the microscope's stage under an objective (Figure 1). With this approach only relatively small, flat objects can be conveniently positioned on the microscope stage.

Obviously, large manuscripts would either not fit under the microscope at all and could therefore not be analysed, or access to the central portions of the manuscript would be limited by the design of the microscope stage. Such objects have to be examined using a different configuration such as that involving a cradle for the manuscript and a support stage for a fibre optic Raman probe. One of the first regular uses of this configuration occurred during the analysis of the Gutenberg Bibles (Chaplin *et al.* 2005, 3611) at the British Library between 2000 and 2001 (Figure 2). This new system allowed for the analysis of awkwardly sized objects, although the use of fibre optics meant that its performance was not as brilliant as that of a traditional microscope: the Raman signal was weaker, the experiments took much longer, extra vibrations hindered the analysis and some of the weaker Raman scattering materials did not provide a suitable spectrum and therefore could not be identified.

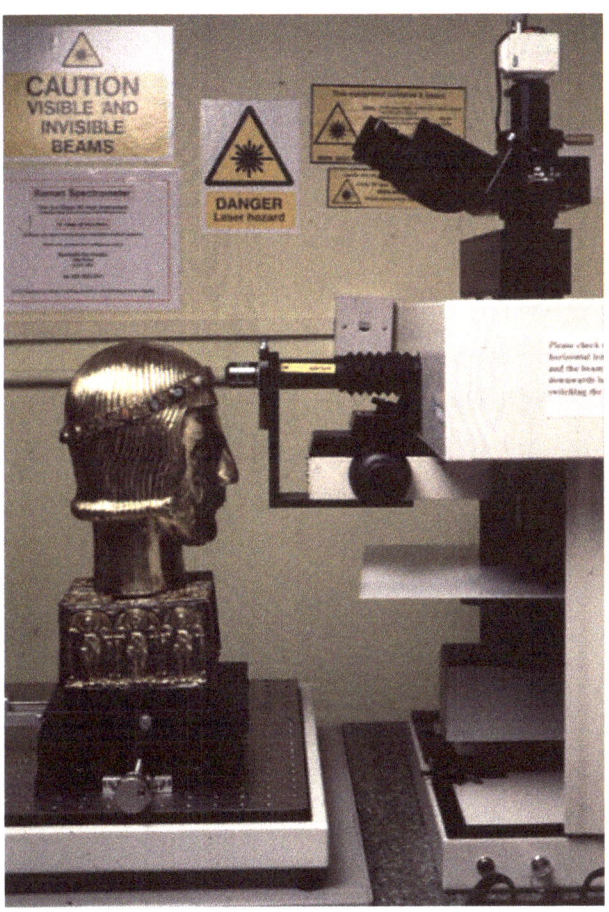

Figure 3: The Horiba Raman microscope used at the British Museum, London, equipped with a horizontal objective (image courtesy of Horiba Jobi Yvon Ltd)

Figure 4: The Renishaw spectrometer used at the Getty Conservation Institute, equipped with a horizontal objective (image courtesy of K. Trentelman and the Getty).

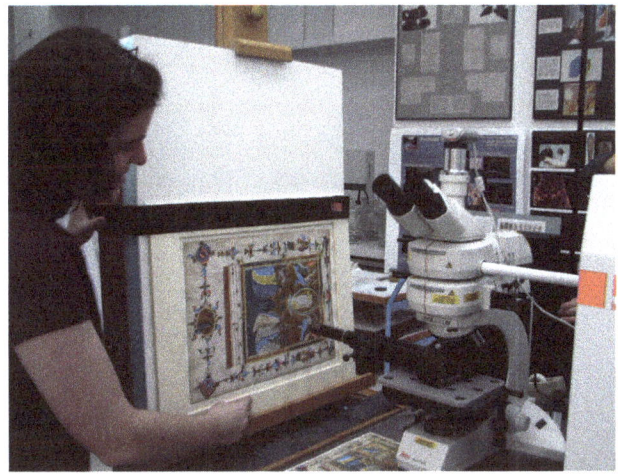

Figure 5: The Bruker Senterra in its open architecture configuration (image courtesy of G.D. Smith)

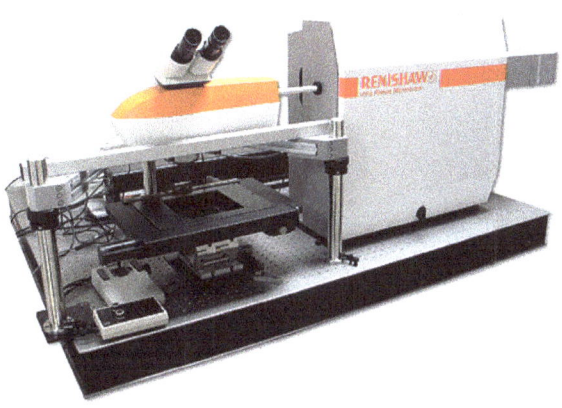

Figure 6: The Renishaw inVia in its free space configuration (image courtesy of Renishaw plc).

As the cultural heritage community warmed to the usage of Raman microscopy for the analysis of art objects and became aware of the limitations of conventional Raman microscope configurations, and the drawbacks of Raman fibre optic probes, new configurations were proposed. A few of these are now being offered as a regular option by Raman manufacturers. These involve either a horizontal objective mounted on the microscope head (Figures 3 and 4), which is very good for the analysis of single folios but not for whole manuscripts, or an open architecture or free space system (Figures 5 and 6). The Bruker Senterra system is particularly flexible as its microscope is mounted on a gantry-type support.

Advantages of Raman microscopy

The advantages afforded by the use of Raman microscopy for the analysis of materials on manuscripts were briefly mentioned earlier. Now they will be discussed more in depth and practical examples will be provided.

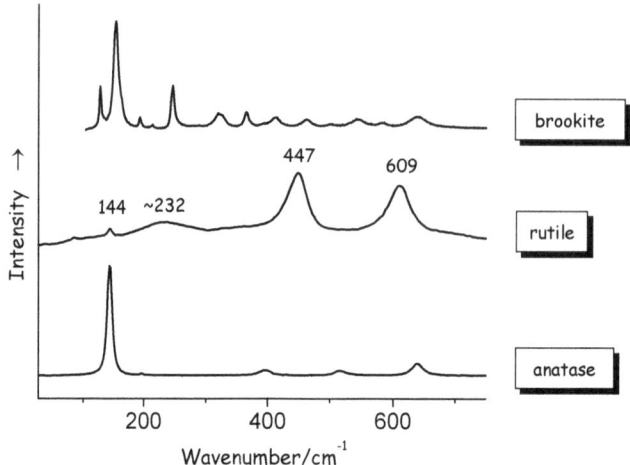

Figure 7: Visible Raman spectra of the three titanium dioxide polymorphs, rutile, brookite and anatase (the spectrum of brookite was kindly provided by Danilo Bersani, University of Pavia, Italy).

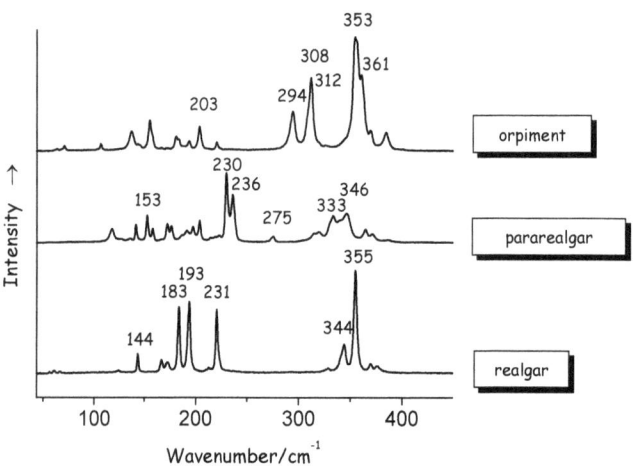

Figure 8: FT-Raman spectra of arsenic-containing species (1064 nm excitation): orpiment, realgar and pararealgar.

In situ analysis

The immediate appeal of Raman microscopy is that it can be used on the manuscript itself, and no samples need to be taken from the books. Nowadays even lectionaries or other large sized manuscripts can be analysed with the use of an open architecture system, a probe or any other microscope modification. If a long working distance microscope objective is used, the analysis can be performed through glass or other transparent protective layers, as the analysis of a 13th century B.C. Egyptian papyrus from the British Museum illustrates (Burgio and Clark 2000, 395). For more details on the latter see under 'Case Studies' below.

Specificity

Raman microscopy allows almost instantaneous recognition of pigments and dyes by providing a molecular fingerprint for the sample under observation. This means that different compounds give rise to different and distinguishable Raman spectra. Even compounds with the same chemical formula yield different Raman spectra, provided their molecular structure is not the same. For example, the three most common polymorphs of titanium dioxide, rutile, anatase and brookite, all with the same chemical formula TiO_2, give rise to very different Raman spectra (Burgio and Clark 2001, 1491). This is very important when modern pigments containing either rutile or anatase or both are investigated (Figure 7), or when they are found in supposedly historical artefacts (Burgio and Clark 2001, 1491; Brown and Clark 2002, 3658; Clark 2004, 2423).

Raman microscopy also allows discrimination between different forms of arsenic sulfide without ambiguity. Until this technique became a routine tool for the analysis of pigments and minerals, there was some confusion about the identity of yellow materials containing arsenic on art work. It was almost always assumed that the yellow material was orpiment (arsenic sulfide, As_2S_3), a natural occurring mineral that has been used as a pigment since antiquity (Fitzhugh 1997, 47). However, it

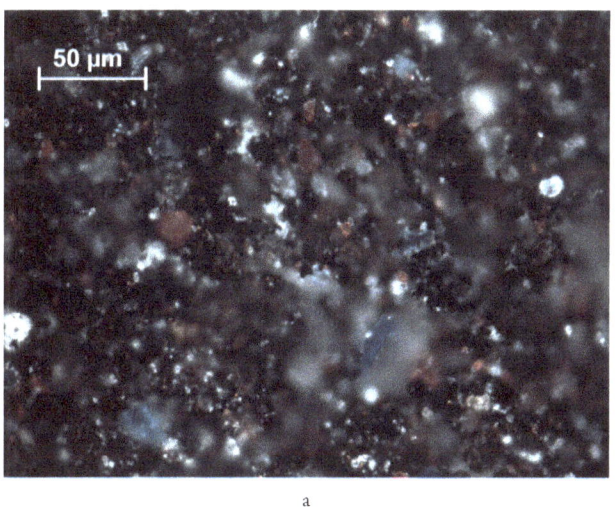
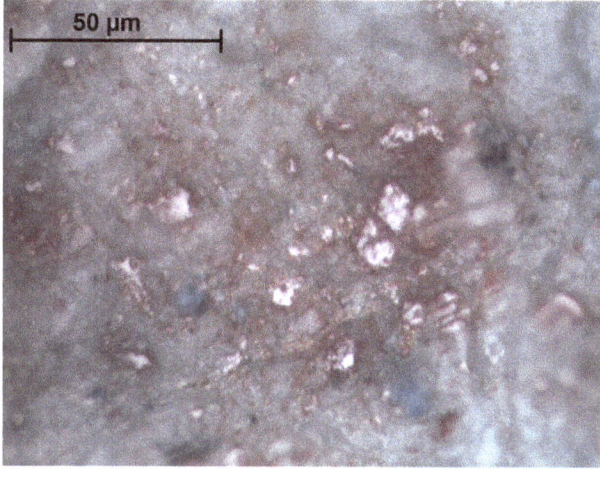

Figure 9: Pigment mixtures on the Nativity by Jean Bourdichon (E.949-2003) viewed under a microscope.

has been proved recently that very often the yellow material is pararealgar (a polymorph of realgar, a different form of arsenic sulfide, As_4S_4), used intentionally as a yellow pigment (see Figure 8 and Clark and Gibbs 1997, 1003; Trentelman et al. 1996, 1755; Clark and Gibbs 1998, 99A; Vandenabeele et al. 2001, 3315; Burgio and Clark 2000, 395).

High spatial resolution

Depending on the laser and the microscope objective used, it is possible to analyse particles that are smaller than 1 µm. If the system used is truly confocal, very little interference from neighbouring particles is experienced. This confocality is particularly useful when finely divided mixtures of pigments are present (see Figure 9). This will be dealt with in more detail within the case studies at the end of this chapter.

Non-destructivity

Raman microscopy is a non-contact technique, and provided the correct experimental conditions are used, the materials under examination are not damaged in any way. The choice of the laser beam is critical: normally visible laser beams are used for the analysis, the most common being in the blue, the green, the red and the far red region of the visible light range. A laser in the near infrared can also be used.

A good rule of thumb is to choose the laser with a colour as similar as possible to that of the specimens under examination, bearing in mind that the intensity of the Raman signal is inversely proportional to the excitation wavelength, i.e. a sample will give a stronger Raman signal if it is analysed with a blue laser than with a red laser because the blue laser light has a shorter wavelength. The Raman effect is based on light scattering and we need to limit as much as possible the absorption of the laser beam by the sample: the more a laser beam is absorbed by the sample the less of it is left for any scattering effect (random reflections). A marked absorption of a laser beam by a pigment or a dye is likely to cause local overheating, i.e. burning of the sample itself under the microscope. This is a very confined damage, as usually the

Laser colour	Laser type	Acronym	Laser Wavelength
Blue	Argon ion	Ar ion	488.0 nm
Green	Argon ion	Ar ion	514.5 nm
	Solid state	-	532 nm
	Neodymium-doped yttrium aluminium garnet $(Nd:Y_3Al_5O_{12})$	Nd:YAG	532 nm
Red	Helium-Neon	He-Ne	632.8 nm
	Solid state	-	633 nm
	Krypton ion	Kr ion	647.1 nm
Far red	Solid state	-	780-785 nm
Near infrared	Neodymium-doped yttrium aluminium garnet $(Nd:Y_3Al_5O_{12})$	Nd:YAG	1064 nm

Figure 10: Table summarising the different Raman lasers which are commonly used for the analysis of manuscripts

burnt area is only a few micrometers across and is invisible to the naked eye, but it is damage nonetheless. The laser-degraded area may also give rise to a Raman spectrum which can be mistaken for a different material (Smith *et al.* 2001, 185). There are of course exceptions to the following 'rules', but in general for a red or orange pigment it would be best to use a He-Ne laser (632 nm) or a Krypton ion laser (647 nm) or any other red solid state laser. It is not normally advisable to use a green laser. For blue pigments it is best to use a blue (Argon ion laser, 488 nm) or a green laser (Argon ion, 514.5 nm; Nd:YAG, 532 nm; or any other solid state green laser). White and yellow pigments can usually be analysed with any type of laser. Far red (solid state lasers usually between 780 and 785 nm) and near infrared lasers (Nd:YAG, 1064 nm, usually found on FT-Raman spectrometers) are particularly suitable for dyes and organic materials, but tend to burn dark inorganic materials as the latter absorb rather than scatter such laser radiation. Figure 10 summarises the most common laser lines used for the analysis of manuscripts.

It is also advisable to do a preliminary test on the specimen under the microscope using a very low laser power (well below 1 mW). The laser power can be progressively increased as needed to obtain a good spectrum once it is clear that the sample will not be damaged by the laser irradiation. Commercial Raman microscopes usually come equipped with a set of neutral density filters which allow to fine tune the laser power at the sample reducing it from 100% to below 1% of the output.

Wide range of targets

Many types of compounds usually yield very good Raman spectra. When dealing with cultural heritage items, inorganic pigments were the first class of materials that were found to be very good Raman scatterers (Bell *et al.* 1997, 2159; Burgio and Clark 2001, 1491). Most of them give a recognisable Raman spectrum within a few seconds, and many of the worse scatterers still give a good spectrum within minutes. Very few inorganic materials are bad Raman scatterers (alumino-silicates are such a group). A few of the traditional, historical dyes, such as indigo, are also good Raman scatterers, but most are not (they will be discussed in the "Limitations" section of this chapter). Most modern, synthetic organic colorants also give a good Raman spectrum (Schulte *et al.* 2008, 1455; Scherrer *et al.* 2009, 505), as do most gems and precious stones (Smith 2005, 335; Kiefert *et al.* 2005, 379).

Limitations of Raman microscopy

Although this technique is versatile and ideal in many respects, it does present a few limitations, which will be discussed below.

Fluorescence

The laser beam can excite electronic transitions that may mask the Raman signal: if any Raman peaks are visible at all, they appear as if they are just coming out of a very bumpy or hilly baseline. In some cases, the fluorescence can be reduced by using a laser beam with a longer wavelength (see the spectra of indigo taken with three different lasers in Figure 11).

However, the fluorescence could also be caused by oil, dirt and impurities present in the sample: it is a well known fact that the Raman analysis of oil paintings can be painfully difficult because of the interference of the fluorescence caused by the medium or varnish. In this respect the analysis of manuscripts is a lot easier because water-based media such as gum Arabic or animal glue rarely give rise to fluorescence. Occasionally, the laser beam itself 'burns off' the dirt or the impurities that cause the fluorescence within the sample; after the first few seconds or minutes of laser irradiation the fluorescent background visibly decreases and the proper Raman bands become clearer.

Coupled with their intrinsic low Raman sensitivity, the fluorescence of natural organic pigments or dyes containing anthraquinones (such as madder and carmine) and flavonoids (such as lueteolin and quercetin) usually prevents a successful Raman analysis. However, surface-enhanced Raman spectroscopy (SERS) and surface-enhanced resonance Raman spectroscopy (SERRS) can help overcome the problem. These techniques involve depositing minute amounts of metal

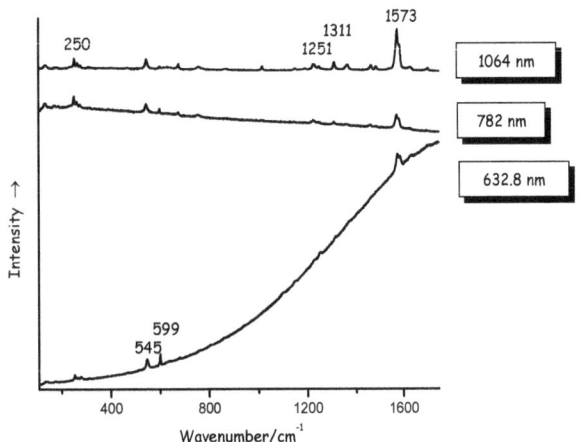
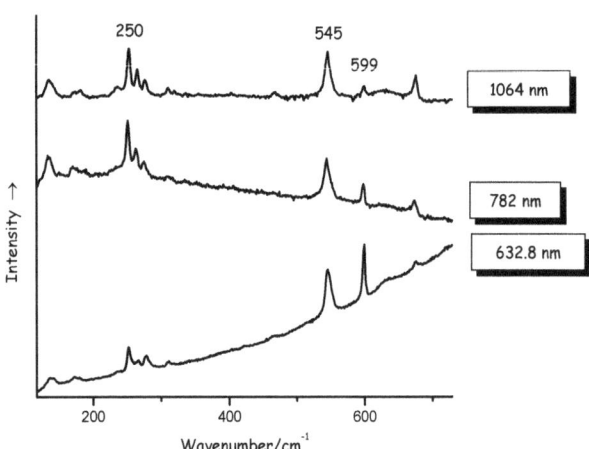

Figure 11: Raman spectra of indigo taken with various laser excitations. The intensity of the fluorescent background decreases and more spectral features appear when a longer wavelength is used.

Figure 12: An Indian miniature being analysed with a Dilor LabRam at the V&A. The page is stabilised with carefully positioned weights.

microscope. Unless the page under observation is kept still, any air movement or floor vibration can alter the position of the page under the microscope. It is critical to a successful outcome of the Raman analysis that the single particle under observation is kept in focus at all times. To avoid vibrations, or at least reduce them as much as possible, a variety of aids can be used. These include padded snake weights, glass weights and so on, which can be positioned on the page under analysis as close as possible to the microscope objective in order to keep the area under observation flat and still. Normally clean lens tissue or acid free paper is positioned between the surface of the page and the aids, to avoid any mechanical damage and transfer of material from one spot of the page to another (Figure 12).

Size restrictions

If only a traditional microscope set up is available for the analysis, then only relatively small manuscripts can be analysed because large ones simply cannot fit under the microscope. However, even if the manuscript or folio is too large, its edges can still be analysed. If the manuscript is too thick, then occasionally the microscope stage can be removed and the manuscript can be fitted under the objective, although its positioning by hand may be tricky. These problems are more easily overcome if an open architecture system is available (such as the Bruker Senterra's – see Figure 5) or if a fibre optic probe can be used, as discussed at the beginning of this chapter.

Miscellaneous limitations

As mentioned earlier, a Raman microscope using visible excitation is not particularly suitable for the analysis of binding media, because the spectrum obtained is usually very weak and is covered by that of the pigments or dyes. The technique is also of limited usefulness with many very dark materials which absorb most of the incident light, as they are prone to local overheating and laser-induced degradation.

nanoparticles (usually silver) onto the surface which is being analysed (a good introductory article by Mukhophadhyay (2010, 44) recently appeared on Chemistry World). These particles are invisible to the naked eye, but result in the amplification of the Raman signal (Leona and Lombardi 2007, 853; Leona 2009, 14757; Berrie 2009, 15095). Unfortunately, these techniques are not usually allowed for the analysis of manuscripts because they involve the contamination, albeit minute, of the object's surface.

Stability and focusing issues

One of the most annoying practical aspects in the Raman analysis of manuscripts is the loss of focus during the analysis, due to the shift of the parchment or paper under the

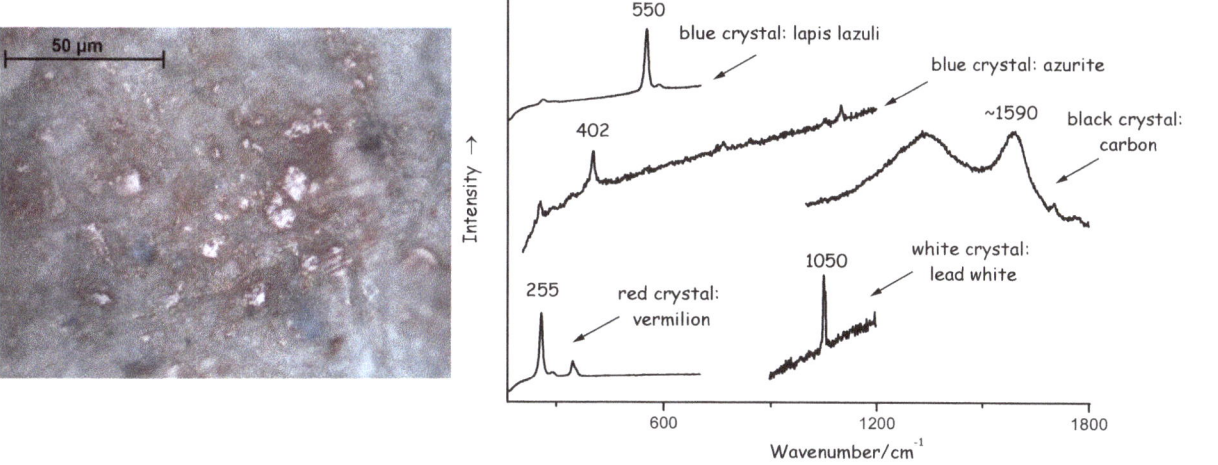

Figure 13: Photomicrograph of the carnation of the Virgin on the Nativity by Jean Bourdichon (left) and Raman spectra from the red, white, blue and black crystals in the carnation mixture. The crystals were analysed with a 633 nm HeNe laser through a x50 objective. The power at the sample never exceeded 1 mW and the laser irradiation of each crystal lasted not more than 20 seconds.

Case studies

Analysis of mixtures

One of the first great advantages of Raman microscopy to be picked up by the heritage community at the end of the 1980s was its ability to record individual spectra from tiny particles of pigments in a complex mixture, normally without interference from nearby particles (see for example Figure 9). Figure 13 shows the Raman spectra taken from a carnation skin area of the Virgin Mary on the 15th century miniature by Jean Bourdichon, the Nativity (V&A accession number E.949-2003; see Trentelman and Turner 2009, 577; Burgio *et al.* 2009a, 611). These spectra show that distinct pigment particles yield very clear Raman spectra which are not normally affected by the presence of several other materials in the mixture, i.e. there are no overlapping bands from nearby pigments.

Things can get a bit more complex when a manuscript contains fine mixtures of very strong and very weak Raman scatterers, i.e. compounds that yield a very good Raman spectrum quickly and a weak one slowly, respectively: in this case it is possible that only a noisy spectrum will be recorded from the weak Raman scatterer whilst bands from the stronger scatterer will be prominent.

Identification of unusual materials

The number of traditional pigments and dyes routinely found on scrolls, manuscripts and paper-based materials from antiquity until the 18th century is relatively small, normally between five and ten on a single object, and in total not more than 25-30 compounds. Many are of mineral origin or are the synthetic reproduction of minerals, for example cinnabar and vermilion (Gettens *et al.* 1997, 159), or azurite and blue verditer (Gettens and Fitzhugh 1997a, 23; Gettens and Fitzhugh 1997b, 183). However, every now and again 'new' materials are discovered, and Raman microscopy usually has a prominent role in the discovery. For example, it was found very recently that the French Court painter Jean Bourdichon, active between the end of the 15th and the beginning of the 16th century and mentioned earlier in this chapter, used metallic bismuth in some of his miniatures. This material was detected during the routine analysis of some of Bourdichon's miniatures from the Getty and the V&A (Trentelman and Turner 2009, 577; Trentelman 2009, 585; Burgio *et al.* 2009a, 611). On the Nativity, which was originally part of the Book of Hours made by Bourdichon for the coronation of King Louis XII in 1498, the Raman spectrum of bismuth was recorded from many of the grey areas. On a privately owned miniature originally from the same book, the Flight to Egypt, metallic bismuth was detected on many of the grey areas as well as on the underlying preparatory pencil drawing. Bismuth is a relatively rare metal often found in its native state. It is difficult to say with certainty when bismuth was first discovered, but mining of bismuth was established in Saxony by the middle of the 15th century. There is even a 1384 German manuscript which gives a bismuth-based recipe for a silver ink, showing that bismuth was recognised as an artist's material, albeit a rare one (Mayr 1984, 153).

The detection of bismuth by Raman microscopy on Bourdichon's miniatures enhanced our knowledge about the materials available to artists at the end of the 15th century, and suggests that Bourdichon may have come across metallic bismuth in his own travels or via merchants bringing wares out of Germany.

Fakes and forgeries

Raman microscopy has often being used to help in the detection of fakes and forgeries, because it can easily expose the presence of date-markers, i.e. materials that, due to their first known date of manufacture, are incompatible with the supposed date of the object under observation. A recent application of Raman microscopy in this field is the analysis of five miniatures by the so-called 'Spanish Forger', which were acquired by the Victoria and Albert Museum in 2008. Believed to be authentic medieval miniatures until the mid-twentieth century, they are now considered to have been painted around the end of the nineteenth and the beginning of the twentieth century on stylistic grounds. Traditional medieval painting materials such as vermilion, carbon black, red lead, lead white and indigo were indeed detected on the miniatures, but many modern and synthetic pigments were also found, such as chrome yellow, Scheele's green, emerald green and ultramarine blue. This was the first systematic study ever carried out to identify in detail the actual painting materials used by the Spanish Forger, and it proved that his forgeries can be consistently and readily detected on scientific as well as stylistic grounds (Burgio *et al.* 2009b, 2031).

Another interesting case is represented by the analysis of six Egyptian papyri belonging to a private collection and brought to London from Egypt in January 1998 for auction. Five of the papyri were said by the owner to be from the period of Ramses II, who was a Pharaoh in the 13th century B.C. The sixth papyrus was said to be a contemporary portrait of the Egyptian Queen Cleopatra who lived in the first century B.C. Part of the authentication procedure required by the auction house was to establish the palette on each papyrus and, in particular, whether any modern pigments were present. Therefore, the pigments on each papyrus were analysed *in situ* by Raman microscopy (Burgio and Clark 2000, 395). For comparison, an authentic papyrus from the Petrie Museum dating from the 18th dynasty (that of Ramses II) was also studied, and was shown to be decorated with a very restricted range of mineral pigments. This papyrus had recently been conserved by the British Museum and placed under glass, and the Raman study was performed without removal of the glass, further emphasising the non-intrusive nature of this technique.

The palette of the six papyri to be auctioned was composed mainly of modern pigments: the white pigment anatase (post 1923), the blue synthetic pigments phthalocyanine blue (post 1936) and Prussian blue (post 1704), the green synthetic pigment phthalocyanine green (post 1936), the yellow pigment Hansa Yellow PY 6 (post 1909) and the red pigment b-naphthol PR 112 (post 1939), all of which can only be produced with technology that was not available in ancient Egypt. Although the papyrus substrate itself was not dated, all the evidence gathered by Raman microscopy lead to the conclusion that (i) the six papyri were not ancient, and (ii) they were painted sometime after the 1939.

Acknowledgements

The author gratefully acknowledges Richard Hark, Juniata College, Pennsylvania for his very helpful comments and Karen Trentelman, Greg Smith, Horiba Jobin Yvon Ltd, Renishaw plc and Bruker Optics Ltd for allowing the use of their images. Danilo Bersani also generously provided the Raman spectrum of brookite.

References

Bell, I. M., Clark, R. J. H. and Gibbs, P. J. 1997 Raman Spectroscopic Library of Natural and Synthetic Pigments (pre- ~1850 AD). *Spectrochimica Acta Part A* **53**, 2159-2179

Berrie, B. 2009 An improved method for identifying red lakes on art and historical artifacts. *Proceedings of the National Academy of Sciences of the United States of America (PNAS)* **106** (36), 15095–15096

Brown, K. L. and Clark, R. J. H. 2002 Analysis of Pigmentary Materials on the Vinland Map and Tartar Relation by Raman Microprobe Spectroscopy (Reprint). *Analytical Chemistry* **74**, 3658-3661

Burgio, L., Ciomartan, D. A. and Clark, R. J. H. 1997a Raman microscopy study of the pigments on three illuminated mediaeval Latin manuscripts *Journal of Raman Spectroscopy* **28**, 79-83

Burgio, L., Ciomartan, D. A. and Clark, R. J. H. 1997b Pigment identification on medieval manuscripts, paintings and other artefacts by Raman microscopy: applications to the study of three German manuscripts. *Journal of Molecular Structure* **405**, 1-11

Burgio, L. and Clark, R. J. H. 2000 Comparative Study of Six Modern Papyri and an Authentic One by Raman Microscopy and Other Techniques. *Journal of Raman Spectroscopy* **31**, 395-401

Burgio, L. and Clark, R. J. H. 2001 Library of FT-Raman spectra of pigments, minerals, pigment media and varnishes, and supplement to existing library of Raman spectra of pigments with visible excitation, *Spectrochimica Acta Part A* **57**, 1491–1521

Burgio, L., Clark, R. J. H., Hark, R. R, Rumsey, M. S. and Zannini, C. 2009a Spectroscopic investigations of Bourdichon miniatures: masterpieces of light and color. *Applied Spectroscopy* **63**, 611–620.

Burgio, L., Clark, R. J. H. and Hark, R. R. 2009b Spectroscopic investigation of modern pigments on purportedly medieval miniatures by the 'Spanish Forger', *Journal of Raman Spectroscopy* **40**, 2031–2036

Chaplin, T. D., Clark, R. J. H., Jacobs, D., Jensen, K. and Smith, G. D. 2005 The Gutenberg Bibles: analysis of the illuminations and inks by Raman microscopy. *Analytical Chemistry* **77**, 3611-3622

Clark, R. J. H. 1995 Raman microscopy: application to the identification of pigments on medieval manuscripts. *Chemical Society Reviews* **24**, 187-196

Clark, R. J. H. 2004 The Vinland Map - Still a 20th Century Forgery *Analytical Chemistry* **76**, 2423

Clark, R. J. H. and Gibbs, P. J. 1997 Identification of Lead(II) Sulfide and Pararealgar on a 13th Century Manuscript by Raman Microscopy, *Chemical Communications* **11**, 1003-1004

Clark, R. J. H. and Gibbs, P. J. 1998 Raman microscopy of a 13th century illuminated text. *Analytical Chemistry* **70**, 99A-104A.

Clark, R. J. H., Gibbs, P. J., Seddon, K. R., Brovenko N. M. and Petrosyan, Y. A. 1997 Non-destructive in situ identification of cinnabar on ancient Chinest manuscripts. *Journal of Raman Spectroscopy* **28**, 91-94

Coupry, C., Lautie, A., Revault, M. and Dufilho, J. 1994 Contribution of Raman spectroscopy to art and history. *Journal of Raman Spectroscopy* **25**, 89-94

Davey, R., Gardiner, D.J., Singer, B. W. and Spokes, M. 1994 Examples of analysis of pigments from fine art objects by Raman microscopy *Journal of Raman Spectroscopy* **25**, 53-57

Ferraro, J. R., Nakamoto, K. and Brown, C. W. 2003 *Introductory Raman Spectroscopy*. Academic Press, London

Fitzhugh, E. W. 1997 Orpiment and realgar. In E. W. Fitzhugh (ed.) *Artists Pigments: A History of Their History and Characteristics volume 3,* 47-79. Oxford University Press 1997

Gettens, R. J., Feller, R. L. and Chase, W. T. 1997 Vermilion and Cinnabar. In A. Roy (ed.) *Artists Pigments: A History of Their History and Characteristics volume 2*, 159-182. Oxford University Press.

Gettens, R. J. & E. Fitzhugh 1997a Azurite and blue verditer. In A. Roy (ed.) *Artists Pigments: A History of Their History and Characteristics volume 2*, 23-36. Oxford University Press.

Gettens, R. J. & E. Fitzhugh 1997b Malachite and green verditer. In A. Roy (ed.) *Artists Pigments: A History of Their History and Characteristics volume 2,*183-202 Oxford University Press.

Guineau, B. 1984 Analyse non destructive des pigments par microsonde Raman laser: exemples de l'azurite et de la malachite. *Studies in Conservation.* **29**, 35-41

Guineau, B. 1989 Non-destructive analysis of organic pigments and dyes using Raman microprobe, microfluorometer or absorption microspectrophotometer. *Studies in Conservation* **34**, 38-44

Kiefert, L., Chalain, J. P., and Haberli, S. 2005 Diamonds, gemstones and pearls: from the past to the present. In H.G.M. Edwards and J.M. Chalmers (eds) *Raman Spectroscopy in Archaeology and Art History,* 379-402. Royal Society of Chemistry, Cambridge

Leona, M. 2009 Microanalysis of organic pigments and glazes in polychrome works of art by surface-enhanced resonance Raman scattering. *Proceedings of the National Academy of Sciences of the United States of America (PNAS)* **106** (35), 14757-14762

Leona, M and Lombardi, J. R. 2007 Identification of berberine in ancient and historical textiles by surface-enhanced Raman scattering *Journal of Raman Spectroscopy* **38**, 853-858

Mayr, K. 1984 Wismutmalerei. *Restauratorenblatter* 7 153–172.

Mukhophadhyay, R. 2010 The art of Raman. *Chemistry World* **January 2010**, 44-47.

Scherrer, N. C., Stefan, Z., Francoise, D., Annette, F. and Renate, K. 2009 Synthetic organic pigments of the 20th and 21st century relevant to artist's paints: Raman spectra reference collection, *Spectrochimica Acta Part A* **73**, 505-524

Schulte, F., Brzezink, K. W., Lutzenberger, K., Stege, H. and Panne, U. 2008 Raman spectroscopy of synthetic organic pigments used in 20th century works of art. *Journal of Raman Spectroscopy* **39**, 1455-1463

Smith, D. C. 2005 Jewellery and precious stones. In H.G.M. Edwards and J.M. Chalmers (eds) *Raman Spectroscopy in Archaeology and Art History*, 335-378. Royal Society of Chemistry, Cambridge

Smith, G. D., Burgio, L., Firth, S. and Clark, R. J. H. 2001 Laser-induced degradation of lead pigments with reference to Botticelli's *Trionfo d'Amore*. *Analytica Chimica Acta* **440** (2), 185-188

Trentelman, K. 2009 A note on the characterization of bismuth black by Raman microspectroscopy *Journal of Raman Spectroscopy* **40**, 585-589

Trentelman, K., Stodulski, L. and Pavlosky, M. 1996 Charaterization of pararealgar and other light-induced transformation products from realgar by Raman microspectroscopy. *Analytical Chemistry* **68**, 1755-1761

Trentelman, K. and Turner, N. 2009 Investigation of the painting materials and techniques of the late-15th century manuscript illuminator Jean Bourdichon. *Journal of Raman Spectroscopy* **40**, 577–584

Vandenabeele, P., Von Bohlen, A., Moens, L., Klockenkamper, R., Joukes, F., and Dewispelaere, G. 2001 Spectroscopic examination of two Egyptian masks: a combined method approach. *Analytical Letters* **33**, 3315-3332.

Chapter 10

Non-destructive Ion Beam Analysis Techniques for Book and Manuscript Studies

Geoffrey W. Grime

Ion Beam Centre, University of Surrey

Introduction

Ion beam analysis using beams of high energy protons is a well established method for determining the elemental composition of ink, pigments and papers used in the manufacture of historically interesting books and manuscripts. Using various interactions, elemental concentrations of regions less than 100 micrometres in diameter can be determined with good quantitative accuracy and with very good sensitivity. This is normally carried out using a beam extracted into air, so that entire objects can be analyzed without the need to remove samples. This paper outlines the techniques, highlights some successful book and manuscript projects which have been performed using the method, and critically examines the often repeated statement that the method is 'non-destructive'.

Ion beam analysis

Ion beam analysis (IBA) using a probe beam of high energy light ions (typically 3 MeV protons) has a well-established role in the characterisation of archaeological and historical objects (Mahnke *et al.* 1990). The analytical interactions available offer significant advantages over more conventional methods. The most used IBA technique, proton induced X-ray emission, or PIXE (Johansson *et al.* 1995) is similar to other X-ray analysis methods such as X-ray fluorescence (XRF) or electron probe microanalysis (EPMA or EDX) in that it offers simultaneous detection of all elements in the sample with an atomic number greater than that of sodium. Crucially, the physics of proton interactions gives two advantages: the non-specific background radiation created is two to three orders of magnitude smaller, which allows detection limits in the part-per-million region to be achieved, and the X-ray yield per incident proton is very high, which means that analysis can be carried out in a short time with very low incident currents. Analysis typically takes a few minutes using currents of 100 to 500 picoamperes. The physics of the PIXE process is well understood, so that in favourable cases, concentrations can be determined to high accuracy (5 – 10 %) without a high dependence on standard reference materials (Gomez-Morilla *et al.* 2006).

PIXE is often used in conjunction with Rutherford backscattering (RBS), where the energy of primary beam particles recoiling from direct 'billiard ball' collisions with the nuclei of atoms in the sample is measured. This can provide information on the mass and depth of the target nucleus. The interpretation of RBS data is less straightforward than for X-ray spectra (Grime 1999), but it provides useful complementary information on light element concentrations and in some cases can determine the depth profile of the elemental composition allowing the possibility of determining the thickness of coatings and corrosion layers or determining the profile of elements diffused into the surface.

The combination of part-per-million trace element sensitivity and quantitative accuracy offered by the techniques of proton induced X-ray emission (PIXE) in combination with Rutherford backscattering (RBS) (Mahnke *et al.* 1990) presents a solution to many problems involving the study of artefacts and raw materials.

Using a suitable micro-focusing system, IBA can be carried out in vacuum with a spatial resolution of less than $1\mu m$[1] (e.g. Grime *et al.* 1991, Watt *et al.* 1994), but this is often inappropriate for archaeological and historic objects. This is due to the nature of the materials, which are often heterogeneous, containing particulate inclusions with diameters of less than 100 micrometres. The long penetration depth of MeV light ions averages the signal over the range of the ions (tens of micrometres) and so unless thin samples are used, it is not possible to analyse small inclusions separately from the matrix and the advantage of using micron or sub-micron beams is lost. Another practical disadvantage of high resolution microbeam facilities for archaeological applications is the requirement to place the sample in an evacuated chamber. For most archaeological or historical objects this would require samples to be removed, which may be highly undesirable for precious, delicate objects.

The long range of MeV ions in air offers the possibility of analysing large or fragile objects in air with no sampling required by extracting the beam from the high vacuum of the beamline into laboratory environment. The beam diameter is degraded by collisions with gas molecules (by approximately 10 μm per mm of air path), but as discussed above, this is not a major problem for archaeological samples and by careful design, a spatial resolution of less than 50 μm can be achieved.

The external beam system developed at the University of Surrey Ion Beam Centre (Merchant *et al.* 2005) is shown in Figures 1 and 2. The key to high performance of this type of system is to minimize the distance between the exit of the beam from the vacuum and the sample. This reduces beam scattering and also reduces the absorption of the emitted signals. The beam emerges into air through an 8μm Kapton window. A magnetic lens focuses the beam to a diameter of around 10 μm and crucially, allows the beam to be magnetically scanned across the sample, permitting elemental mapping.

---

[1] 'μm' is the symbol for micrometers, or microns; one micron is a thousandth of a millimetre.

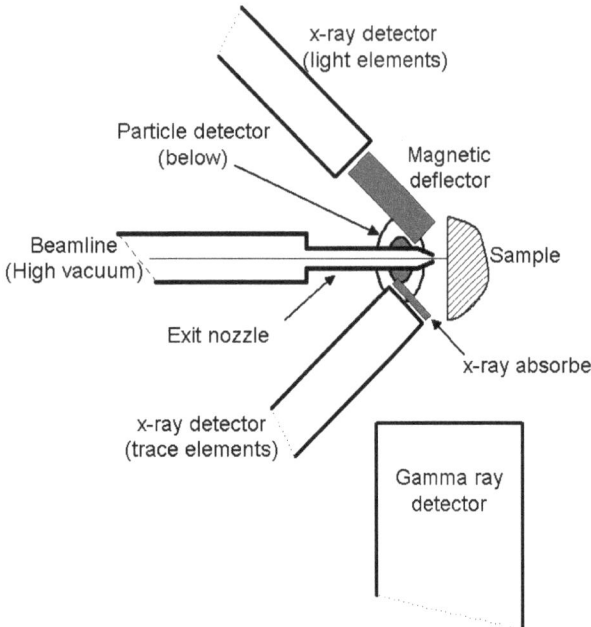

Figure 1. Schematic diagram of the Surrey external beam system. The beam emerges from the high vacuum beamline through a thin window (typically 8 mm Kapton foil) and impinges on the sample mounted at a distance of 4 mm from the window. The analytical signals are recorded by an array of radiation detectors depending on the type of analysis to be performed. These can include one or two X-ray detectors (one is shown here fitted with a magnetic deflector to exclude backscattered particles), a detector mounted below the beam to measure the energy of backscattered particles (for RBS), and a semiconductor gamma ray detector.

Figure 2. Photograph of the Surrey external beam system being used to analyse a glass vessel. The beam nozzle is in the left centre of the image. Two X-ray detectors can be seen (in the retracted position) and the particle detector is located below the beam nozzle. A light guide for sample illumination enters from the top left of the photograph.

The sample is mounted at approximately 4mm from the window, allowing a resolution of 40-50 μm to be achieved on the sample. Detectors for X-rays, recoiling protons and gamma rays allow analysis using PIXE, RBS and also proton induced gamma-ray emission (PIGE) analysis for the detection of light elements such as lithium and fluorine. This allows virtually the entire periodic table to be covered in a single measurement. The region surrounding the sample, exit nozzle and detectors is usually flushed with helium gas. The initial motivation for doing this was to reduce the absorption of light X-rays by the nitrogen in air, but as we will see later, the helium gas flow also provides an important cooling mechanism for sensitive samples.

Systems such as this are in use in a number of laboratories around the world, the most active of these in the field of document analysis being the AGLAE facility at the Centre de Récherche et Restauration des Musées de France in the Louvre Museum in Paris[2] and Laboratorio di Tecniche Nucleari per i Beni Culturali at the University of Florence.[3]

Ion beam analysis applied to book studies

External beam analysis of manuscripts has been one of the niche applications for PIXE analysis since its inception. The first high profile application of the method was the work carried out at the University of California, Davis, in which the signatures of a Gutenberg Bible were grouped in order of printing according to the compositional 'fingerprint' of the metal based inks used. This early example of a successful collaboration between scientists and historians was producing publications over a period of several years in the 1980s (e.g. Kusko et al. 1984).

Around this time the group at the University of Florence led by Pier-Andrea Mandó began to apply external beam analysis to the study of the pigments used in miniatures in illuminated manuscripts (e.g. MacArthur et al. 1990). Another study carried out by the Florence group was their ingenious method of determining the time sequence of notes written in the margins of Galileo's treatise on motion by comparing the composition of the ink in undated marginalia with that of the ink used in well dated writings such as letters and inventories (Giuntini et al. 1995, Del Carmine et al. 1996)

At C2RMF the external beam at the AGLAE facility has been used to study silverpoint drawings. By analysing the metallic marks on the paper, PIXE can determine not only the major metal of the stylus, but from the lower concentration alloying elements, different styli of the same metal can be distinguished. This has been used for example, to group or discriminate otherwise unattributed silverpoint drawings from the 15th century (Duval et al. 2004).

---

[2] http://www.c2rmf.fr/homes/home_id21888_u1l2.htm
[3] http://labec.fi.infn.it

How non-destructive is non-destructive?

Ion beam analysis is usually presented as "non-destructive". At some level, this is true; the total beam dose used is relatively small and the experience of many workers over decades of PIXE analysis is that the effect of the beam on the majority of inorganic solid samples is difficult to detect. With organic materials, the organic matrix may be damaged or discoloured following long or intense exposure (Watt et al. 1988), but the inorganic composition (which is what is measured in PIXE) is not changed – the experiment may be repeated many times with the same result for the trace element concentrations. In addition, in external microbeam analysis, the analysed area is small (usually less than 1 mm in diameter), so the visual impact of any beam marking is usually not noticeable to a visual inspection.

However, paper and other manuscript substrate materials present a different challenge. The materials are often fragile and whitened to enhance the contrast of the ink, which makes the objects particularly sensitive to discolouration. The growing awareness of the fact that books and manuscripts require special consideration is highlighted in three quotations from papers published by the Florence group over a period of twelve years:

In 1995, using a beam current density of 11,000 pA mm^{-2} (pico-amperes per square millimetre), we read that 'Under the conditions at which we operate, we have never detected visible damage in the examined documents.' (Giuntini et al., 1995). A year later, in 1996, with a beam current density of 3,000 pA mm^{-2}, '... the risk of damage to the documents is absolutely negligible.' (Lucarelli and Mando, 1996). Finally, in 2007, '... the density of beam charge delivered in this case (250 pA/mm^2) might not always be allowed on these kind of target [documents], owing to the requirements of non-damage.' (Grassi et al. 2007). Coming from one of the leading research groups in this field, this clearly indicates that the subject of beam effects on analysed documents needs to be taken seriously.

A high energy beam of charged ions such as protons can affect the substrate materials of documents through three main mechanisms: the deposition of thermal energy leading to heating and thermal decomposition; structural degradation resulting from collisions of the fast ions with the atoms of the sample, leading to the breaking of long polymer chains in the cellulose or collagen framework, and optical effects caused by the modification of the structure of organic or inorganic pigments, which can lead to detectable changes in the infra-red or ultra-violet as well as in the visible spectrum.

Thermal effects

The amount of thermal energy which could be absorbed from a proton beam is easy to calculate. The electrical power in a typical analysis beam of 3MeV protons at 100 pA is 300 μW, and if the beam stops in the target, all this power is deposited. If we assume a beam diameter of 100 μm and a penetration depth of 50 μm, this corresponds to a power density of around 800 mW mm^{-3}. If this heat were not dissipated, it would lead to a temperature increase in a typical solid organic material of the order of 500 °C per second! Of course there are physical mechanisms for dissipating this heat: conduction through the material, infra-red radiation to the surroundings and convection to the surrounding gas. Unfortunately calculating the magnitude of these effects is a complex mathematical problem which depends on a detailed knowledge of the physical properties and microstructure of the sample and its environment. This makes it impossible to model any real situation, especially for complex materials like paper, and we have to fall back on order of magnitude estimation and experiment. It was realised right from the early days of document analysis that the dominant mechanism for heat dissipation is transfer to the surrounding gas. The cooling is especially effective with light gases such as helium, which fortuitously is also the optimum environment from the point of view of reducing x-ray absorption. Cooling with a jet of helium gas is essential to the safe analysis of documents.

Structural degradation

It is well known that bombardment with high energy ions can displace atoms within crystal lattices or large organic molecules leading to changes in the mechanical and chemical properties of the target materials. This effect is indeed exploited in the newly emerging microfabrication method of proton beam writing (Watt et al. 2007) in which a finely focused ion beam is used to change the solubility of polymer materials to allow the production of microscopic three-dimensional structures.

It is to be expected that a similar effect will occur in the structural molecules of paper and other document substrates. This has been investigated by Cheng et al. (1998), who exposed a 2mm wide rectangular region located laterally across the centre of a strip of paper (250 mm x 25 mm) to varying fluxes of high energy protons. The relative tensile strength was determined by measuring the longitudinal force required

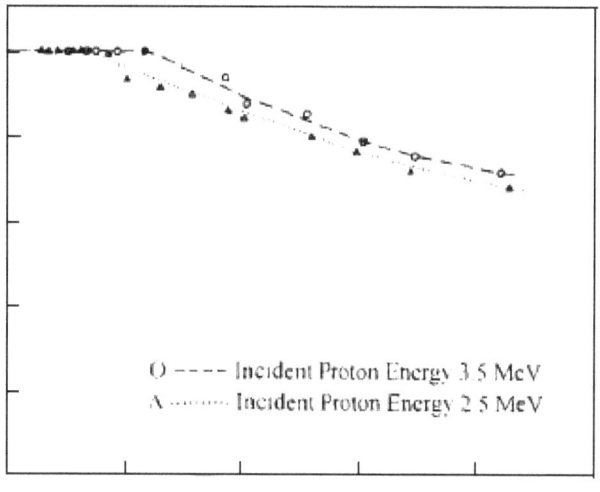

Figure 3. Dependence of relative tensile strength of paper following exposure to different fluxes of protons with energies of 2.5 MeV (triangles) and 3.5 MeV (circles). From Cheng et al. 1998.

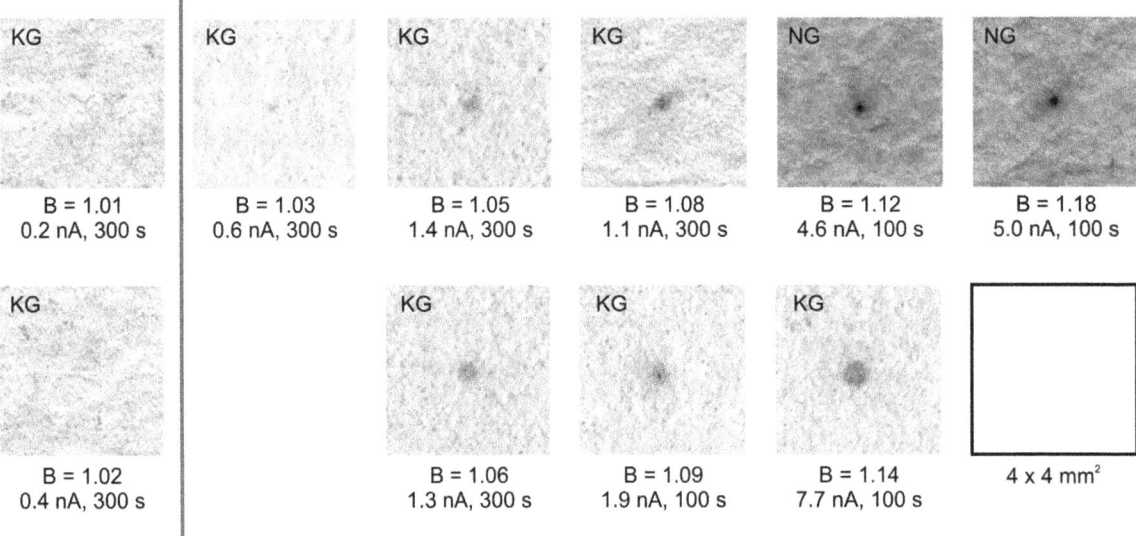

Figure 4. Enlarged images of irradiated paper areas after accelerated ageing, ordered by increasing exposure to protons. NG is ungrounded rag paper, KG is grounding with bone white. The so-called black-value B (essentially the ratio between the gray-scale values of a spot and its environment) indicates the amount of beam-induced discoloration. For the leftmost figures with B up to 1.02, separated from the rest by a vertical line, no effect is visible. From Milota *et al.* 2008.

to rupture the paper strip. Figure 3 shows the reduction in tensile strength as a function of the incident beam flux. The curves show clearly that the strength of the paper is degraded by exposure to the proton beam, but it is interesting that there is a threshold dose below which no effect is observed and that the value of the threshold dose increases at higher beam energy. The latter effect is presumably related to the fact that higher energy ions have a smaller linear energy transfer (or LET) and so create less damage per unit length than lower energy ions.

The values of the threshold flux observed in the experiments of Cheng *et al.* (1998) are of the order of 1 $\mu C\ cm^{-2}$ (microcoulombs per square centimetre). To put this in perspective, using a beam of 100 pA focused to 100 μm diameter, it would take about 20 minutes to reach this flux, and 2000 minutes if the beam is 1 mm in diameter. Both these times are significantly longer than the typical run time for PIXE analysis, which suggests that structural damage to the paper is not a significant problem in ion beam analysis, especially given the small area of the analysis points.

Optical effects

It is well known that ion irradiation of solids can induce changes in their optical properties due to atomic displacements following ion collisions. The effects can be seen as changes in optical absorption (darkening or discoloration), enhanced ultra-violet fluorescence or enhanced polarizing activity. The latter effect can be seen strongly in transparent polymer films, but is not really relevant to document substrates.

These effects can be measured over a wide range of wavelengths from infra-red to ultra-violet and can be particularly noticeable in document substrates which are anyway light in colour and may have been treated with mineral grounds to further enhance the whiteness.

In organic molecules such as cellulose, ion bombardment, even at currents below the beam densities required to induce thermal charring, can desorb hydrogen and lead to carbonization of the material with a resultant discoloration. In crystalline materials such as mineral pigments the optical effects are caused by lattice damage such as vacancies or dislocations created by collisions with the high energy ions. These can be optically active, creating absorption centres which can be seen as discoloration or fluorescence centres which render the beam impact point visible under ultra-violet illumination. In some materials the lattice defects are metastable so that the effect may decay slowly with time due to room temperature thermal annealing, but often the effects are permanent.

There have been few systematic studies of the discoloration resulting from the ion beam analysis of paper. A recent paper (Milota *et al.* 2008) reports the marking of two types of artificially aged rag paper (with a bone ground and with no ground) resulting from exposure to MeV protons under a variety of conditions. Figure 4, taken from this paper shows a typical set of observations. The authors conclude that provided that the exposure conditions are kept below certain criteria, no visible marking is observed, even after a process of humidity and temperature cycling aimed to simulate ageing of around 100 years.

It is worth emphasizing that effects which are not visible to the eye may still be visible in the ultra-violet or infra-red regions of the spectrum. In an unpublished study by staff at the Bodleian Library, Oxford, papers which had been exposed to Ion Beam Analysis were observed to show strong fluorescence when exposed to ultra violet light even when the visible marking was virtually undetectable (McKay, 1995).

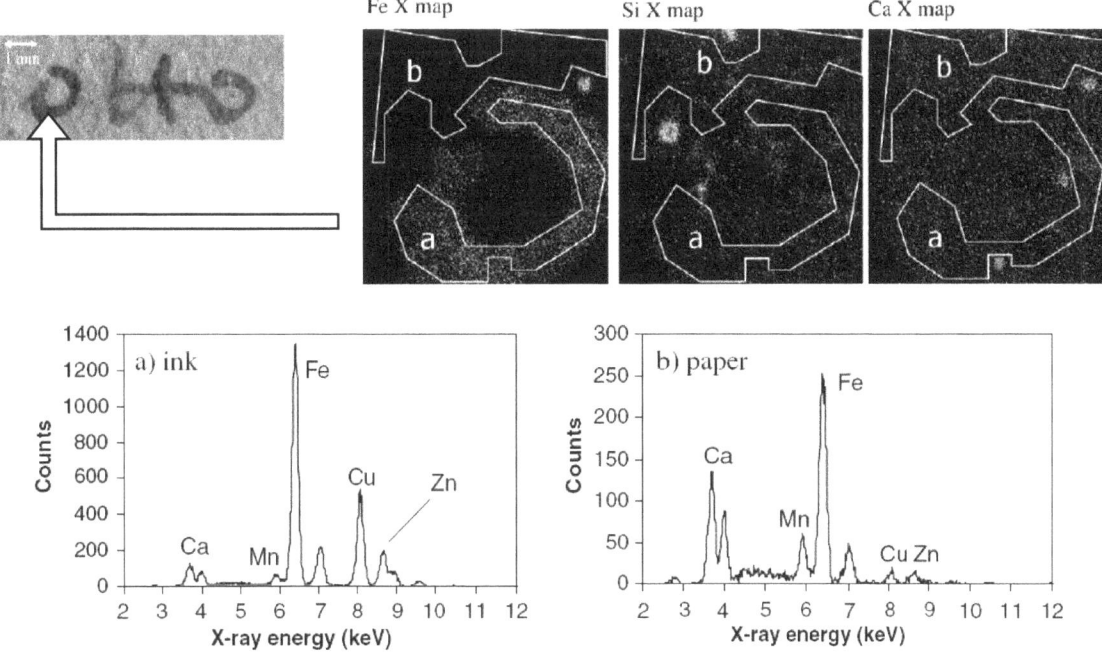

Figure 5. An example taken from Grassi *et al.* 2007 showing the use of scanning analysis to determine the composition of the ink used in the letter 'o' shown in the photograph in the top left. The X-ray maps show the distribution of iron, silicon and calcium X-rays in a 2 mm square region of the sample. From these it is possible to identify the ink and also areas of particulate contamination. Using suitable software, spectra corresponding to the two selected areas of ink (a) and uncontaminated paper (b). These are shown as spectra (a) and (b) below.

Spreading of the damage

One issue which is sometimes raised is whether paper damage or discolouration initially confined to a small region may with the passage of time spread as a result of some slow 'chain reaction'. There is no obvious physical mechanism by which any beam induced damage could spread; the effects discussed above have a relatively high activation energy (as in the MeV primary beam) and such energies are not available under normal storage conditions. Furthermore exposure to beams of this energy does not induce any long-lived radioactivity in the samples; such nuclear reactions as do occur are short-lived and rare and it is not possible to detect any radioactivity after the analysis. There are no reports in the literature or anecdotally of any damage spreading beyond the original impact point, though the technique has now been in use in many institutions for several decades. This is further confirmed by the accelerated ageing study of Milota *et al.* referred to above.

Minimising sample damage in ion beam analysis

The discussion above points us to a number of guidelines for developing strategies for minimising sample damage in ion beam analysis: (a) avoid heat build-up in the sample, e.g. by using cooling gas as already discussed, (b) minimise the total beam dose required for the analysis and (c) minimise the current density on the sample (by increasing the impact area) to avoid localised effects. These are probably obvious, but it is worth examining some of the ways in which these are being implemented in modern facilities.

Reducing the total beam dose

It is clear that the analysis should be carried out using the absolute minimum beam exposure necessary to obtain the data with the desired precision. The yield of potentially detectable photons or particles is ultimately determined by the physics of the ion-atom interaction, and here the use of PIXE provides a clear advantage, since the number of X-rays emitted related to the deposited energy in typical situations is significantly higher than analogous techniques such as X-ray fluorescence or electron microprobe analysis. The total required dose to generate sufficient X-rays to provide a result with the desired level of confidence can be further reduced by improving the collection efficiency of the X-ray detectors. This can be achieved by careful design of the detector mounting arrangements to maximize the solid angle of detection. The use of two detectors simultaneously can halve the required beam dose.

A further beam dose reduction can be achieved by noting that all radiation detection systems have a so-called deadtime following the detection of a photon or particle. During this period, the system cannot accept any more data and beam falling on the sample contributes only to damage and not to analysis. Dead time periods are typically measured in tens of microseconds per data pulse, this sounds short, but it can represent up to 50% or more of the total analysis time at high count rates. Using a very fast beam switch it is possible to stop the beam during the deadtime periods so that the sample is not exposed during this time. This technique is known as on-demand beam pulsing (ODBP) and can permit high count rates with the minimum beam exposure.

Reducing the current density by scanning the beam

The power density and hence the visual impact of any beam induced damage can be reduced by spreading the beam over a larger area of the sample. This is undesirable if the features of interest are small, such as in the latest generation of microbeam analysis facilities, where a key advantage is the ability to select small features for analysis (or to avoid areas of obvious contamination). Microbeams can be employed to best advantage by using an electrostatic or magnetic deflection system to sweep the beam rapidly over the features of interest on the sample and recording the data in 'list mode', where the position of each detected event is recorded as well as its energy. Then, using suitable off-line software, the analytical data of a selected region (for example the outline of a letter on the paper) can be extracted separately from that corresponding to the blank paper or any contaminants, such as dust particles. A further advantage of this method is that by moving the beam continuously, the thermal energy deposited at any individual point has time to dissipate before the beam returns on the next sweep, thus the temperature rise is negligible. In addition, the average current density over the whole analysis region is much lower that it would be in a fixed spot, thereby reducing the flux well below the threshold for discoloration.

This method is being pioneered by the Florence group (Grassi et al. 2007), and Figure 5, which is taken from this paper shows how the iron and calcium elemental maps are used to select regions corresponding to ink and blank paper while also avoiding the dust particle visible in the silicon map. The data was obtained in five minutes with the relatively high beam current of 1 nA, which if the beam were stationary would leave a visible (albeit small) mark.

Conclusions

In-air ion beam analysis is a powerful method for determining trace element concentrations with part per million detection limits in microscopic areas of documents without the necessity of removing samples. Results from such measurements have yielded historical insights which could not be obtained in any other way. Although the technique is widely quoted as being 'non-destructive', a more careful study of the literature shows that there can be a serious risk of damage or discoloration to paper samples through a number of physical and chemical effects. However, it is widely accepted by workers in the field that provided that suitable experimental protocols are followed, and the beam dose is maintained below a certain threshold, permanent visible marking can be avoided. However these conditions cannot easily be predicted for any particular situation and a very strong recommendation is to carry out trials using unimportant samples before exposing historically important material.

With modern microbeam instruments, using advanced methods for minimizing dose and current density, damage or discoloration is unlikely; even if it should occur, it is localised to a very small region (sub-millimetre), compared with the damage created by physically removing samples for conventional analysis. The risks from ion beam analysis of books and manuscripts may now be seen to be outweighed by the benefits of its unique analytical capability.

External beam analysis is now available as a service at a number of European laboratories, and in many cases access to these facilities can be supported through initiatives of the European Commission such as SPIRIT[4] or CHARISMA.[5] In the UK, external beam analysis can be carried out at the University of Surrey Ion Beam Centre.[6]

References

Cheng, H., Yanfang, D., Wenquan, H. and Fujia, Y. 1998 Non-destructive analysis and appraisal of paper-like objects. *Nuclear Instruments and Methods in Physics Research Section B: Beam Interactions with Materials and Atoms* **136-138**, 897-901.

Del Carmine, P., Giuntini, L., Hooper, W., Lucarelli, F. and Mando, P. A. 1996 Further results from PIXE analysis of inks in Galileo's notes on motion. *Nuclear Instruments and Methods in Physics Research Section B: Beam Interactions with Materials and Atoms* **113**, 354-358.

Duval, A., Guicharnaud, H. and Dran, J. C. 2004 Particle induced X-ray emission: a valuable tool for the analysis of metalpoint drawings. *Nuclear Instruments and Methods in Physics Research Section B: Beam Interactions with Materials and Atoms* **226**, 60-74.

Giuntini, L., Lucarelli, F., Mando, P. A., Hooper, W. and Barker, P. H. 1995 Galileo's writings: chronology by PIXE. *Nuclear Instruments and Methods in Physics Research Section B: Beam Interactions with Materials and Atoms* **95**, 389-392.

Grassi, N., Giuntini, L., Mandò, P. A. and Massi, M. 2007 Advantages of scanning-mode ion beam analysis for the study of Cultural Heritage. *Nuclear Instruments and Methods in Physics Research Section B: Beam Interactions with Materials and Atoms* **256**, 712-718.

Grime, G. W. 1999 *High Energy Ion beam Analysis Method and Background*. In *Encyclopedia of Spectroscopy and Spectrometry* (Eds, Lindon, J. C., Tranter, G. E. and Holmes, J. L.),750-760. Academic Press, Chichester.

Grime, G. W., Dawson, M., Marsh, M., McArthur, I. C. and Watt, F. 1991 The Oxford submicron nuclear microscopy facility. *Nuclear Instruments & Methods in Physics Research Section B-Beam Interactions With Materials and Atoms* **54**, 52-63.

Gomez-Morilla, I., Simon, A., Simon, R., Williams, C.T., Kiss, A.Z. and Grime, G.W. 2006 An evaluation of the accuracy and precision of X-ray microanalysis techniques using BCR-126A glass reference material. *Nuclear Instruments and Methods in Physics Research Section B-Beam Interactions With Materials and Atoms* **249**, 897-902

Johansson, S.A.E., Campbell, J.L. and Malmqvist, K.G. 1995 *Particle-Induced X-ray Emission Spectrometry (PIXE)*. Wiley, New York

---

[4] http://www.spirit-ion.eu/
[5] http://www.charismaproject.eu/
[6] http://www.surreyibc.ac.uk/

Kusko, B. H., Cahill, T. A., Eldred, R. A. and Schwab, R. N. 1984 Proton milliprobe analyses of the Gutenberg Bible. *Nuclear Instruments and Methods in Physics Research Section B: Beam Interactions with Materials and Atoms* **3**, 689-694.

Lucarelli, F. and Mando, P. A. 1996 Recent applications to the study of ancient inks with the Florence external-PIXE facility. *Nuclear Instruments and Methods in Physics Research Section B: Beam Interactions with Materials and Atoms* **109-110**, 644-652.

Mahnke, H.-E., Andrea Denker, A. and Salomon J. 2009 Accelerators and x-rays in cultural heritage investigations, *Comptes Rendus Physique* **10**, 660-675.

MacArthur, J. D., Carmine, P. D., Lucarelli, F. and Mandò, P. A. 1990 Identification of pigments in some colours on miniatures from the medieval age and early Renaissance. *Nuclear Instruments and Methods in Physics Research Section B: Beam Interactions with Materials and Atoms* **45**, 315-321.

McKay, A. 1995 *Proton beam exposure tests and results.* Unpublished Bodleian Library Internal Report.

Merchant, M. J., Mistry, P., Browton, M., Clough, A. S., Gauntlett, F. E., Jeynes, C., Kirkby, K. J. and Grime, G. W. 2005 Characterisation of the University of Surrey Ion Beam Centre in-air scanning microbeam. *Nuclear Instruments and Methods in Physics Research Section B: Beam Interactions with Materials and Atoms* **231**, 26-31.

Milota, P., Reiche, I., Duval, A., Forstner, O., Guicharnaud, H., Kutschera, W., Merchel, S., Priller, A., Schreiner, M., Steier, P., Thobois, E., Wallner, A., Wünschek, B. and Golser, R. 2008 PIXE measurements of Renaissance silverpoint drawings at VERA. *Nuclear Instruments and Methods in Physics Research Section B: Beam Interactions with Materials and Atoms* **266**, 2279-2285.

Watt, F., Grime, G. W. and Perry, C. C. 1988 The damage effects of a 1-micron proton-beam on a single pollen grain. *Nuclear Instruments & Methods in Physics Research Section B-Beam Interactions With Materials and Atoms* **30**, 331-336.

Watt, F., Orlic, I., Loh, K.K., Sow, C.H., Thong, P., Liew, S.C., Osipowicz, T., Choo, T.F. and Tang, S.M. 1994 The National University of Singapore nuclear microscope facility. *Nuclear Instruments and Methods in Physics Research B-Beam Interactions With Materials and Atoms* **85**, 708-715

Watt, F., Breese, M. B. H., Bettiol, A. A. and van Kan, J. A. 2007 Proton beam writing. *Materials Today* **10**, 20-29.

Chapter 11

Provenancing Parchment, Leather and Paper using Stable Isotopes

A.M. Pollard & Fiona Brock

Research Laboratory for Archaeology and the History of Art
University of Oxford

Introduction

In addition to needing to know *when* a manuscript was produced, it is also important to be able to say *where* it was produced. Scientific approaches to dating the organic components of historical manuscripts (e.g., parchment, leather and paper) are discussed in Chapter 12. The use of radiocarbon dating necessitates the measurement of $\delta^{13}C$, the ratio of the isotopes ^{13}C to ^{12}C expressed relative to the ratio in an international standard (see technical appendix at the end of this chapter). This chapter develops the idea of using the isotopic ratio of this and other light elements (in particular nitrogen, oxygen, and hydrogen, but possibly also sulphur) as a means of locating the place of origin of the plant or animal from which library materials were derived.

Stable isotopes in animal and plant tissues

Both parchment and leather are made up of collagen, a protein which contains primarily carbon, nitrogen, oxygen and hydrogen, whilst paper, papyrus and bark are plant tissues composed of cellulose, a carbohydrate material which is made up of carbon, hydrogen and oxygen. All of these 'light' elements exist in different isotopic[1] forms. The relative abundance of these isotopes for a particular element will, however, vary geographically because environmental factors can alter the ratio as the element is cycled through the various geological and biological processes which are involved in supporting plant and animal life on Earth (more information is provided in the technical appendix at the end of this chapter). These isotopic ratios are fixed into plants at the bottom of the food chain, and are transmitted through to animals. Organic library materials derived from plants such as papyrus and paper, and also material from animals such as parchment and leather, will therefore have isotope ratios which are potentially indicative of the geographical origin of the material.

The use of a range of stable isotopes (in some cases along with heavier isotopes and trace elements) is now well-established in the field of food chemistry to authenticate the source of origin of foodstuffs, including oil, meat and dairy products (Kelly *et al.* 2005), showing that products derived from living organisms can be isotopically provenanced. Some work has been done on the isotopic composition of wool, such as the study of the provenance of woollen carpets from Turkey (Hedges *et al.* 2005), and more similar research is currently underway. Nothing systematic has yet been done on the geographical significance of stable isotopes in parchment or leather, although a number of carbon isotope measurements on parchments have been published as a result of radiocarbon dating on, for example, the Dead Sea Scrolls (Bonani *et al.* 1992) and the Vinland Map (Donahue *et al.* 2002). We present below some measurements on modern parchments which indicate that there is substantial variation in the isotopes of carbon and nitrogen which might be related to geographical origin, but it should be emphasized that the ideas presented here are largely speculative in terms of their systematic application to library material.

Using isotopes to provenance wool and parchment

The best published analogy for the use of isotopes to provenance historical biological material is the study by Hedges *et al.* (2005), in which the authors use wool from modern sheep collected from 13 carpet-producing sites from three regions in western and central Turkey. Wool is a biopolymer consisting largely of the protein keratin, and is therefore likely to reflect variation in other biopolymers, such as the collagen which is present in parchment and leather. Hence data from wool and skin products should be closely related.

Measurements of carbon, nitrogen and sulphur stable isotope ratios (abbreviated as $\delta^{13}C$, $\delta^{15}N$ and $\delta^{34}S$ respectively) showed significant variation between the three regions sampled. These regions were 'coastal' (three sites around Bergama, c. 70 km north of Izmir), 'western' (six sites around Gordes, c. 125 km northeast of Izmir) and 'central' (four sites around Aksaray, c. 160 km ENE of Konya). $\delta^{13}C$ showed a significant increase (from c. -25‰ to -20‰)[2] when the sites are plotted from west to east (see Figure 1). The same trend is apparent in the $\delta^{15}N$ values (from c. 4‰ to 9‰), but with some substantial deviation in the case of two sites (Bergama and Gordes-Eski, both identified as 'urban sites', with the sheep grazing between houses), attributed to anthropogenic enhancement of $\delta^{15}N$, presumably as a result of manuring.

The values for $\delta^{34}S$ also show significant variation (from 3.5‰ to 9.5‰), with some evidence of a trend from coastal to inland, but not as clear as in the carbon isotopes. This was slightly surprising to the authors, since carbon and nitrogen in protein both reflect the dietary input (i.e., underlying variation in vegetation values), whereas $\delta^{34}S$ is affected by underlying geological factors, with the additional possibility of coastal sites showing enhanced values as a result of sea-spray. The paper concludes by stating that there appears to be good

---

[1] Isotopes are atoms of an element which have a different number of particles called neutrons within their nucleus. They have the same chemical properties, but differ in weight.

[2] The symbol '‰' means 'per mil' or 'parts per thousand'.

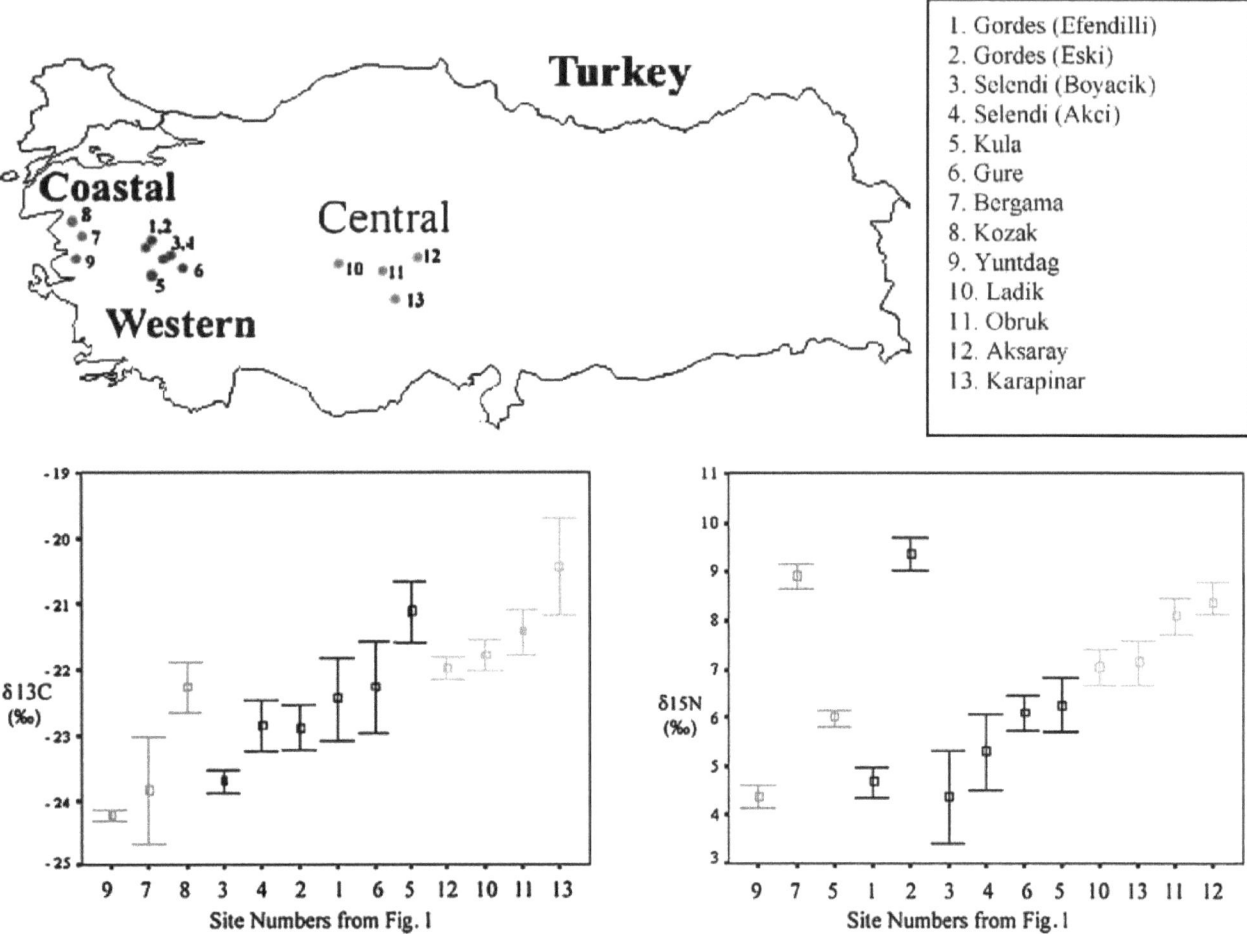

Figure 1. Map of wool sampling sites in Turkey, and plots of average values of $\delta^{13}C$ and $\delta^{15}N$ for each site (from Hedges *et al.* 2005 figures 1-3).

Sample No.	Species	Origin
C1	Calf	unknown
C2	Calf	unknown
C3	Calf	USA
C4	Calf	Germany
C5	Calf	Brazil
G1	Goat	unknown
G2	Goat	unknown
G3	Goat	unknown
G4	Goat	Brazil
G5	Goat	Brazil
G6	Goat	France
G7	Goat	Czech Rep
P1	Pig	Germany
R1	Reindeer	Finland
RD1	Red Deer	Germany
D1	Deer	unknown

Figure 2. Modern parchment samples used during the pilot study

potential for the use of stable isotope measurements on wool as an indicator of the provenance of carpets.

Subsequently, Dr Fiona Brock in Oxford has carried out a pilot study on a selection of modern parchment samples provided by Z.H. De Groot (Netherlands), listed in Figure 2. Samples were defatted prior to analysis to remove fats that have a slightly different isotopic signature to collagen, and stable isotope measurements were made in triplicate on untreated and defatted subs-samples of all samples listed. The full experimental procedure is detailed in the technical appendix at the end of this chapter.

Pilot study results

The data obtained in this pilot (following defatting of the samples) are plotted in Figures 3 (by species) and 4 (by provenance).

These figures show a very wide range of variation in both isotopes. Figure 3 shows that goats can exhibit very high values of $\delta^{15}N$ (around 20‰), which might be an indication of living in an arid environment. Any samples with a $\delta^{13}C$ value greater than (i.e., less negative than) -17‰ almost certainly

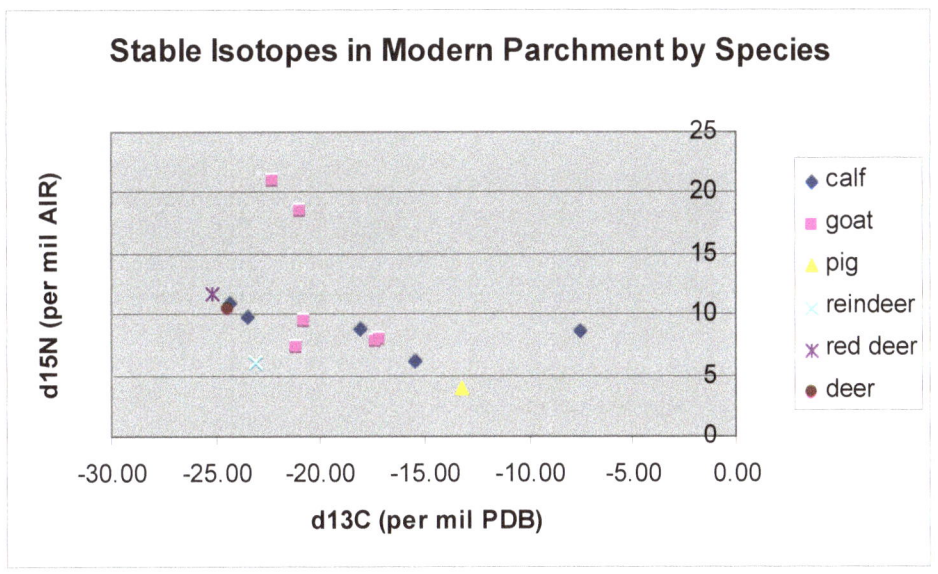

Figure 3. δ^{13}C vs. δ^{15}N for modern parchment samples by species

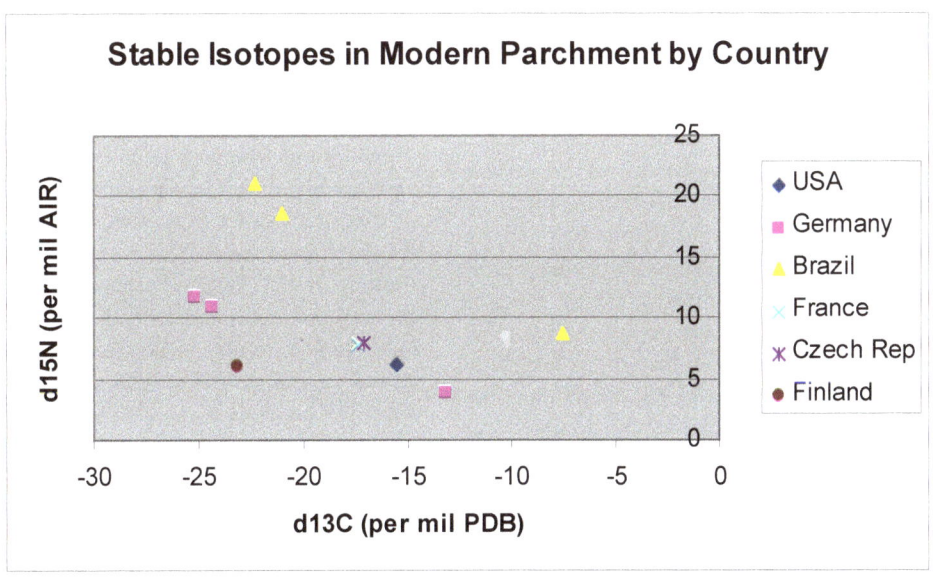

Figure 4. δ^{13}C vs. δ^{15}N for modern parchment samples by origin.

have a dietary protein source rich in C_4 plants[3] – most likely, in modern material, the result of maize foddering. Thus at least one sample each from the USA, Brazil and Germany (Figure 4) can be seen to have a C_4 input – something we would not expect to see in historic material.

Conclusion

There is ample reason to expect that the stable isotopes in plant material (δ^2H, δ^{13}C, and δ^{18}O), and in animals which depend on these plants (δ^2H, δ^{13}C, δ^{15}N, δ^{18}O and δ^{34}S), will show measurable geographical variation on a continental scale. The best predictor of this variation is likely to be the annual precipitation map – areas of steep rainfall gradient should show large differences, whereas those of constant rainfall may be difficult to differentiate. At least for the isotopes of carbon and nitrogen, these isotopes are easily measured using a few milligrams of material. The pilot study has shown significant variation in modern parchments – albeit most likely dominated by the presence of C_4 dietary protein, which should be absent from historic material. It seems highly worthwhile to follow this up with an investigation of the use of these isotopes as a geographical indicator on a range of historic manuscript parchments, starting with objects of known provenance from a wide range of sources. It is possible that questions such as

---

[3] 'C_4' refers to the particular mechanism used in certain plants for carbon fixation during photosynthesis, the process whereby plants manufacture energy using sunlight. There are two other mechanisms of carbon fixation used by plants, and those which use the C_4 mechanism are in the minority. C_4 plants in general are grasses adapted to hot dry climates.

'where does this parchment come from?' can be answered, at least on a regional scale. More highly-focused questions, such as 'do all the parchments in the same volume come from the same geographical area (or even from the same animal)?', or 'does a single scriptorium use the same source of material for all its parchments?' might also be addressable. Equally interesting would be a similar study of historic paper.

Technical appendix

Light stable isotopes [δD ($\delta^2 H$), $\delta^{13}C$, $\delta^{15}N$, $\delta^{18}O$ and $\delta^{34}S$]

Most light elements (e.g., hydrogen and oxygen) occur naturally in more than one isotopic form. For example, the most abundant stable isotope of oxygen is ^{16}O, with eight protons and eight neutrons in the nucleus; however, two other heavier stable isotopes exist - ^{17}O, with nine neutrons, and ^{18}O, with ten neutrons. The lightest isotope is by far the most abundant (99.76% of all atoms of oxygen are ^{16}O), with the natural abundance of ^{17}O being 0.04%, and that of ^{18}O slightly higher at 0.2%. A similar pattern is exhibited by most other light stable isotopes. Isotope systematics of these lighter elements have been extensively studied because of their importance in understanding a wide range of environmental, earth science and bioscience processes (Peterson and Fry 1987; Pollard and Heron 2008, 352). For example, as water is cycled around the Earth's system (from the atmosphere to rivers to ocean and back to the atmosphere), the ratios of both $^2H/^1H$ and $^{18}O/^{16}O$ change. This is because the increased mass of the heavier isotope renders it slightly less likely to take part in processes such as evaporation, enriching slightly the remaining liquid in the heavier isotope whilst depleting the resulting vapour of the same isotope. Modern maps of these isotopes in precipitation show that the geographical variation in these ratios is controlled by temperature and continentality. Such processes are termed *fractionation*, and the magnitude of the effect depends on the mass difference between the two isotopes. Hydrogen, therefore, shows the largest fractionation, since the heavier isotope is twice the mass of the lighter, whereas in oxygen, it is only heavier by 12.5%. Even for hydrogen, however, the effects are small. The average abundance ratio of ^2H to ^1H is 0.000156, and therefore any changes due to fractionation are only detected in the last digit. In order to magnify these small but important effects, isotope geochemists have adopted the d notation, which is defined for hydrogen as follows:

In this notation, the ratio of ^2H to ^1H in the sample is compared to the same ratio in an internationally agreed standard material. If the ratio in the sample is identical to that in the standard, then the d value ($\delta^2 H$, or dD, where D stands for deuterium) is zero. If the sample is isotopically heavier than the standard, the $^2H/^1H$ ratio in the sample is greater than that in the standard, and d becomes positive. If the sample is isotopically lighter, then the top line becomes negative, and d becomes negative. The units (because of the multiplication by 1000) are known as 'per mil' (or 'parts per thousand'), symbolised as ‰. The standard used for hydrogen isotopic measurements in water is SMOW (standard mean ocean water). The equations for $\delta^{13}C$, $\delta^{15}N$, $\delta^{18}O$ and $\delta^{34}S$ are identical to that given above, with the appropriate isotope ratio (e.g., $^{18}O/^{16}O$) replacing that of hydrogen.

Carbon has two stable isotopes: ^{12}C, with six protons and six neutrons, and ^{13}C, with seven neutrons. Isotopic fractionation of carbon as it is cycled has been studied in great detail for many years. The internationally agreed standard for carbon is related to the CO_2 produced from a Cretaceous belemnite rock in South Carolina, called the Peedee Formation (PDB). Measurements of $\delta^{13}C$ have become particularly important in archaeology for two reasons. One is that $\delta^{13}C$ measurements are used to correct radiocarbon dates obtained on organic material for fractionation effects. The other is because $\delta^{13}C$ measurements (often combined with $\delta^{15}N$) made on skeletal and dental collagen can be used to reconstruct the diet and mobility of an animal or a human (Pollard and Heron 2008, chapter 10).

Geographical variation in light stable isotopes

There has been a growing interest in the geographical and temporal variation of light stable isotopes in biological material over the past 20 years, largely as a result of the suggestion that such variation in bone, teeth and wood can be used as a climate proxy. Although oxygen and hydrogen isotopes are most likely to contain climate information (because of their relationship to the water cycle), the largest data sets that actually exist are those of carbon and, to a much lesser extent, nitrogen, because these have been compiled in support of radiocarbon dating. They are also much easier to measure routinely in organic systems than $\delta^2 H$, $\delta^{18}O$ and $\delta^{34}S$. On a continental scale, it has been shown that $\delta^{13}C$ measurements on Holocene bone collagen, charcoal and wood samples from across Europe show a trend from north to south and east to west, which can be linked to latitudinal (north-south) differences and oceanic (east-west) influences on climate (van Klinken *et al.* 1994). The variation for $\delta^{13}C$ in bone collagen across Europe is shown in Figure 5. The average value of $\delta^{13}C$ for archaeological bone samples from Spain is -18.9‰ compared with -20.8‰ for Sweden. Similar trends are reported for charcoal. The same publication shows plots of $\delta^{13}C$ from bone collagen, charcoal and wood against modern day mean July temperatures, sunshine, humidity and precipitation, which show significant correlations (e.g., r = 0.84 between bone collagen $\delta^{13}C$ and total July sunshine).

Similar studies have been made on bone collagen data from modern bird and mammal samples, which confirm the tendency of some isotopic data to vary with latitude. For example, $\delta^{13}C$ of bone collagen from carnivorous terrestrial mammals has a correlation of $r^2 = 0.75$ with latitude (Kelly 2000), although other animal groups show much less significant correlation (e.g., African elephant, $r^2 = 0.28$).

This variation in faunal values is most likely to be due to variations in the isotopic value of plant tissue at the base of the food chain. There is now substantial evidence in the plant physiology literature to suggest that the principal control on the value of $\delta^{13}C$ in plant tissue is the water use efficiency (WUE) during photosynthesis, which is related to rainfall and/or water availability (e.g., Ehleringer *et al.* 1993). There is also some evidence to suggest that the level of $\delta^{15}N$ in the biosphere is related to the aridity of the environment (Schwarcz *et al.*

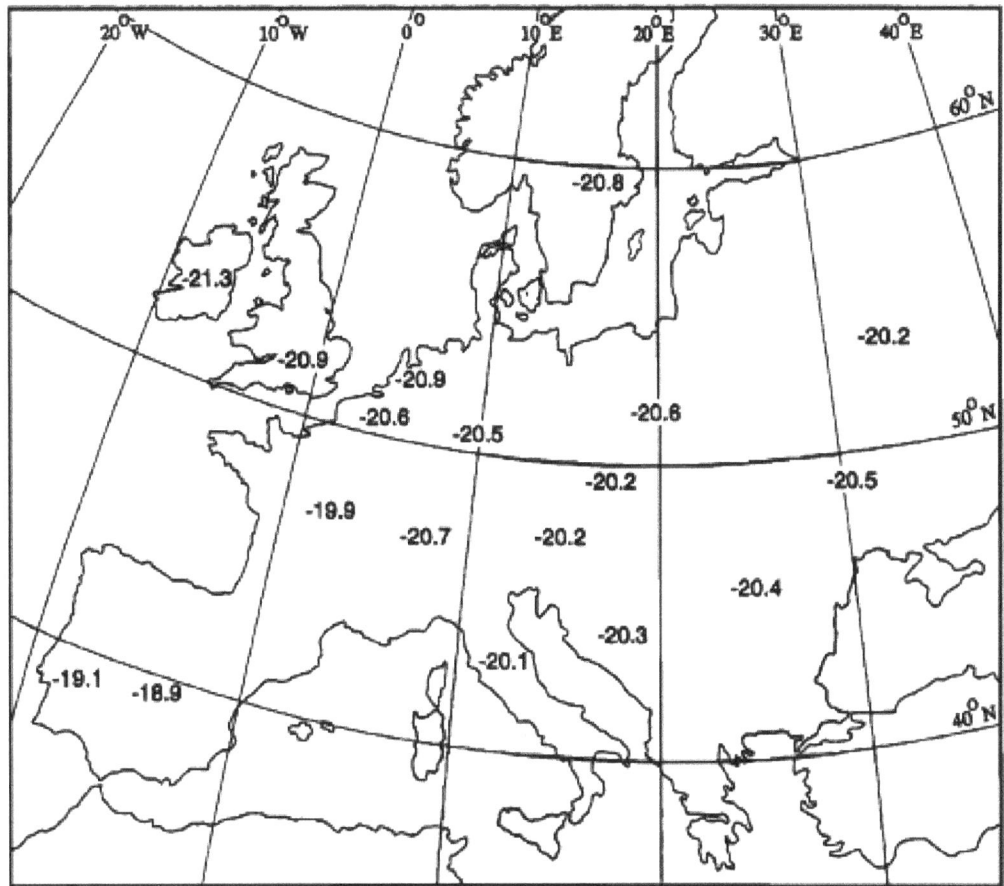

Fig. 5. The pattern of $\delta^{13}C$ variation across Europe as measured in bone collagen. Figures are averages for each region (from van Klinken *et al.* 1994, figure 2).

1999). In the terrestrial environment, therefore, we envisage an isotopic system in which the stable isotopes of carbon and nitrogen in the plants at the base of the food chain have values which are related primarily to water availability. We therefore expect geographical variability in these isotopes in plants (and therefore material derived from them, such as papyrus and paper), and the animals grazing upon these plants (and hence in the parchment and leather made from the skins of these animals).

Such measurements are now becoming relatively routine in the food industry, to ensure that products which are said to come from a particular area do indeed come from that area. Indeed, such monitoring is now a major compliance test in the European Union Protected Food Name Schemes (Kelly *et al.* 2005). Specific examples include olive oil [Camin *et al.* (2010), using δ^2H, $\delta^{13}C$ and $\delta^{18}O$, plus trace elements], lamb meat [Camin *et al.* (2007), using δ^2H, $\delta^{13}C$, $\delta^{15}N$ and $\delta^{34}S$, and Perini *et al.* (2009), using δ^2H, $\delta^{13}C$, $\delta^{15}N$, $\delta^{18}O$ and $\delta^{34}S$], beef [Nakashita *et al.* (2008), using $\delta^{13}C$, $\delta^{15}N$ and $\delta^{18}O$] and dairy products [Karoui and De Baerdemaeker (2007), using a wide range of diagnostic tests, including δ^2H, $\delta^{15}N$, $\delta^{18}O$ and $\delta^{34}S$]. These studies are sufficient to show that the light stable isotope ratios do show geographical variation on a continental scale, sufficient to potentially provide some general guide to the provenance of the animal or plant from which the material is derived.

Measurement of stable isotopes in parchment: pilot study procedure

Stable isotope measurements on all of the modern parchment samples listed in Figure 2 were made in triplicate on untreated and defatted subs-samples. Samples were soaked in a 1:1 mixture of chloroform and methanol overnight to remove fats that have a slightly different isotopic signature to collagen, and allowed to air-dry completely before analysis. De-fatting resulted in average weight losses for each sample of up to 9%, and untreated versus defatted measurements showed a small systematic enrichment in $\delta^{13}C$ (average of sixteen measurements = -0.37‰, maximum difference -1.71‰) and a variable change in $\delta^{15}N$ (ranging between -0.29 and +0.86‰). Additional measurements were taken from part of three of the samples where the parchment had turned opaque and brittle, and was assumed to have been partially gelatinized during the parchment-making process. Comparison of results from normal versus 'gelatinized' data showed a random change, of less than ± 0.5‰ in both $\delta^{13}C$ and $\delta^{15}N$, which is insignificant.

A sub-group of six samples also underwent a solvent wash (acetone, methanol, chloroform) followed by an acid-base-acid-bleach pre-treatment which is standard prior to radiocarbon dating of parchments at Oxford University (Brock *et al.*, 2010), and stable isotope measurements were taken in triplicate after each step to test the effect of different sample preparation procedures. Fully pre-treated samples recorded a maximum change in $\delta^{13}C$ of up to -0.95‰ and up to -1.17‰ in $\delta^{15}N$ from the untreated parchments. No one particular step of the pre-treatment process significantly affected the $\delta^{13}C$, but the largest shifts in $\delta^{15}N$ were observed after bleaching. Since there is as yet no agreed protocol for the isotopic analysis of such materials, further investigation is needed to define a standard measurement protocol, especially when considering that historic parchments are often degraded and may be already partially gelatinized by age (e.g. Weiner *et al.*, 1980). Also necessary prior to extending such a study to historic parchments and library materials is the determination of a 'minimum' sample size, in order to minimise the aesthetic impact on any sampled library materials.

References

Bonani, G., Ivy, S., Wolfli, W., Broshi, M., Carmi, I. and Strugnell, J. 1992 Radiocarbon dating of 14 Dead Sea Scrolls. *Radiocarbon* **34**, 843-849.

Brock, F., Higham, T. and Bronk Ramsey, C. 2010 Pre-screening techniques for identification of samples suitable for radiocarbon dating of poorly preserved bones. *Journal of Archaeological Science* **37**, 855-865.

Camin, F., Bontempo, L., Heinrich, K., Horacek, M., Kelly, S.D., Schlicht, C., Thomas, F., Monahan, F.J., Hoogewerff, Rossmann, A. 2007 Multi-element (H,C,N,S) stable isotope characteristics of lamb meat from different European regions. *Analytical and Bioanalytical Chemistry* **389**, 309-320.

Camin, F., Larcher, R., Nicolini, G., Bontempo, L., Bertoldi, D., Perini, M., Schlicht, C., Schellenberg, A., Thomas, F., Heinrich, K., Voerkelius, S., Horacek, M., Ueckermann, H., Froeschl, H., Wimmer, B., Heiss, G., Baxter, M., Rossmann, A. and Hoogewerff, J. 2010 Isotopic and elemental data for tracing the origin of European olive oils. *Journal of Agricultural and Food Chemistry* **58**, 570-577.

Donahue, D.J., Olin, J.S. and Harbottle, G. 2002 Determination of the radiocarbon age of parchment of the Vinland Map. *Radiocarbon* **44**, 45-52

Ehleringer, J.R., Hall, A.E. and Farquhar, G.D. (eds.) 1993 *Stable Isotopes and Plant Carbon-Water Relations*. Academic Press, London.

Hedges, R.E.M., Thompson, J.M.A. and Hull, B.D. 2005 Stable isotope variation in wool as a means to establish Turkish carpet provenance. *Rapid Communications in Mass Spectrometry* **19**, 3187-3191.

Karoui, R. and De Baerdemaeker, J. 2007 A review of the analytical methods coupled with chemometric tools for the determination of the quality and identity of dairy products. *Food Chemistry* **102**, 621-640.

Kelly, J.F. 2000 Stable isotopes of carbon and nitrogen in the study of avian and mammalian trophic ecology. *Canadian Journal of Zoology* **78**, 1-27.

Kelly, S., Heaton, K. and Hoogewerff, J. 2005 Tracing the geographical origin of food: the application of multi-element and multi-isotope analysis. *Trends in Food Science and Technology* **16**, 555-567.

Nakashita, R., Suzuki, Y., Akamatsu, F., Iizumi, Y., Korenaga, T. and Chikaraishi, Y. 2008 Stable carbon, nitrogen and oxygen isotope analysis as a potential tool for verifying geographical origin of beef. *Analytica Chimica Acta* **617**, 148-152.

Perini, M., Camin, F., Bontempo, L., Rossmann, A. and Piasentier, E. 2009 Multielement (H, C, N, O, S) stable isotope characteristics of lamb meat from different Italian regions. *Rapid Communications in Mass Spectrometry* **23**, 2573-2585.

Peterson, B.J. and Fry, B. 1987 Stable isotopes in ecosystem studies. *Annual Review of Ecology and Systematics* **18**, 293-320.

Pollard, A.M. and Heron, C. 2008 *Archaeological Chemistry* (2nd revised edition), Royal Society of Chemistry, Cambridge

Schwarcz, H.P., Dupras, T.L. and Fairgrieve, S.I. 1999 ^{15}N enrichment in the Sahara: in search of a global relationship. *Journal of Archaeological Science* **26**, 629-636.

van Klinken, G.J., van der Plicht, H. and Hedges, R.E.M. 1994 Bone C-13/C-12 ratios reflect (palaeo-)climatic variations. *Geophysical Research Letters* **21**, 445-448.

Weiner, S., Kustanovich, Z., Gil-Av, E. and Traub, W. 1980 Dead Sea Scroll parchments: unfolding of the collagen molecules and racemization of aspartic acid. *Nature* **287**, 820-823.

Chapter 12

Scientific Approaches to Dating Historical Documents

A.M. Pollard

*Research Laboratory for Archaeology and the History of Art,
University of Oxford*

Introduction

One of the important properties of a historical document is the date of the material upon which the text or image is inscribed, and also the date of the binding and construction media for a book. 'Date' can mean different things to different researchers. It is important to appreciate that in most of what follows the word 'date' for materials derived from living organisms is intended to mean the calendrical date of death of the organism, which must pre-date the preparation of the object. In many cases it is likely to be only shortly before (perhaps months or a few years), but in the case of wood it could be several years – possibly much more if the wood is re-used. The same is true of parchments and other writing surfaces, which may have been re-used or amended over time, whilst current manuscript bindings may, of course, have been used to replace original bindings at a later date. Thus the date of the material is an *important* parameter when considering the date of the content of a manuscript, but does not necessarily date that content. This is particularly the case, as shown below, in disputes relating to authenticity when the date of the object is not necessarily proof of the authenticity of the content. This chapter is intended to discuss in a non-technical manner some of the dating techniques widely used in archaeology which might be of value in the study of historical documents. Some, such as radiocarbon dating, have already been used in some studies; others are more speculative. Further information on scientific approaches to archaeological dating in general can be found in Aitken (1990) and Taylor and Aitken (1997).

It is widely accepted that one of the greatest contributions made by science to archaeology in the last 60 years has been the development of scientific methods of dating. Foremost amongst these has been radiocarbon dating, developed in the 1950s. The fortunate combination of its wide applicability (because of the ubiquity of organic carbon) and its convenient timescale, in theory approximately 0 - 50,000 years Before Present (BP),[1] has meant that radiocarbon dating has revolutionised archaeology in the last thirty years. The need to date archaeological artefacts which were made more than 50,000 years BP has necessitated the development of other methods, mostly borrowed from geology – e.g., potassium–argon dating, uranium series dating, luminescence techniques. These are unlikely to be of any importance for dating historical documents, but some possible exceptions are discussed briefly at the end of this chapter.

Like all scientific methods of dating, radiocarbon dating has an associated uncertainty (unhelpfully referred to as an 'error'), which inevitably limits the precision of the date. Most radiocarbon laboratories normally give a radiocarbon date with an age range of around ± 20-30 years (which usually gets bigger after calibration – see below). Thus it is not realistic to expect a single radiocarbon date to be able to date a historical manuscript to a particular calendar year, or even to within a few decades – hence it can never compete on these terms with a historical date. However, dating multiple objects with a known chronological sequence can reduce these uncertainties drastically, and could conceivably produce a date which is useful in a historical context, as illustrated below. There is, however, another technique developed for historical and archaeological material which can produce dates of historical precision, if suitable material is available – that is dendrochronology. This requires a piece of wood upon which can be measured the thickness of around a minimum of 50 annual growth rings. By matching this pattern against a 'master series' of measured ring-widths, the date of cutting of the timber can sometimes be determined to a particular year, and sometimes to within a specific season. Thus, wooden bindings may be suitable targets for dating with a method which has annual resolution.

Radiocarbon dating

Principles

Radiocarbon (^{14}C or carbon-14) is a radioactively unstable isotope[2] of carbon, which is produced in the atmosphere as a result of the interaction of cosmic rays with nitrogen. It is extremely rare (one part in a million million of all carbon) and has a half-life of 5730 years.[3]

Despite being rare, it is important because this radioactive carbon in the atmosphere is taken up into living organisms, initially by photosynthesis into plant tissue, but from there by entering the food chain. Thus all living creatures absorb small

---

[1] 'present', in radiocarbon terms is taken to be AD 1950, since this pre-dates a huge increase in atmospheric carbon-14 which was artificially induced by atomic testing during the 1960s

[2] Isotopes are atoms of an element which have a different number of particles called neutrons within their nucleus. Most chemical elements exist in several isotopic forms, and these may be stable or unstable. Unstable isotopes are radioactive and emit radiation (sometimes in the form of particles such as electrons) in order to become more stable, in a process known as 'radioactive decay'. This process often changes the isotope into an atom of a different chemical element.

[3] The 'half life' refers to the time taken for half of the original quantity of a radioactive substance to 'decay' into another, more stable, substance. A 'half life' of 5730 years means that, after 5730 years, half of the original quantity of radiocarbon will have converted back to nitrogen as a result of radioactive decay, and another half of what remains in a further 5730 years, and so on.

quantities of radiocarbon. Whilst they are alive, biological processes ensure that radiocarbon neither accumulates nor diminishes – the organism is in equilibrium with atmospheric radiocarbon. On death, however, the radiocarbon is not replenished and the amount diminishes according to the laws of radioactive decay – half is lost in one half life, a further half in the second, etc. Thus, if we measure the amount of radiocarbon present in the remains of a once-living organism, we can calculate how much has been lost. This tells us how many half-lives have passed, giving the time elapsed since the death of the organism. Further details of the radiocarbon method are given in Bowman (1990).

Procedure

Any material which derives from a living organism is likely to be suitable for radiocarbon dating. This includes much of the material used to make historical documents – papyrus, parchment, paper, leather, glues and gums, and some pigments such as lamp black. In the early days of radiocarbon dating, large quantities of carbon were necessary to produce a date, but developments in accelerator mass spectrometry (AMS) during the 1980s meant the sample requirement has been drastically reduced. Most laboratories can now produce a date from a few milligrams of carbon. The actual amount of sample required depends on the carbon content of the sample, and the amount of chemical pre-treatment necessary to produce a clean sample. For most materials of interest here, this is unlikely to be more than a few tens of milligrams of original sample. The sample is, however, destroyed by the process, although most labs will archive or return any unused sample submitted. As part of the routine measurement, most laboratories also produce the stable carbon isotope value of the sample – this is the ratio of carbon-13 to carbon-12 in the sample, expressed relative to the value in a standard, where a value of zero implies the sample has the same ratio as the standard. This ratio (called $\delta^{13}C$) is used during the calculation of the date, and some labs will also quote the $\delta^{15}N$ value (the ratio of nitrogen-15 to nitrogen-14 in the sample). Although beyond the scope of this discussion, these values are useful because they can be compared with the expected values for the class of material dated, and are indicators of contamination and therefore of reliability. Additionally, they are used to determine the extent of marine contribution to the diet of the organism, and hence the extent of any marine reservoir correction that might be needed (for further information see the technical appendix at the end of this chapter). The use of carbon and nitrogen isotopes to determine the provenance of skin-based material is discussed further in Chapter 11.

Calibration

As described above, the radiocarbon dating process is relatively simple – it is based on a comparison of the amount of ^{14}C left with the amount that would have been present when the organism was alive. Unfortunately, we do not know exactly how much that was, so the simplest estimate is to say that it is the same as that present in modern living organisms. This assumes that the rate of production of radiocarbon has been constant, and also that rates of assimilation have been uniform over time. Neither of these assumptions can be completely relied upon. Indeed, in establishing the radiocarbon method during the 1960s, it became increasingly clear that there was a systematic difference between the radiocarbon age and the 'true' or 'calendrical' age of dated historic material. This discrepancy, which is caused by a combination of factors, is now overcome by a process known as 'calibration'. For this, a radiocarbon date, which is usually expressed as a single value and a symmetrical 'error term', e.g., 570 ± 30 years Before Present (BP), is converted into a (non-symmetric) calendrical age range (as shown in the technical appendix at the end of this chapter). Without such calibration, any radiocarbon age is likely to be an underestimate of the true age of an object, and will certainly be wrong.

Calibration is carried out by comparing the radiocarbon age of the object with the radiocarbon age of something for which we independently know the true age, and assuming that if the radiocarbon ages are comparable then the true ages will also be comparable. Fortunately we have an excellent calibration system available for the past 10,000 years, consisting of a continuous sequence of annual tree rings produced by dendrochronology (see below). Unfortunately, however, the calibration process introduces some complications. The calibration curve is not a regular shape, meaning that a single uncalibrated radiocarbon date does not necessarily correspond to a single calendrical date or date range. There may, therefore, be several possibilities for the actual calendrical date of the material. In many cases it may only be possible to provide an age range of several decades, or at worst several possible age ranges (see the technical appendix at the end of this chapter for an example).

There is much to be learned about the potential applicability of radiocarbon dating to a particular time period by studying the calibration curve. Essentially the shape of the calibration curve at any particular time is the most important factor in dictating the likely usefulness of the radiocarbon date. The last 800 years of the curve is shown in Figure 1. The inflection of the curve around the 14th Century may result in a single uncalibrated date giving rise to more than one calendrical date; a radiocarbon age of 600 years ± 15 BP, for example, could relate to any of three different positions on the calibration curve, which correspond to three different 14th Century date ranges. One might equally expect such a result around AD 1600. The main issue, however, is the nature of the calibration curve post- AD 1650, where it becomes almost flat, meaning that any object with a real age between about AD 1650 and 1950 will give the same radiocarbon age. Consequently, radiocarbon is incapable of giving a real age between these dates. Thus, radiocarbon is likely to be ineffective for this crucial 300 year period in the history of written manuscripts. It should be noted, however, that the possibility exists of producing a finite number of possible calibrated date ranges within this period, provided the radiocarbon date is measured to very high precision, which can be done if sufficient sample is available and the machine is left to count for long enough. For example, a radiocarbon date of 170 ± 5 BP produces calibrated ages of AD 1660 – 1690, 1730 – 1810, or 1930 – 1950; conceivably in some circumstances this might be helpful.

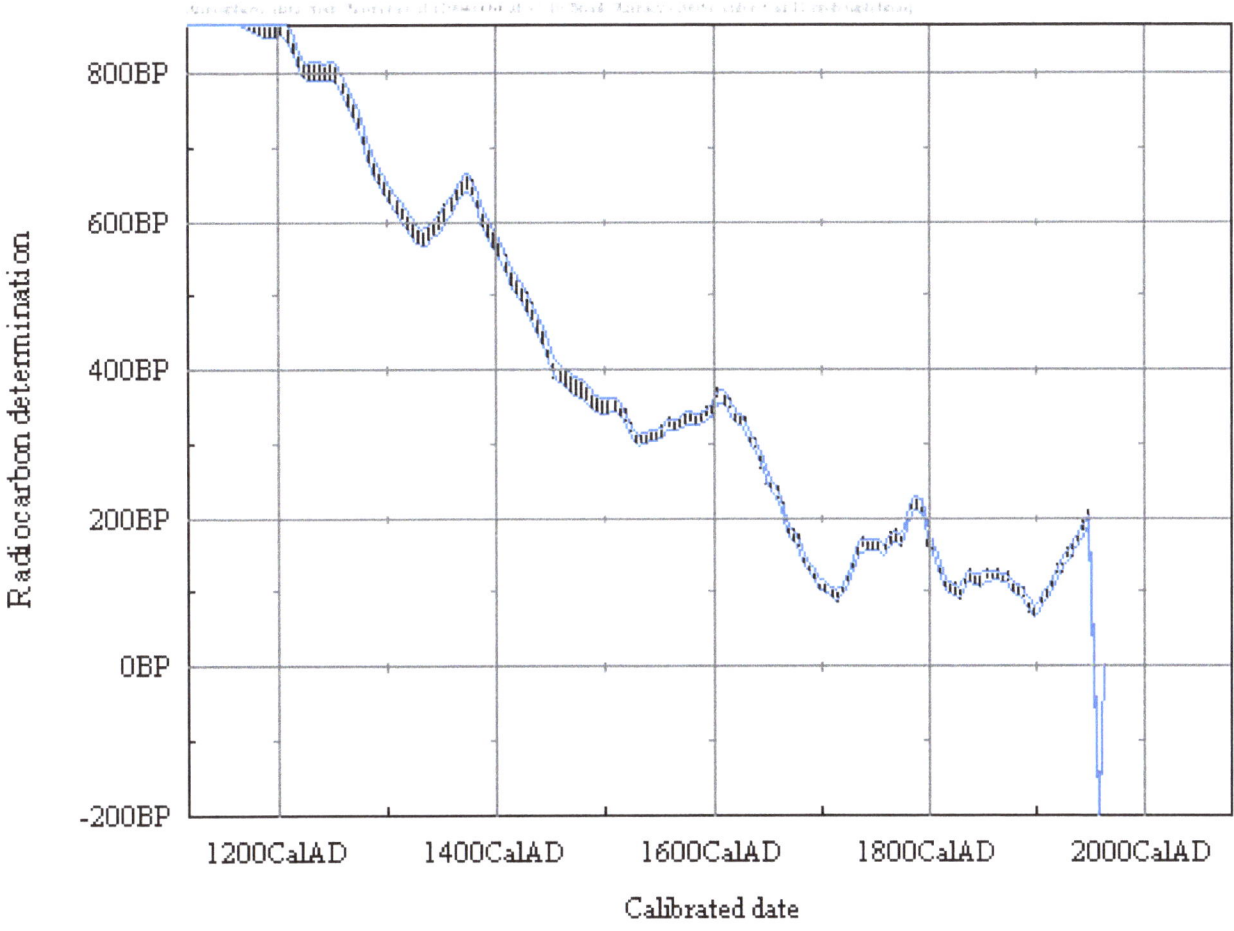

Figure 1. The radiocarbon calibration curve from c. AD 1200 to AD 1950

Sequence dating

As discussed above, radiocarbon dating of organic materials which are part of a physical book or manuscript has the ability to date the materials which make up the object, but probably only to within several decades at best. Only in the most extreme of cases, where the date of an object is not known to better than a few centuries, is this likely to be of much value to the historian. However, new developments in the manipulation of radiocarbon data, using a mathematical approach known as Bayes' Theorem, offer new levels of precision by combining the radiocarbon evidence with other sources of information [see Bayliss (2009) for an overview of the application to archaeology, and Bronk Ramsey (2009) for the mathematical formulation]. Thomas Bayes (c. 1701 – 1761) was a Presbyterian minister and a mathematician. The theorem which now bears his name was published posthumously in 1764 by the Reverend Richard Price (Bayes and Price 1763), in the form of a letter which Price found amongst Bayes' papers. In non mathematical terms, this formulation allows the calculation of the probability of some event happening to be modified by the inclusion of prior knowledge. In both archaeological and codicological research, the most valuable piece of prior information is likely to be the sequence in which a series of events happened.

Consider a situation in which three manuscripts (labelled A, B and C) are known to have been published in this order, but the dates are unknown. If each is radiocarbon dated, then this will produce a date, the distribution of which, after calibration, is likely to be too broad to satisfy the historical researcher. To illustrate this (upper part of Figure 2), we have simulated three radiocarbon dates, which, after calibration (using Oxcal[4]) give date ranges of:

MANUSCRIPT A
Radiocarbon age: 400 ± 28 BP
Calibrated calendrical date: AD 1436-1516 or AD 1593-1624.

MANUSCRIPT B
Radiocarbon age: 380 ± 28 BP
Calibrated calendrical date: AD 1445-1524, AD 1560-1565 or 1570-1632.

MANUSCRIPT C
Radiocarbon age: 360 ± 28 BP
Calibrated calendrical date: AD 460-1530 or AD 1541-1636.

---

[4] 'Oxcal' software allows computerised calibrations to be carried out online, and can be accessed for free at https://c14.arch.ox.ac.uk/login/login.php?Location=/oxcal/OxCal.html.

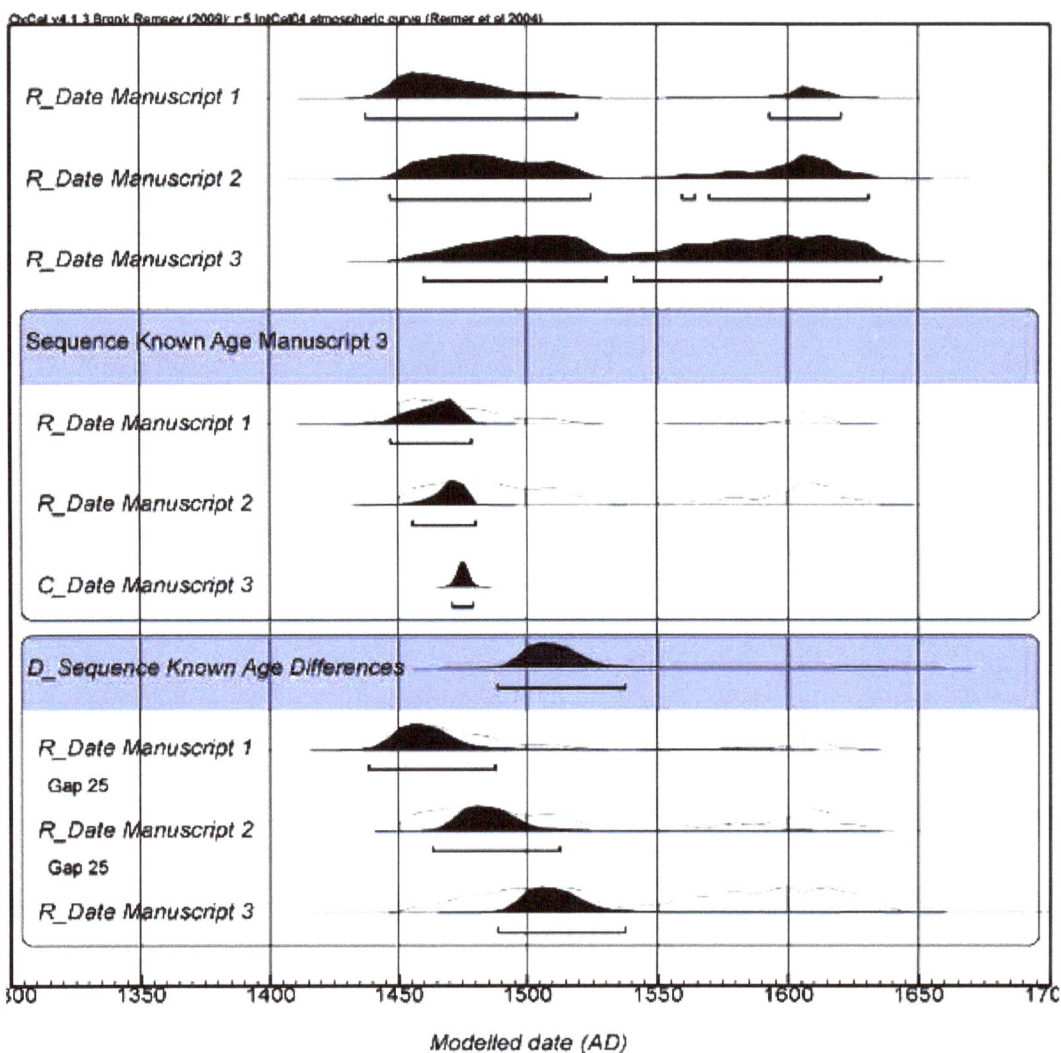

Figure 2. 'Sequence dating' of three manuscripts (see text).

It is immediately obvious that these ranges are far too broad to convey anything of value. However, by knowing that A must be older than B which must be older than C, and that if (by some other means) we are able to find out that manuscript C was produced in AD 1475 (plus or minus two years), we can significantly constrain these age ranges, as shown in middle part of Figure 2. The calendrical date estimates now become:

Manuscript A – AD 1439 – 1471
Manuscript B – AD 1452 –1478
(Manuscript C – AD 1471 – 1479, as defined in the model).

If, to take a different example, we do not know the absolute calendrical date of any of them, but know that each was produced 25 years apart (a 'generation'), then we can constrain the calendrical dates as follows (lower part of Figure 2):

Manuscript A – AD 1435 – 1491
Manuscript B – AD 1460 – 1516
Manuscript C – AD 1485 – 1541.

Although still not precise by historical standards, it can be seen that by the application of other forms of scholarship the initially quite uninformative individual radiocarbon dates can be constrained to something more helpful. Careful construction of a model from existing knowledge, combined with good quality radiocarbon dating, has the potential to contribute to some aspects of manuscript scholarship.

Dendrochronology

Dendrochronology is the procedure whereby wooden timbers can be dated by cross-matching the tree ring patterns. It is well known that many temperate species of trees produce an annual growth ring, the thickness of which is dependant on a range of factors, including climatic conditions during the growing season. An individual living tree can be aged by simply counting the number of annual growth rings starting at the bark edge and moving inwards towards the heartwood. The reliability of this process depends to some extent on the species – some, such as oak, produce annual rings almost without fail, whereas other species can occasionally fail to produce a ring, leading to an underestimate of the age.

More usefully, however, the variation in ring width over a period of time produces a pattern which is both distinctive and more-or-less replicated by the same species of tree across large regions of the world. This pattern forms a 'bar code' which can be used to identify the time period covered. Using a process known as cross-matching, which starts with living trees and gradually progresses back in time by overlapping the sequence with ever older trees, a continuous chronology has been developed using European oak to cover the last 10,000 years. This is the very same sequence that has been used to calibrate radiocarbon dates, as described above, but it also provides a 'master chronology' of ring width variation against which any piece of oak can be cross-matched to give a date which is accurate to a single year [see Baillie (1982, 1995) for an overview of chronology building and the application to archaeology].

Although essentially very simple, the process of matching an unknown sequence with this 'master curve' to produce a date requires a great deal of experience. The unknown sequence needs to contain ideally more than 50 individual consecutive rings, and certainly no less than 30. The matching process is essentially a statistical exercise – what is given is the number of significant date matches. In the simplest case, only one significant match is given, in which case the date is fixed precisely and unambiguously. Not infrequently, however, more than one match might be given – each with an associated probability – and it is up to the researcher to decide which of the dates is the most likely, either on archaeological/historical grounds, or using the probabilities.

The date given is that of the last ring (i.e., the youngest) in the sequence. This may or may not be the date of cutting of the timber, depending on how the wood was cut. Felling dates can only be securely given if sapwood and (ideally) bark are present, but most wood preparation removes these rings. If absent, a sapwood correction has to be applied (usually by adding 25 years for oak: Baillie, 1982: 55). Equally, this date may or may not be the date of use of the timber. It is extremely common to find old timbers being re-used for structural or other purposes. Thus, the interpretation of the significance of the date can depend on a whole range of other observations relating to woodworking techniques and context. Although the master sequence for the last 10,000 years consists solely of oak, it is not impossible to date other species of wood, ideally using a shorter master sequence for that particular species (if it exists), or, if necessary, by comparison of the non-oak species with the oak chronology.

Dendrochronology is now widely used to date the timber elements of standing and historic buildings, and also in archaeology, where certain preservation conditions allow the survival of wood. The most relevant application, however, is its use to date the oak boards upon which 'Old Master' paintings were painted, with obvious implications for the dating and authenticity or otherwise of the associated paintings (Fletcher 1982). These particular oak boards can be dated non-destructively because the ring-width pattern is visible on the narrow edges, allowing the required measurements to be made by simply lightly cleaning the edge and counting using a microscope. If similar wooden boards were used as part of the bookbinding (of sufficient size to retain 30-50 rings), then it should be possible to date these boards by the same completely non-destructive methodology. If successful, this could potentially be of more use than radiocarbon, at least in terms of historical precision.

Other possibilities for dating historical documents

It is possible that some other (as yet untried) methods of dating might prove useful in some circumstances – most likely in distinguishing modern (post-1950) from more ancient material. What follows, however, is pure speculation!

Lead-210 dating

The element lead has four stable isotopes (used for geochemical provenancing of lead ore sources, including identifying the source of lead pigment: e.g., Fortunato *et al.* 2005), but it also has a number of radioactive isotopes. One of these is ^{210}Pb, which has a half life of 22 years (Olsson, 1986: 298-303). This provides a useful chronometer on a timescale of between 1 and 150 years. It seems possible that ^{210}Pb might provide a useful chronometer for dating the use of lead-containing pigments – the necessary assumptions would be that the preparation of the pigment isolates the sample from the radioactive isotopes present in the ore deposit, and that the quantity of ^{210}Pb present at this time is then reduced by radioactive decay only. If so, then the amount of ^{210}Pb remaining in the sample is related to the date of manufacture of the pigment.

Other short lived isotopes

Nuclear testing in the 1960s produced other radioactive nuclei in addition to radiocarbon which have since found there way into the biosphere (Glasstone and Dolan, 1977) - tritium (^{3}H, half-life 12.4 years), strontium-90 (^{90}Sr, half-life 28 years) and cesium-137 (^{137}Cs, half-life 35 years). Although the rate of generation of these isotopes as a result of nuclear testing has been reduced by the Test Ban Treaties, radioactive emissions from nuclear power plants may continue to enhance their concentration at levels above natural background for the foreseeable future (Glasstone and Jordan, 1980). Furthermore, nuclear accidents such as Chernobyl in 1986 have been responsible for significant spikes in the concentration of artificial radioisotopes in both the atmosphere and in rainfall (Furukawa and Kojima, 1991). Although, with the exception of the work of MacLaughlin-Black *et al.* (1992), little research into these isotopes has been done from either the forensic or the archaeological point of view, it seems likely that enhancements may be detectable in recent remains which may help to distinguish between material derived from organisms living before or after 1950 AD.

Cesium-137 activity, for example, showed a peak in the northern hemisphere in 1963, which had reduced to a third of that value by 1965. Any organism growing in the post-1960s period is likely to contain enhanced levels of these artificial radionuclides. Thus, paper, parchment, bone, ivory, leather and organic pigments should exhibit higher levels than the same materials produced pre-bomb (allowing for the natural radioactive decay). The biological behaviour of strontium-90 has been intensively studied since the 1950s, because it is a bone-seeking element, and once stored in bone tissue it is not easily lost. The total amount of ^{90}Sr in the stratosphere reached a peak in 1962, but levels were kept high by subsequent nuclear testing (Glasstone and Dolan, 1977, pp604-609). Although subsequent changes in radiostrontium activity have not been as closely monitored as that of radiocarbon, it seems likely that ^{90}Sr could provide a useful dating marker in biological tissue studies. This has been demonstrated to be possible by the work of MacLaughlin-Black et al. (1992), which reported enhanced levels of ^{90}Sr in three fresh post-mortem bone samples, compared with three mediaeval archaeological bone samples.

Amino acid racemization of parchment

As an alternative to radiocarbon dating, it is possible that collagen-containing materials such as parchment or leather could be dated by amino acid racemization [AAR – see Pollard and Heron (2008), chapter 8]. The structure of parchment is discussed in more detail in Chapter 7, but both parchment and leather are made up of collagen. Collagen contains amino acids, which are molecules that exhibit a phenomenon known as chirality – they can exist as two chemically identical but structurally different configurations, corresponding to the left- and right-handed forms of a mirror image pair. In life, most proteins are constructed from amino acids which are formed and maintained in the left-handed form only, but after death, the process of racemization occurs by which the left-handed converts to the right-handed form, until such a time as the protein contains equal amounts of both forms – a racemic mixture. The rate at which this transformation occurs is controlled by many factors, of which temperature is one of the most important. Thus, if the ratio of left- to right-handed forms can be measured, and the rate of racemization is known, then the time elapsed since the death of the organism can be calculated.

This technique should work well on parchment and leather, since skin is rich in collagen, which contains relatively large amounts of the fastest-racemizing amino acids (aspartic acid, etc.). In most circumstances, however, it is difficult to see why AAR would be preferred over radiocarbon, since the sample requirements are likely to be similar, the error terms similar, and radiocarbon is intrinsically more reliable. However, recalling the problems of radiocarbon post-AD 1650, it might be worth considering AAR for material from this period.

Some published case studies on the scientific dating of historical manuscripts

The Dead-Sea Scrolls

The Dead Sea scrolls are a generic name for a collection of more than 1200 manuscripts (some fragmentary, others complete scrolls) found in the hills on the western shore of the Dead Sea from 1947 onwards. The first find was made in a cave near Khirbet Qumran, from which was eventually excavated 800 manuscripts written in Hebrew and Aramaic on either papyri or parchment. None of these Qumran scrolls bear a date, but are palaeographically dated to between the mid-4th Century BC through to the 1st C AD. Some of the other scrolls from the area do carry their dates of copying (Bonani et al. 1992).

Prior to the development of Accelerator Mass Spectrometry (AMS), radiocarbon required too much sample for the scrolls themselves to be dated. Some related objects were dated, indicating an age as expected of around 2000 years (Bonani et al. 1992). Subsequently 34 samples of the Dead Sea scrolls were radiocarbon dated using AMS (requiring much smaller samples), of which Bonani et al. (1992) have dated 14. Of these 14, in most cases the calibrated age ranges included the expected date from palaeographic evidence (the calibrated dates are quoted in the original paper at 65% confidence: good practice would now suggest that calibrated dates should be quoted at the 95% confidence level).

In three cases there was a discrepancy:

Sample #2
calibrated range 388-353, 309-235 BC expected age 100 – 75 BC

Sample #7
calibrated range 169-93 BC   expected age 30-1 BC

Sample #12
calibrated range AD 28-122   expected age AD 130-131

Sample #12 (a papyrus) is marginally too young, but, when recalibrated at 95%, covers the age range AD 1 – 220, comfortably including the expected age.

In samples 2 and 7 (both parchment) the radiocarbon age is older than the expected date, but when re-calibrated and quoted at 95% confidence, the following results are obtained:

Sample #2
2240 ± 39 BP; calibrated 400 – 200 BC (95.4% confidence)

Sample #7
2086 ± 28 BP; calibrated 200 – 40 BC (95.4% confidence).

In both cases the ages are still too old. Re-use of an older parchment in sample 2 (the Testament of Qahat) was dismissed by infrared examination of the text.

Bonani et al. (1992) concluded that there is some evidence of a systematic difference of 35 years between the expected age and the calibrated age range, with the calibrated ages being older. In the conclusion they speculated that the modern practice of using castor oil to aid the visibility of the text might have introduced a shift in the age of the sample if it was not removed by the chemical pre-treatment of the sample, but this would have made the parchment appear younger. Subsequent statistical analysis of the same data (Rodley, 1993) concluded that the apparent discrepancy was due to the way in which the calibrated dates were quoted, and that the general accuracy of the dates was ± 25 years.

In a later analysis, Carmi (2002), using a larger dataset of radiocarbon dates containing 34 samples, tested the hypothesis that castor oil might have systematically shifted the scientific dates. Using recalibrated dates and the 95% confidence level, this paper concluded that there was no problem in the dataset resulting from castor oil contamination. Despite this, 10 of the 27 samples with independent dating evidence did not agree, suggesting that there may be a problem with the palaeographic dating. This debate continues (Rasmussen *et al.* 2003).

The Vinland Map

Even more controversial has been the debate over the authenticity of the Vinland Map. If genuine, this is the earliest depiction of the north American continent, and it is conventionally dated to the Council of Basle (AD 1431-1449), thus pre-dating by at least half a century the voyage of Columbus. The map states that 'the Island of Vinland' was 'discovered by Bjarni and Leif in company'. It clearly has implications for the antiquity of knowledge of land in the western North Atlantic, and that Columbus may have had knowledge of the existence of North America. A sample of 28.8 milligrams was removed from the map in 1995, and was dated by AMS radiocarbon dating (Donahue *et al.* 2002). The calibrated calendrical age range (95% confidence) was quoted as AD 1411-1468, supporting the alleged historical date, and clearly pre-dating the voyage of Columbus. In accordance with good scientific practice, the original 28.8 mg sample was sub-sampled into 6 samples, each of which was dated separately, and subjected to sample pre-treatments of increasing stringency. Other samples of known-age parchments were also dated to check the accuracy of the procedure.

The conclusion of this paper is important: 'the measurements described here determine only the age of the parchment of the Vinland Map and not that of the map itself'. Further: 'Our dating research does not prove that the Vinland Map is authentic. We have introduced new evidence that should be addressed in future discussions of the map's authenticity'. This debate is certainly ongoing, much of it focussing on the apparent presence of traces of titanium in the ink, allegedly in the form of anatase crystals, which only became commercially available in the 1920s (Harbottle 2008).

Dating some Japanese papers

In a series of research papers, Oda *et al.* (2000, 2003, 2004, 2007) have dated Japanese sutras written on paper made from wood fibres, and covering a wide range of dates from the Nara period (AD 729-766) to AD 1689. The importance of these papers, apart from resolving some issues about the dating of certain Japanese sutras, is to show that paper made from wood fibres is a suitable material for radiocarbon dating, and that the dates are consistent with the expected dates. As expected, however, the dates of papers attributed to the 17th Century AD show multiple probabilities, including some coming through to the 20th Century. The implication of the concordance between the earlier dates and the corresponding expected ages is that Japanese paper was not made using old wood.

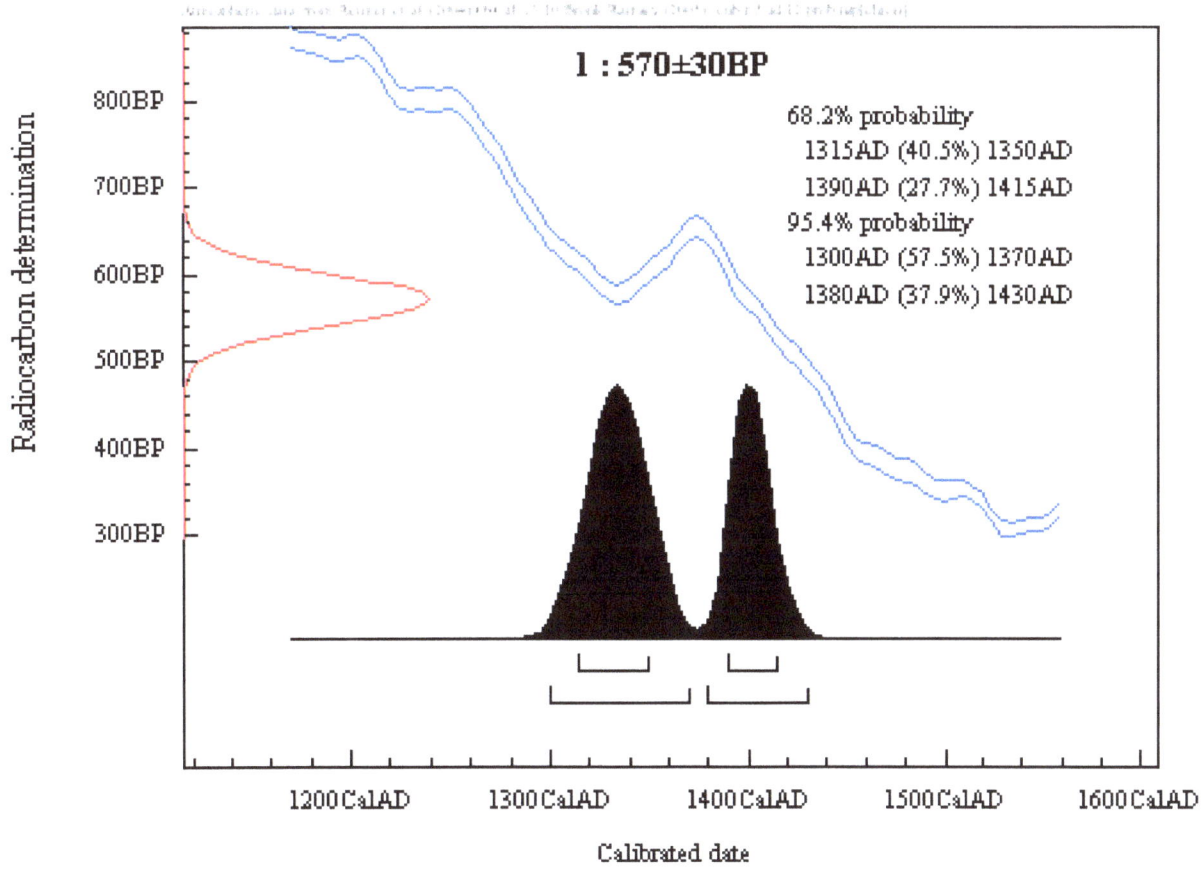

Figure 3. The calibration using OxCal of an age of 570 ± 30 radiocarbon years Before Present (BP)

Conclusion

As has been shown by the case studies, radiocarbon dating is applicable to historical manuscripts written on or bound using organic material (e.g., parchment, papyrus, paper, leather) prior to the 17th Century AD, using milligram size samples. The pre-treatment chemistry appears to be satisfactory in removing any likely contaminants. In the cases quoted, the calibrated age range estimates are of sufficient accuracy to enable meaningful historical interpretations to be made (although the saga of the Vinland map clearly shows that dating the parchment alone cannot resolve a long-term issue of authenticity). What the simulated set of radiocarbon dates also hopefully demonstrate is that by combining historical and scientific dating methods in a statistical (Bayesian) model, it is possible in some cases to provide dating evidence on a known sequence of manuscripts which is much more accurate than the individual radiocarbon dates.

Post c. AD 1650, the calibrated radiocarbon date is likely to ambiguous (because of the flattening of the calibration curve), but may still be useful in resolving gross issues of dating. The following ideas may also be worth investigating, either as supplementary to radiocarbon dating prior to AD 1650, or as techniques suitable to specific classes of problems:

- Dendrochronology of wooden book-bindings should be explored;
- Amino acid racemization might be useful post-AD 1650 for the dating of parchment and leather;
- The use of lead-210 as a dating method for lead-based pigments over the last few centuries;
- The investigation of the use of strontium-90 to distinguish between pre- and post-1950 materials

Radiocarbon Dating: Technical Appendix

Calibration

A radiocarbon age starts life as a single value and a symmetrical 'error term', e.g., 570 ± 30 years Before Present (BP). When calibrated, it becomes a 'probability distribution', which may be very irregular in shape and possibly even discontinuous. This has to be interpreted as a 95% confidence level age range rather than a single value. For an uncalibrated radiocarbon age of 570 ± 30 BP there are two possible calendrical dates, as shown in Figure 3. These are expressed as 'AD 1300 – 1370 (57.5%), AD 1380 – 1430 (37.9%)'. In words, this means that the material being analysed most likely dates to between AD 1300 and 1370 (with a 57.5% probability), but it could also date to the period AD 1380 – 1430, with a 37.9% probability. Thus, what appears to be a simple result (570 BP, i.e., AD 1380, with an error range of ± 30 years) appears to have become much less tractable, and with a much extended age range. This is an inevitable consequence of the physics and chemistry of radiocarbon dating. Fortunately, at least, such calibrations can be carried out online using the OxCal software, which can be accessed for free at https://c14.arch.ox.ac.uk/login/login.php?Location=/oxcal/OxCal.html.

Bomb Carbon

When using the standard radiocarbon calibration curve to determine a calendrical age, the flattening of the curve from 1650 onwards can make it difficult to provide a useful date for objects made after this point in time. An exception to this rather unhelpful picture has been the use of the so-called 'bomb carbon' curve. During and after the Second World War, atmospheric testing of nuclear weapons caused a significant increase in the rate of production of atmospheric ^{14}C, which

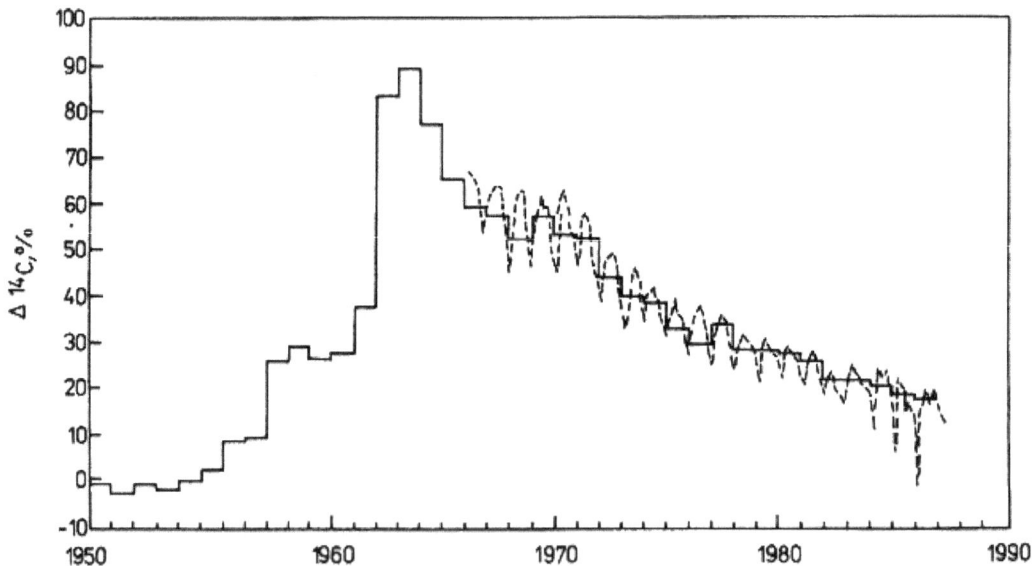

Thermonuclear bomb-produced ^{14}C variations in samples of annually produced Georgian wines (~38° N, ~45° E) and in monthly samples of atmospheric CO_2 in Bratislava (~48° N, ~17° E)
—— = wines; - - - - = CO_2

Figure 4. The 'Bomb carbon' effect, as measured in Georgian wines (from Burchuladze *et al.*, 1989 Figure 1)

has been gradually dispersed throughout the whole of the biosphere via the carbon cycle. Figure 4 shows the change in ^{14}C concentration since 1950, as measured in single year vintage wines from Georgia, compared to the concentration of atmospheric carbon dioxide (Burchuladze *et al.*, 1989). The ^{14}C concentration reached a peak in 1963 at approximately twice the level of 1950, and has been declining steadily ever since, but in 1989 was still 15% above the 1950 level. It is evident, therefore, that organic material between 1950 and present can be dated quite accurately if a sufficiently precise measurement of the amount of bomb-produced radiocarbon present is made – albeit, however, that there will always be two possible dates given – one prior to 1963 (on the way up) and one, less accurate, post 1963 (on the way down). Such an approach has in fact been used in forensic contexts when it has been necessary to date the skeleton of a human thought to have died sometime during the second half of the 20th Century (Ubelaker *et al.* 2006).

Marine Carbon

One further caveat is necessary in the context of using radiocarbon to date historic written material – the so-called 'marine correction'. The discussion above assumed that the ^{14}C produced in the atmosphere entered the terrestrial biosphere via plant photosynthesis. Equally important, however, is the carbon that enters the marine food chain via photosynthetic phytoplankton or as dissolved carbonates. Much of this marine carbon enters the deep oceans, where it has a long residence time due to the poor mixing of the oceans. The result is that modern marine carbon, and any organisms in equilibrium with it, can have an apparent radiocarbon age of several hundred years. The modern-day value of this marine reservoir correction is derived from ^{14}C measurements on contemporary marine organisms (e.g., Ascough *et al.* 2009), and is known to vary geographically across the Earth's oceans from between ~200 and ~750 radiocarbon years.[5] The average global marine reservoir correction is around 400 radiocarbon years. Thus, a date produced on material derived from a marine organism will appear to be about 400 years older than it actually is.

Identifying which samples are derived from marine organisms, and which therefore require the application of a marine reservoir correction, is not always easy. Clearly any tissue from a marine organism will obviously require correction, but it is more ambiguous in the case of human bone, for instance, when the diet might contain a proportion of marine input. As described above, the values of the stable isotopes of carbon and nitrogen are often used to estimate the importance of marine protein in the diet, and the degree to which correction is necessary. In the context of historical manuscripts, however, such considerations are unlikely to be necessary, and the materials requiring marine correction should be reasonably obvious, including bindings made from fish or marine mammal skin, and also fish glues.

References

Aitken, M.J.1990 *Science-based Dating in Archaeology*. Longman, London.

Ascough, P.L., Cook, G.T. and Dugmore, A.J. 2009 North Atlantic marine 14C reservoir effects: implications for late-Holocene chronological studies. *Quaternary Geochronology* **4**, 171-180.

Baillie, M.G.L. 1982 *Tree-ring Dating and Archaeology*. Chicago University Press, Chicago.

Baillie, M.G.L. 1995 *A Slice through Time: Dendrochronology and Precision Dating*. Batsford, London.

Bayes, T. and Price, R. 1763 An essay towards solving a problem in the doctrine of chances. *Philosophical Transactions* **53**, 370-418

Bayliss, A. 2009 Rolling out revolution: using radiocarbon dating in archaeology. *Radiocarbon* **5**, 123–147.

Bonani, G., Ivy, S., Wolfli, W., Broshi, M., Carmi, I. and Strugnell, J. 1992 Radiocarbon dating of 14 Dead Sea Scrolls. *Radiocarbon* **34**, 843-849.

Bowman, S. E. 1990 *Radiocarbon Dating*. British Museum Publications, London.

Bronk Ramsey, C. 2009 Bayesian analysis of radiocarbon dates. *Radiocarbon* **51**, 337–360.

Burchuladze, A. A., Chudy, M., Eristavi, I. V., Pagava, S. V., Povinec, P., Sivo, A. and Togonidze, G. I. 1989 Anthropogenic C-14 variations in atmospheric CO_2 and wines. *Radiocarbon* **31**, 771-776.

Carmi, I. 2002 Are the C-14 dates of the Dead Sea Scrolls affected by castor oil contamination? *Radiocarbon* **44**, 213-216.

Donahue, D. J., Olin, J. S. and Harbottle, G. 2002 Determination of the radiocarbon age of parchment of the Vinland Map. *Radiocarbon* **44**, 45-52.

Fletcher, J. 1982 Tree-ring dating of Tudor portraits. *Proceedings of the Royal Institution of Great Britain* **52**, 81-104.

Fortunato, G., Ritter, A., and Fabian, D. 2005 Old Master's Lead White pigments: investigations of paintings from the 16th to the 17th century using high precision lead isotope abundance ratios. *Analyst* **130**, 898-906.

Furukawa, M. and Kojima, S. 1991 Time variations of artificial radionuclide concentrations in the air over Japan since 1974. *Radiochimica Acta* **54**, 109-112.

Glasstone, S. and Dolan, P. J. (eds.) 1977 *The Effects of Nuclear Weapons*. U.S. Dept. of Defense, Washington.

Glasstone, S. and Jordan, W. H. 1980 *Nuclear Power and Its Environmental Effects*. American Nuclear Society, La Grange Park, Ill.

Harbottle, G. 2008 The Vinland map: a critical review of archaeometric research on its authenticity. *Archaeometry* **50**, 177-189.

MacLaughlin-Black, S. M., Herd, R. J. M., Willson, K., Myers, M. and West, I. E. 1992 Sr-90 as an indicator of time since death - a pilot investigation. *Forensic Science International* **57**, 51-56.

Oda, H., Yoshizawa, Y., Nakamura, T. and Fujita, K. 2000 AMS radiocarbon dating of ancient Japanese sutras. *Nuclear Instruments and Methods in Physics B* **172**, 736-740.

---

[5] see global database at http://intcal.qub.ac.uk/marine/

Oda, H., Masuda, T., Niu, E. and Nakamura, T. 2003 AMS radiocarbon dating of ancient Japanese documents of known age. *Journal of Radioanalytical and Nuclear Chemistry* **255**, 375-379.

Oda, H., Ikeda, K., Masuda, T. and Nakamura, T. 2004 Radiocarbon dating of Kohitsugire (paper fragments) attributed to Japanese calligraphists in the Heian-Kamakura period. *Radiocarbon* **46**, 369-375.

Oda, H., Ikeda, K. and Nakamura, T. 2007 Radiocarbon age of the kohitsugire calligraphy and the kiwamefuda certificate. *Nuclear Instruments and Methods in Physics B* **259**, 374-377.

Olsson, I.U. 1986 Radiometric dating. In Berglund, B.E. (ed.) *Handbook of Holocene Palaeoecology and Palaeohydrology*, 273-312. John Wiley, Chichester.

Pollard, A. M. and Heron, C. 2008 *Archaeological Chemistry*. Royal Society of Chemistry, Cambridge.

Rasmussen, K. L., van der Plicht, J., Doudna, G., Cross, F. M. and Strugnell, J. 2003 Reply to Israel Carmi (2002): "Are the C-14 dates of the dead sea scrolls affected by castor oil contamination?". *Radiocarbon* **45**, 497-499.

Rodley, G. A. 1993 An assessment of the radiocarbon dating of the dead-sea-scrolls. *Radiocarbon* **35**, 335-338.

Taylor, R. E. and Aitken, M. J. (eds.) 1997 *Chronometric Dating in Archaeology*. Plenum Press, New York.

Ubelaker, D. H., Buchholz, B. A. and Stewart, J. E. B. 2006 Analysis of artificial radiocarbon in different skeletal and dental tissue types to evaluate date of death. *Journal of Forensic Sciences* **51**, 484-488.

www.ingramcontent.com/pod-product-compliance
Lightning Source LLC
Chambersburg PA
CBHW061544010526
44113CB00023B/2789